Hyb-IT-up!

Azusa Nakata • Ana Balula
Paulo J. M. Santos • Hanna Järvenoja
António Moreira • Armin Weinberger
Editors

Hyb-IT-up!

Designing Effective Hybrid Teaching and Learning

HYB'IT.UP

Co-funded by
the European Union

Springer

Editors
Azusa Nakata
University of Oulu
Oulu, Finland

Ana Balula
University of Aveiro
Aveiro, Portugal

Paulo J. M. Santos
Saarland University
Saarbrücken, Germany

Hanna Järvenoja
University of Oulu
Oulu, Finland

António Moreira
University of Aveiro
Aveiro, Portugal

Armin Weinberger
Saarland University
Saarbrücken, Germany

ISBN 978-3-031-99742-6 ISBN 978-3-031-99743-3 (eBook)
https://doi.org/10.1007/978-3-031-99743-3

This Springer imprint is published by the registered company Springer Nature Switzerland AG
The registered company address is: Gewerbestrasse 11, 6330 Cham, Switzerland

A Preface for Hyping Up Hybrid Learning

Upgrading Hybrid Learning!

The Erasmus+ funded project Hyb-IT-up (Upgrading higher education teachers' and students' hybrid learning competences) was launched during the time when the Covid-19 pandemic was still strongly influencing our lives.

The project idea was initiated from the long-term collaboration history of a jointly organized course *Computer-Supported Collaborative Learning (CSCL)* among some of the project partners. The course organizers witnessed the value of learning activities in which higher education students can learn together across their degree programs and study countries. Meanwhile, the pandemic brought "new normal," shifting the way of learning, working, and meeting people toward online and eventually toward hybrid. This also changed our mind toward thinking that the future of higher education will move beyond any one model of online or co-present education but will eventually embrace the potential of hybrid teaching and learning.

Literatures already acknowledge both positive and negative aspects of hybrid teaching and learning. In pandemic emergency situations, many teachers had difficulty in shifting to online teaching and hesitated to implement hybrid teaching. Here, we would like to emphasize that the goal of the project was not driven by the urgency of providing education in an online/hybrid manner caused by the pandemic. Instead, we were seeking to intentionally design hybrid learning for the future of education and were focusing on the potential of this unique teaching approach over the challenges. We sought out to explore how educators can enhance the richness of learning experiences by combining physical and digital worlds.

To achieve our goals, namely, upgrading higher education teachers' and students' hybrid learning competence, the project has conducted several studies and produced various useful tools. We applied co-design approaches to create our solutions with various stakeholders, including researchers, teachers, students, and technology companies. For instance, we have organized a workshop in EC-TEL 2023 in Aveiro, Portugal, to identify challenges and potentials, reimagine hybrid practices, and co-design hybrid teaching and learning approaches. Through these co-design and collaboration activities, we have connected to various people studying and encouraging the implementation of hybrid learning. This made us think that it might be valuable to collect all the project findings and experiences of collaborators and to compile them into one book.

How We Define Hybrid Teaching and Learning

Hybrid learning is defined in this book (and the project) as a "mode of teaching which is implemented flexibly as online and face-to-face mode, covering the situations where students can participate in the same activities either in class or in distance" (Hyb-IT-up, n.d.). As another Springer Nature book about hybrid learning, *Hybrid Learning Spaces*, states, hybrid learning "adopts an interdisciplinary perspective, which combines pedagogy, technology and space design …" (Gil et al., 2022, p. 2). We acknowledge the complexity and find the need for covering these different elements into the book. We also believe that involving simultaneous in-person and online learning, mediated by digital technology, makes it increasingly relevant to reflect on the "pedagogical aspects" from both the teacher's and learner's perspectives. Hence, while we offer some insight into technology use and classroom design in this book, our main focus remains on pedagogical approaches to take advantage of hybrid mode and make learning experience more unique, impactful, and enjoyable. This book, therefore, addresses the increasing trend of hybrid teaching and learning, putting forward some of its main advantages and hurdles as well as best practices.

The Structure of the Book and Chapter Outlines

The book consists of three parts: Part "*Conceptual Pillars of Hybrid Teaching and Learning in Higher Education*"; Part "*Unlocking the Potential of Hybrid Teaching and Learning in Higher Education Through Co-design*"; and Part "*Experience-Based Cases of Hybrid Teaching and Learning*".

With a focus on hybrid higher education, Part "*Conceptual Pillars of Hybrid Teaching and Learning in Higher Education*" of this book introduces some central concepts for the understanding and practice of hybrid learning and instruction.

Chapter "A Social Perspective on Hybrid Learning" investigates the notion of social presence, underlining its essential influence on communication and learning dynamics in hybrid learning contexts. It discusses how social presence—conceptualized as the perception of others as physical "real" persons in technology-mediated communication—allows the formation of dynamics that are central to effective hybrid education. Specifically, it highlights the importance of supporting remote students to feel involved in classroom, lecture, or group learning activities and in making students attending in person perceive their remote peers as actively present and engaged.

Chapter "Teacher Educators' Digital Competence for Hybrid Teaching" delves into teachers' and learners' hybrid learning competencies, offering an analysis of the skills and knowledge that help them navigate hybrid teaching and learning effectively. Emphasizing the need for a solid theoretical foundation, this chapter proposes directions for further investigations on the role of teacher and learner competencies for hybrid education.

Chapter "Regulation of Learning: Cognition, Motivation and Emotion" aims to clarify the understanding of hybrid learning by taking a situative perspective on the regulation of learning. The chapter discusses the concept of regulation of learning—the strategic management of one's own learning process (self-regulation of learning) and that of others (co- and socially shared regulation of learning)—focusing on cognition, motivation, and emotion at the heart of it all. The chapter also explores the relevance of regulating these processes within the specific contexts of time and place afforded by hybrid scenarios. By examining the interplay between self-regulation and the contextual dynamics of hybrid learning, this chapter sheds light on how to optimize one's learning process in hybrid educational settings.

Finally, **Chapter "Orchestration Load of Hybrid Teaching"** introduces the concept of orchestration load considering the multifaceted challenges faced by educators engaging in hybrid teaching. This chapter reflects on the balance between technological, pedagogical, and content demands, emphasizing the importance of a holistic approach to sustain effective teaching and meet students' needs.

In response to the growing integration of digital technology in higher education settings, Part "*Unlocking the Potential of Hybrid Teaching and Learning in Higher Education Through Co-design*" of this book seeks to fulfil the need to better understand the affordances, obstacles, and optimal ways of designing and implementing hybrid teaching and learning that come along such digitalization.

Chapter "Constructing a Hybrid Learning Design Framework: A Group Concept Mapping Study" focuses on constructing a framework for the design of hybrid learning and teaching. This framework is based on a group concept mapping methodology and includes ideas gathered from experts on hybrid learning and a literature review, which includes AI tools. The ideas were systematically structured through sorting and rating and quantitatively analyzed using multidimensional scaling and hierarchical cluster analysis. The resulting principles for organizing and orchestrating hybrid learning, teaching, and assessment; supporting collaboration and connectedness; fostering engagement and motivation; as well as technical prerequirements and teacher and student digital competences are described.

Chapter "Competence-Driven Guidelines for Hybrid Teaching" is grounded in three types of competences that teachers should master to fully develop, manage, and navigate hybrid teaching environments, i.e., generic, contextual, and transformative competences. It also provides guidelines for developing hybrid teaching in higher education, which were defined following a co-design approach, involving teachers, students, and researchers in the educational area. The focus is on empowering higher education teachers to harness the full potential of hybrid teaching, based on a set of guidelines that were co-designed with educators, researchers, and practitioners.

Following this line of thought and given its relevance in today's educational landscape, **Chapter "Enhancing Hybrid Teaching with Collaborative Online International Learning"** delves into a practical approach to enhance hybrid teaching with Collaborative Online International Learning (COIL). Given that COIL refers to the integration of online collaboration between students from different parts of the world, integrating this approach into hybrid teaching provides students with opportunities to interact with peers from diverse cultural backgrounds. This collaborative approach brings an international dimension to the hybrid learning experience, ensuring cross-cultural understanding and expanding the boundaries of traditional education. Hence, this chapter outlines the main pillars of a COIL life cycle, particularly in terms of planning, operationalization, and evaluation, while also acknowledging its key limitations and potential.

Finally, in **Chapter "Co-designing a Micro-Course on Hybrid Learning Competencies for Higher Education Students"** from the students' perspective, the focus is on the learner's motivation as well as cognitive and emotional (self-) regulation. The discussion then moves on to a collaborative development of an MOOC with higher education students, aimed at improving their skills to navigate hybrid learning settings. The approach starts from integrating key competencies from established frameworks and systematically incorporating students' perspectives and shaping the learning experience to their needs. Such collaboration underscores initiatives aimed at understanding and involving students in educational design, with the goal of enhancing the effectiveness of hybrid learning strategies.

Overall, these chapters collectively advocate for innovative co-design approaches for hybrid higher education, emphasizing collaboration, student engagement, and integration of digital technology to create dynamic and effective learning scenarios.

The last part of the book, Part "*Experience-Based Cases of Hybrid Teaching and Learning*", compiles "sample cases" of various scenarios presenting good practices of implementing hybrid learning. The aim of the part is to stimulate the inspiration of the readers to design and develop their own application of hybrid education. The cases are collected from various countries in Europe, including Finland, Estonia, Austria, Belgium, the Netherlands, and Portugal, within a variety of educational contexts. We lay out practical examples using a systematic template to make it more graspable and applicable for the readers.

Chapter "Hybrid Problem-Based Learning with Work-Life Clients: A Context of the Educational Technology Project Course" implements a hybrid learning approach in the Educational Technology Project Course held at the University of Oulu, Finland. The course aimed at cultivating students' collaborative problem-solving skills with real clients from the industry and education sector, expanding the opportunities to work with external clients located in other parts of Finland or even abroad by using hybrid approaches.

Chapter "Collaborative Hybrid Learning in Developing Health Sciences Competence" presents the practical insights into organizing hybrid courses at the Faculty of Medicine in the Health Sciences degree program. Students from different areas of Finland participated in small classes of 10–20 students and large classes of 30–50 students. The chapter provides a structured framework for higher education educators on designing and implementing hybrid teaching in the health science field, focusing on students' core competences and interactions as well as educators' workload and well-being.

Chapter **"Hybrid Teaching and Learning in the Context of Vocational Secondary Education"** provides the case of Waldviertel Business Academy, a collaboration of four vocational secondary schools in Lower Austria. Hybrid teaching allowed the local students to freely choose the topic, such as international logistics, health management and sports, e-business entrepreneurship, and food and wood, enabling them to study it without commuting to another school. Lessons combined various learning activities such as synchronous and asynchronous activities, passive and active learning, and interactions with teachers, peers, and media.

Chapter **"Connecting in All Ways: A Case on Synchronous Hybrid Education Using a Flipped Classroom Approach"** introduces Professor Thomas Elias Cocolios's journey of hybrid teaching in multilocation classrooms at KU Leuven. A flipped classroom approach and well-equipped classrooms effectively supported classroom activities of General Physics III, including lecturing and group learning. The chapter also provides lessons learnt and practical tips from his challenging journey.

Chapter **"A Next Generation Hybrid Classroom: Facilitating Mixed-Modality Collaborative Learning in a Hybrid Context"** showcases the new "hybrid collaborative classroom" at KU Leuven. This innovative classroom was designed based on the deep knowledge and experiences of KU Leuven's hybrid learning implementation and research. The classroom is equipped with multiple screens, cameras, and audio equipment to make a mixed modality (i.e., mixture of in-person and online interactions) collaboration possible.

Chapter **"Shaping Sustainable Urban Landscapes Through Picturebooks: An Interdisciplinary COIL Journey"** presents an interesting international project called "Collaborative Online International Learning project (COIL)." The project connects Padova (Italy), Aveiro (Portugal), and Gdansk (Poland), and the students from these countries learned together sustainable urban landscapes by analyzing the design and landscapes of children's picture book. Hybrid and blended learning approaches nicely supported an intercultural collaborative learning project.

Chapter **"Fostering Tourism and Hospitality Students' Language and Career Skills: A Blended and Hybrid Approach"** explores the use of a hybrid learning approach to address the importance of career skills and enhance students' employability by inviting external HR managers and recruiters. The course also integrated a variety of digital tools and a learning management system to enhance blended learning experiences, providing opportunities for students to practice for creating personal digital portfolios for a future working life. The course contributed to updating the curricular to meet current and future societal and market demands.

Chapter **"Telepresence Robots and Chatbots in Hybrid Teaching and Learning: A Case of Interdisciplinary Focused Environment"** provides an interesting case of hybrid teaching using telepresence robot (TPR) in Tallinn University,

Estonia. The case describes a situation where a teacher appears through TPR, moves around freely, and communicates with the students in the remote classroom using a power of robot. The course also implemented a chatbot to support students 24/7, enhancing the experience of remote and hybrid learning.

Chapter "Experimenting with Hybrid Learning in Distance Education: Experiences, Results, and Lessons Learned" demonstrates a pilot project of implementing hybrid learning as a fully distant educational institution. The pilot included five classes ($N = 90$) of hybrid condition and four classes ($N = 64$) of online condition and compared the students' learning experiences at the end. Especially as the pilot took place during the pandemic time, most of the students appreciated hybrid learning more owing to the social interactions in a (half) physical environment.

Chapter "Hybrid Classroom Scenarios and Academic Teaching Spaces" presents varying example configurations of hybrid learning settings and optimal environment arrangements, including audio, light, and screen settings, to successfully implement hybrid learning. The chapter provides several industrial standards, which are useful in designing a hybrid classroom based on the hybrid classroom project conducted in the Hague, Netherlands.

These examples highlight the diverse possibilities that hybrid teaching and learning can offer. For instance, Chapters "Hybrid Problem-Based Learning with Work-Life Clients: A Context of the Educational Technology Project Course" and "Fostering Tourism and Hospitality Students' Language and Career Skills: A Blended and Hybrid Approach" showcase collaborations with private companies and local schools, helping students develop essential skills for the future workforce. Chapters "Collaborative Hybrid Learning in Developing Health Sciences Competence", "Hybrid Teaching and Learning in the Context of Vocational Secondary Education", and "Connecting in All Ways: A Case on Synchronous Hybrid Education Using a Flipped Classroom Approach" demonstrate how hybrid learning effectively shares teacher resources and expertise, expanding students' access to lectures beyond their local area by connecting classrooms across different regions. Chapter "Shaping Sustainable Urban Landscapes Through Picturebooks: An Interdisciplinary COIL Journey" further extends this idea internationally, illustrating the potential for cross-border collaboration. Chapters "A Next Generation Hybrid Classroom: Facilitating Mixed-Modality Collaborative Learning in a Hybrid Context", "Telepresence Robots and Chatbots in Hybrid Teaching and Learning: A Case of Interdisciplinary Focused Environment", and "Hybrid Classroom Scenarios and Academic Teaching Spaces" introduce advanced technical arrangement to facilitate hybrid learning and enhance both students' and teachers' social presence. Meanwhile, Chapter "Experimenting with Hybrid Learning in Distance Education: Experiences, Results, and Lessons Learned" highlights a key insight—although online courses offer convenience in today's fast-paced world, people generally prefer hybrid learning over fully remote formats due to the increased interactivity with peers and instructors.

Finally, **Chapter Toward an Integrated Understanding of Designing for Hybrid Learning and Teaching** synthesizes the preceding chapters and reflects on the need for conceptual understanding, diverse stakeholder involvement, and practical implementation from a micro-ecological perspective on learning to design to support the design of effective hybrid learning scenarios. Addressing the rapidly changing landscape in higher education, the chapter concludes with future directions for this emerging field, highlighting the importance of conceptual clarity and more experimental, evidence-based research. Overall, the book provides insight into the strategies for enhancing social presence of teachers and learners, managing cognitive load, promoting self-regulated learning skills, and addressing emotional well-being in hybrid educational scenarios. These theoretical aspects are reflected and discussed in real-world cases. The provided examples illustrate the flexibility and inclusivity of hybrid learning, demonstrating its ability to foster a dynamic and engaging teaching and learning environment. As mentioned in the beginning, our focus has been to seek and promote effective pedagogy in hybrid teaching, rather than addressing technological aspects. This is because the psychological mechanisms of human learning may remain the same while technology rapidly changes. In the future, hybrid learning experience might be upgraded with cutting-edge AI technology and extended reality (XR). The boundary or conceptualization of physical and virtual spaces might become increasingly blurred in a metaverse environment. However, we believe that the core principles of learning will remain the same—the value of social presence, interactions, regulation of learning, and pedagogical options to support these elements will be important in future hybrid teaching and learning. Therefore, the book is designed to support readers in designing and applying hybrid leaning activities in their unique contexts regardless of the available technology and classroom settings. We hope that this book inspires readers to view hybrid teaching and learning not just as a response to emergencies, but also as a valuable and forward-thinking approach to the future of education.

References

Gil, E., Mor, Y., Dimitriadis, Y., & Köppe, C. (2022). *Hybrid learning spaces*. Springer.

Hyb-IT-up. (n.d.). What is Hybrid Learning? https://hybitup-project.eu/about/

Oulu, Finland — Azusa Nakata
Aveiro, Portugal — Ana Balula
Saarbrücken, Germany — Paulo J. M. Santos
Oulu, Finland — Hanna Järvenoja
Aveiro, Portugal — António Moreira
Saarbrücken, Germany — Armin Weinberger

Acknowledgements

Our sincere appreciation goes to Professor Annelies Raes for her generous contribution to this book. Her expertise in hybrid learning and her insightful discussion enriched our understanding, strengthened the arguments, and enhanced coherence across the chapters.

We warmly thank all the chapter authors for the collaborative effort. It has been a privilege to work with scholars beyond the project consortium and to get new insight into hybrid learning across diverse educational, cultural, and institutional contexts.

We are grateful to the reviewers of the book chapters for their invaluable feedback and insights. Their constructive comments significantly improved the quality of the contributions, and we appreciate the time and expertise they devoted to the process.

Finally, the editing of this book has been supported by Finnish National Agency within Erasmus+ Key Action 2, Cooperation Partnerships in Higher Education project "Upgrading higher education teachers' and students' hybrid learning competences—Hyb-IT-up!" (No. 2022-1-FI01-KA220-HED-000086605). We are deeply thankful for this support.

Reviewers (alphabetical order) Aaron Peltoniemi (University of Jyväskylä, Finland)

Andreas Gegenfurtner (University of Augsburg, Germany)
Andreas Korbach (Saarland University, Germany)
Anni Silvola (University of Oulu, Finland)
Cecília Guerra (Universidade do Porto, Portugal)
Diogo Casanova (Universidade Aberta, Portugal)
Franziska Perels (Saarland University, Germany)
Giedrė Valūnaitė Oleškevičienė (Mykolas Romeris University, Lithuania)
Isabel Huet (Universidade Aberta, Portugal)

Joni Lämsä (University of Oulu, Finland)
Kati Mäenpää (Oulu University of Applied Science, Finland)
Pantelis Papadopoulos (University of Twente, Netherlands)
Riikka Tumelius (University of Oulu, Finland)
Rita Costa (University of Aveiro, Portugal)
Sandra Vieira Vasconcelos (Polytechnic of Porto, Portugal)
Sara Ahola (University of Oulu, Finland)
Sarah Malone (Saarland University, Germany)
Sari Pramila-Savukoski (University of Oulu, Finland)
Sebastian Strauß (Ruhr University Bochum, Germany)
Tomohiro Nagashima (Saarland University, Germany)

Editing Assistant Niklas Heikkala (University of Oulu, Finland)

Contents

Experience-Based Cases of Hybrid Teaching and Learning

Discussant

Annelies Raes is an Assistant Professor in Educational Technology at KU Leuven's Centre of Instructional Psychology and Technology, Belgium. Her research agenda comprises two overarching and interconnected topics, namely, (a) the changing role of teachers in an AI-driven world, and (b) synchronous hybrid education. Her research on synchronous hybrid learning environments examines how to effectively combine in-person and remote learning in real-time classroom settings, which has become particularly relevant as educational institutions increasingly adopt hybrid learning models.

Finally, Chapter "Toward an Integrated Understanding of Designing for Hybrid Learning and Teaching" synthesizes the preceding chapters and reflects on the need for conceptual understanding, diverse stakeholder involvement, and practical implementation from a micro-ecological perspective on learning to design to support the design of effective hybrid learning scenarios. Addressing the rapidly changing landscape in higher education, the chapter concludes with future directions for this emerging field, highlighting the importance of conceptual clarity and more experimental, evidence-based research.

About the Editors

Azusa Nakata (ORCID: 0000-0002-2845-3920) is a Project Manager in the Learning and Educational Technology (LET) Research Lab at the University of Oulu and a Coordinator of the Hyb-IT-up project. She has worked on multiple EU projects focusing on the design and implementation of pedagogical approach using digital tools to enhance distance, hybrid, and technology-enhanced learning. Her research focuses on students' negotiation and group regulation processes, exploring their influence on the socio-emotional climate and effectiveness of online collaborative learning environments.

Ana Balula is an Associate Professor (with habilitation) at the University of Aveiro, with expertise in education with a focus on pedagogy and educational technology. Her main research interests include e-assessment, e-teaching evaluation, and integration of digital technologies in education. She is an integrated member of the Research Centre on Didactics and Technology in the Education of Trainers (CIDTFF) and the Laboratory of Digital Contents of the Department of Education and Psychology of the University of Aveiro.

Paulo J. M. Santos holds a master's degree from the Department of EduTech at Saarland University, where he investigated the impact of information sources on attitudes in debates over controversial topics. His research employs mixed-methods approaches to understand how individuals construct arguments and learn, with a particular focus on perspective strategies that support attitudinal changes and learning.

Armin Weinberger is a Full Professor and founder of the Department of EduTech at Saarland University, Germany. His main research areas are educational technology and technology-enhanced and computer-supported collaborative learning. He investigates collaboration scripts, awareness tools, and conversational AI agents facilitating joint attention, transactivity, attitudinal changes, and knowledge convergence in argumentative knowledge construction.

Hanna Järvenoja is a Full Professor and co-leader of the LET Lab at the University of Oulu, Finland. Her research focuses on self-regulated learning, particularly in collaborative learning contexts. She is internationally recognized for her work on the role of motivation and emotions in socially shared regulation of learning and has also contributed to advancing process-oriented methods for studying regulation in collaborative settings. Currently, she leads research projects funded by Finnish Science Foundation and Horizon Europe, being a board member of the University of Oulu's Hybrid Intelligence research program.

António Moreira holds a PhD in Didactics of Foreign Languages (University of Aveiro). His research interests encompass cognitive flexibility in hypertexts and communities of practice. He founded and coordinated the Nónio Século-XXI Local Competence Centre and directed the Digital Content Laboratory at the University of Aveiro, serving as Deputy Coordinator of the Research Centre on Didactics and Technology in the Education of Trainers (CIDTFF), focusing on innovative initiatives in the field of education.

Contributors

Sara Ahola Learning and Educational Technology Research Lab (LET), Faculty of Education and Psychology, University of Oulu, Oulu, Finland

Ishari Amarasinghe National Education Lab AI (NOLAI), Radboud University, Nijmegen, the Netherlands

Universitat Pompeu Fabra, Barcelona, Spain

Ana Balula Águeda School of Technology and Management, CIDTFF, University of Aveiro, Aveiro, Portugal

Małgorzata Cackowska Faculty of Social Sciences, University of Gdańsk, Gdańsk, Poland

Susana Caixinha University of Aveiro, Aveiro, Portugal

Marnie Campagnaro Department of Philosophy, Sociology, Pedagogy and Applied Psychology, University of Padova, Padova, Italy

Thomas Elias Cocolios Department of Physics and Astronomy, Institute for Nuclear and Radiation Physics, KU Leuven, Leuven, Belgium

Yannis Dimitriadis School of Computer Engineering, Universidad de Valladolid, Valladolid, Spain

Vincent Engelen Continuing Medical Education, DeusExMedica, Lanaken, Belgium

Olga Firssova Faculty of Educational Science, Open University of the Netherlands, Heerlen, Netherlands

Marta Fortunato CIDTFF (Centro de Investigação em Didática e Tecnologia na Formação de Formadores), University of Aveiro, Aveiro, Portugal

Sylvia Grommen Tutorial Services, Educational Development and Quality Care, Faculty of Science, KU Leuven, Leuven, Belgium

Cecília Guerra CIDTFF (Centro de Investigação em Didática e Tecnologia na Formação de Formadores), University of Aveiro, Aveiro, Portugal

Peter ten Hacken Faculty of Management Sciences, Open University of the Netherlands, Heerlen, Netherlands

Lubna Hakami Department of Engineering, Universitat Pompeu Fabra, Barcelona, Spain

Maartje Henderikx Faculty of Educational Science, Open University of the Netherlands, Heerlen, Netherlands

Davinia Hernández-Leo Department of Engineering, Universitat Pompeu Fabra, Barcelona, Spain

Hanna Järvenoja Learning and Educational Technology Research Lab (LET), Faculty of Education and Psychology, University of Oulu, Oulu, Finland

Tine Keulemans Centre of Instructional Psychology and Technology, Faculty of Psychology and Educational Sciences, KU Leuven, Leuven, Belgium

Juuso Kojo Faculty of Education and Psychology, University of Oulu, Oulu, Finland

Karel Kreijns Faculty of Educational Sciences, Open Universiteit, Heerlen, The Netherlands

Heli-Maria Kuivila Faculty of Medicine, University of Oulu, Oulu, Finland

Äli Leijen Institute of Education, University of Tartu, Tartu, Estonia

Tobias Ley Center for Digitalization in Lifelong Learning, University for Continuing Education Krems, Krems, Austria

Center for Educational Technology, Tallinn University, Tallinn, Estonia

Maria João Loureiro CIDTFF (Centro de Investigação em Didática e Tecnologia na Formação de Formadores), University of Aveiro, Aveiro, Portugal

Kristiina Mänty Faculty of Education and Psychology, University of Oulu, Oulu, Finland

Kristina Mikkonen Faculty of Medicine, University of Oulu, Oulu, Finland

Alejandra Martínez Monés School of Computer Engineering, Universidad de Valladolid, Valladolid, Spain

António Moreira CIDTFF (Centro de Investigação em Didática e Tecnologia na Formação de Formadores), University of Aveiro, Aveiro, Portugal

Azusa Nakata Learning and Educational Technology Research Lab (LET), Faculty of Education and Psychology, University of Oulu, Oulu, Finland

Femke Nijland Faculty of Educational Science, Open University of the Netherlands, Heerlen, Netherlands

Alejandro Ortega-Arranz School of Computer Engineering, Universidad de Valladolid, Valladolid, Spain

Margus Pedaste Institute of Education, University of Tartu, Tartu, Estonia

Gerti Pishtari Center for Digitalization in Lifelong Learning, University for Continuing Education Krems, Krems, Austria

Frederik Van de plas KU Leuven Learning Lab, KU Leuven, Leuven, Belgium

Sari Pramila-Savukoski Faculty of Medicine, University of Oulu, Oulu, Finland

Northern Well-being and Services, Lapland University of Applied Sciences, Rovaniemi, Finland

Annelies Raes Centre of Instructional Psychology and Technology, Faculty of Psychology and Educational Sciences, KU Leuven, Leuven, Belgium

Ana Margarida Ramos Department of Languages and Cultures, University of Aveiro, Aveiro, Portugal

Blanca Ruiz-del-Pino Edutech Department, Saarland University, Saarbrücken, Germany

Katrin Saks Institute of Education, University of Tartu, Tartu, Estonia

Paulo J. M. Santos Department of Educational Technology, Saarland University, Saarbrücken, Germany

Slavi Stoyanov Open University of the Netherlands, Heerlen, the Netherlands

Rita Tavares CIDTFF (Centro de Investigação em Didática e Tecnologia na Formação de Formadores), University of Aveiro, Aveiro, Portugal

Tiina Törmänen Faculty of Education and Psychology, University of Oulu, Oulu, Finland

Sandra Vieira Vasconcelos UNIAG, ESHT, Polytechnic of Porto, Vila do Conde, Portugal

CIDTFF – Research Centre on Didactics and Technology in the Education of Trainers, University of Aveiro, Aveiro, Portugal

Sirje Virkus School of Digital Technology, Tallinn University, Tallinn, Estonia

Marlene Wagner Center for Digitalization in Lifelong Learning, University for Continuing Education Krems, Krems, Austria

Armin Weinberger Department of Educational Technology, Saarland University, Saarbrücken, Germany

Conceptual Pillars of Hybrid Teaching and Learning in Higher Education

A Social Perspective on Hybrid Learning

Karel Kreijns, Paulo J. M. Santos, and Armin Weinberger

1 Introduction

Prior to the internet, all education was delivered in-person except for distance education that relied on written correspondence communication between teacher and student (Moore & Kearsley, 1996). The advent of the internet made it possible to introduce the online learning mode, predominantly adopted by distance education only to depart from correspondence communication (Moore et al. 2011) and by higher education (HE) institutions that offer MOOCs (Kim, 2016). Other digital delivery forms of education were probed such as blended, and hybrid learning. However, the recent Covid-19 pandemic forced all educational institutions to a rapid shift to hybrid and online learning modes, revealing their benefits but also eliciting a number of issues, one of them is associated with the lack of social presence. Today, blended, hybrid, and fully online learning modalities have become firmly established within the educational landscape.

In the *blended learning mode*, students experience a mix of face-to-face and online learning activities that are typically conducted separately. Thus, students attend physical classes for certain learning tasks while other tasks or coursework are done online. In contrast, the *hybrid learning mode* is a learning situation where both remote and in-person students are mixed when they attend classes, participate in discussions and collaborate on projects together. Typically, remote students live close enough to the educational institution, which allows them to easily switch between on-site and remote participation as needed or preferred (Park et al., 2019).

K. Kreijns (✉)
Faculty Educational Sciences, Open Universiteit, Heerlen, the Netherlands
e-mail: karel.kreijns@ou.nl

P. J. M. Santos · A. Weinberger
Department of Educational Technology, Saarland University, Saarbrücken, Germany

A. Nakata et al. (eds.), *Hyb-IT-up!*,
https://doi.org/10.1007/978-3-031-99743-3_1

Hybrid learning is characterized by real-time, synchronous teaching and learning activities, with video conferencing tools serving as the primary means of connecting remote and in-person students. In contrast, in fully *online learning mode* both teachers and students are remote. While some remote students might live close to the educational institution, the more common case is that they reside far away, possibly in different countries and time zones. In online learning, the teaching and learning activities take place both real-time and asynchronously. While it might appear that the various digital learning modes—in-person, blended, hybrid, and fully online—are distinct, they share several features. For instance, all modes can utilize Learning Management Systems (LMS), such as Moodle, which facilitate distribution of course materials, assessments, and serve as communication hubs for students and teachers, organizing teaching materials and communication. Regarding student location, hybrid learning is not exclusively for those nearby. Both hybrid and fully online modes can accommodate students regardless of distance. Depending on the specific learning mode, not all features of the LMS are necessary or will be utilized. For instance, in-person learning might not require any of the LMS's communication tools. Fully online learning, in contrast, typically uses nearly every component of the LMS, especially the various communication and collaboration tools it offers.

Interest in hybrid learning among primary and secondary schools and HE institutions began to grow after the post-pandemic period. During the COVID-19 pandemic, these educational institutions were forced to adopt online learning because of the lock down (Crawford et al., 2020). While fully online learning offered several operational benefits, the most crucial during the pandemic was its capacity to continue education for many students. However, it also revealed psychological downsides, such as social isolation, boredom, and loneliness (Arslan, 2021; Elmer et al., 2020; Wang et al., 2020). It's important to note that these disadvantages were not solely due to online learning but were exacerbated by the overall pandemic situation, including lockdowns and social distancing measures that drastically reduced opportunities for social interaction both in and outside of school, and the closure of places like theatres, cinemas, museums, and festivals. In the post-pandemic period, as lockdowns and social distancing were lifted, other operational advantages of fully online learning became more apparent; among them are its flexibility in regard to where students choose to be (relaxation of place) (Leinonen & Mäkelä, 2022), when students want to study (relaxation of time) (Leinonen & Mäkelä, 2022) and its accessibility for students with issues such as health concerns (Klunder et al., 2022), special needs (Rachmawati et al., 2022), or being geographically isolated preventing them from in-person learning (Bell et al., 2022) (equity and inclusion). Yet, there was still the issue that online learning may cause feelings of social isolation and detachment from staff, faculty and peers (Algarni & Burd, 2015). The hybrid learning mode would alleviate these kinds of shortcomings of fully online learning.

However, despite its benefits, hybrid learning presents challenges, including limited social interaction within hybrid classes, uneven attention from teachers and in-class students to remote students, and a lack of connectedness between in-person and remote students. Indeed, Peterson and Arnold (2015) found that face-to-face and online students felt less connected to online students and face-to-face students noted less social interaction with the remote students. Huang et al. (2017) reported that remote students felt physically separated from the on-site class and subsequently felt excluded from this class.

Several researchers have hinted that the underlying cause of is in the direction of the lack of the social presence of the involved teacher and students (Cunningham, 2014; Nguyen, 2022; Peterson & Arnold, 2015). Social presence is the perception that the other persons appear to be 'real', as though no communication tools are mediating the interaction, making these other persons to be in proximity rather than at a distance. A more detailed discussion of social presence theory will be provided below. Miller et al. (2021) mentioned research suggesting synchronous online classes may reduce the perception of 'distance' via increased social presence (p. 202). A recent study on the relationship between social presence and hybrid learning revealed that "[e]nhancing social presence in synchronous hybrid classrooms and improving the usability of the technology used can [...] be seen as important steps for maximizing its impact" (Wagner et al., 2023, p. 446). The question, however, arises of how to increase social presence. Zydney et al. (2019), for instance, questioned how video technologies can be effective in maximizing the social presence of remote students (p. 131). Additionally, the question is whether there are other avenues beyond technology to increase social presence.

This specific learning situation imposed by the hybrid learning setting requires a pedagogy that considers its unique characteristics, such as its dependency on technology-mediated communication to connect remote students with in-person students and the teacher (see also this book, chapter "Constructing a Hybrid Learning Design Framework: A Group Concept Mapping Study"). Given the above discussion, such pedagogy must also build on and foster social presence of teachers and students.

2 Configurations of Hybrid Learning Settings

Hybrid learning situations vary in their configuration. For example, in one configuration, the teacher and some students are in the classroom while individual remote students are joining using a video conference software package such as the one built in Microsoft Teams or a standalone one such as Zoom. A big screen is used to display the Microsoft Teams screen; the screen can either be placed in front of the classroom (Fig. 1a) or at the back (Fig. 1b). Raes et al. (2020) referred to this configuration as the Hybrid Virtual Classroom (HVC) thereby following Butz and Stupnisky (2016) and Hastie et al. (2010).

Fig. 1 (**a**) Big screens in front of the classroom. (Picture was AI generated using Midjourney). (**b**) Big screens at the back of the classroom. (Picture was AI generated using Midjourney)

In another configuration, the teacher and students are distributed across different remote locations. Some students may share the same location. Video screens are used to connect remote locations (Fig. 2a and b). Raes et al. (2020) referred to this configuration as the Remote Virtual Classroom (RVC) thereby following Szeto and Cheng (2014).

Fig. 2 (**a**) Connecting remote locations. The teacher is at her desk. (Picture was AI generated using Midjourney). (**b**) Connecting remote locations. The teacher is in the classroom. (Picture was AI generated using Midjourney)

The two examples provided are appropriate for classes, lectures, and presentations but not for group learning where groups have to be formed. Subsequently, we may differentiate between HVC group learning and RVC group learning. In HVC and RVC group learning video conferencing tools are needed where the video streams are displayed on the computer screens of in-person and remote students (Fig. 3a, b). Very well-known are the breakout rooms that can be created in, for instance, MS Teams.

Of course, many other configurations are possible.

Fig. 3 (**a**) HVC group learning where each student has his/her own laptop/desktop. The picture displays only the in-person students; remote members connect from their homes. (Picture was AI generated using Midjourney). (**b**) RVC group learning. The picture shows only one collaborative group. Remote members are at the same location. (Picture was AI generated using Midjourney)

3 Challenges

The hybrid learning mode, as discussed above, helps mitigate some of the drawbacks of fully online learning, such as feelings of social isolation, detachment, and loneliness regarding peer students and staff. It maintains certain operational benefits, such as enabling remote students to participate, thereby promoting equity and inclusion (Rachmawati et al., 2022) and providing the flexibility to choose between attending in person or remotely (Bower et al., 2015). Beyond these operational advantages, hybrid learning also offers several educational advantages. These include enhanced learning quality through the integration of external expertise and a broader range of viewpoints, ensuring continuity by supporting uninterrupted studies in the face of challenges such as illness or relocation. Additionally, hybrid learning adapts to varied student needs with diverse instructional methods and timely interactions, and it builds technology proficiency that prepares students for future careers in a tech-driven world (see further: Fabian et al., 2024; Raes et al., 2020). However, hybrid learning is not without its own challenges. Indeed, we may distinguish between pedagogical, social, and technological challenges.

3.1 Pedagogical Challenges

One important pedagogical challenge is related to the fact that fully in-person learning has undeniable educational benefits when it comes to the social interaction that is much easier to perform than in fully online learning mode (Sprecher & Hampton, 2017) or in hybrid learning mode (Raes et al., 2020). Social interaction is needed for learning transactions and making connections with others. However, in the case of in classroom activities in RVC, the social interaction tends to be confined to the distinct locations with limited interaction between locations. For classroom activities in HVC, the social interaction is primarily centered around the teacher's location, with minimal engagement from remote students. Thus, despite all the communication and collaboration tools made available by the LMS or by the videoconferencing system there is no guarantee that they will be used and if so, whether productive social interaction will arise either in real-time or asynchronously (Kreijns et al., 2023). For example, Raes (2022) reported that for HVC, teachers revealed that "although it was indicated that students could ask questions using the chat, interaction was nearly non-existent" (p. 153). Another issue is that in both RVC and HVC settings, teacher attention and social interaction are usually predominantly focused on in-class students rather than remote participants.

In the context of group work and peer interactions, other issues regarding social interaction may arise making it challenging. For RVC group learning, it may lead to the formation of subgroups. For instance, when the group members are split into two locations, members at each location tend to work together with low attention for remote members. Subsequently, impressions of remote group members and the productivity of them will be negatively affected (cf. Storck & Sproull, 1995). Furthermore, in hybrid learning—especially in HVC—it is common for some remote students to turn off their cameras and audio during class (Castelli & Sarvary,

2021). This results in black tiles on the screen, sometimes displaying only the students' names or a picture (a photo or cartoon). This situation creates the impression that these remote students are not interested in the classroom activities and frustrates the teacher, who receives no feedback on whether these students are paying attention to her or him (Toth et al., 2024).

3.2 Social Challenges

We already mentioned hybrid learning is mitigating some of the drawbacks of fully online learning that relates to the social domain (i.e., isolation, detachment, and loneliness), which means that these drawbacks are not fully removed as they return as feelings of distance and loss of connectedness between in-person students and those who are remote (Cunningham, 2014). Remote students often find it difficult to feel fully integrated into the classroom community because of the physical separation and limited opportunities for spontaneous interactions with their peers and the teacher. In-person students might also perceive remote classmates as less accessible or engaged, leading to reduced collaboration and communication. Research by Butz and Stupnisky (2016) showed that online students report significantly lower levels of relatedness compared to their on-campus peers, and students from both groups feel more capable of developing connections with peers from their own attendance mode. This social divide can hinder the formation of a cohesive learning community, which is essential for effective learning and student satisfaction.

3.3 Technology Challenges

Technological challenges include setting up large presentation screens, connecting them to computers and setup boxes, managing poor internet connections, handling crashes of the video conferencing software, solving malfunctioning cameras, taking care of audio issues, solving software problems and device driver issues (see also: Ramsey et al., 2016; Zydney et al., 2019). These challenges often result in delayed starts for classes or lectures, reducing the available teaching and learning time. While technological challenges may be tackled by either a technical assistant who is available for the duration of the hybrid learning class (Lakhal et al., 2020; Ramsey et al., 2016) or by training the teacher in technical skills (Bower et al., 2015), it remains a source of unpredictable troubles.

4 Social Presence

Social Presence Theory (SPT) is a theory about the social psychological effects of a communication between two or more persons when that communication is happening via technological tools that vary in the number of channels offering different modalities of communication; for instance, text-based communication versus desktop video conferencing that offers visual and audio communication. SPT was devised by Short et al. (1976) to study how interpersonal relationships establish or sustain during a real-time communication episode and how these affect the social influence communication partners exert on each other. They found that the degree to which communication partners were perceived as 'real' persons was central in this all; they designated this perception as social presence. Short et al. saw media attributes as solely determining the degree of perceived social presence. They, therefore, could rank different media according to their degree of social presence and found video conferencing as the medium that produced the highest perception of social presence, followed by audio and telephone. SPT was adopted and further developed by educational researchers to study online behavior of groups involved in group work (Gunawardena, 1995; Tu & McIsaac, 2002). In contrast to Short et al. (1976), however, these educational researchers saw social contextual factors as more important determinants of the degree of social presence rather than media attributes. Thus, in their view, the topic of conversation, the degree of interactivity, and way of conversating were more important in the determination of social presence than media attributes. As for today, quite a number of SPTs exist that differ in the definition of social presence, its antecedents, and how it is measured (see for an overview, Richardson et al., 2017; Kreijns et al., 2022). Table 1 shows six mainstream SPTs that can be identified from the literature (Kreijns et al., 2022).

One popular definition of social presence is formulated by Garrison (2009) who defined it as "the ability of participants to identify with the community (e.g., course or study), communicate purposefully in a trusting environment, and develop interpersonal relationships by way of projecting their individual personalities" (p. 352). Most social presence researchers adhere to this definition. Another definition of social presence is put forward by Kreijns et al. (2022) is "the psychological phenomenon of perceiving other persons in technology mediated communication as 'real' and with whom one can connect" (p. 1). Being 'real' here does not relate to being tangible or visually 'real' (although this certainly may strongly help) but rather relates to being psychologically 'real'. In essence, their definition aligns to what Short et al. (1976) meant with their definition "degree of salience of the other person in the interaction" (p. 65).

This prompts the question of whether the degree of social presence is determined solely by telecommunication technology, or whether teachers and students can establish different degrees of social presence through different communication styles and behaviors. While computer-mediated communication has significantly impacted social presence and played a role in the development of social presence theories, social presence is a psychological concept that can be cultivated through multiple means. These include, apart from technological setups and software, also the specific behaviors and communication strategies employed by teachers and students (Aragon, 2003; Lowenthal et al., 2017). This line of thought is represented in the second mainstream of social presence theories in Table 1.

Although other social presence researchers may see social presence as realness of the other person, they—at the same—time may present interpretations to this realness that, to a greater or lesser extent, have little to do with being 'real'. For example, Sung and Mayer (2012) interpreted realness as "the subjective feeling of being connected and together with others during computer mediated communication" (p. 1739). However, Kreijns et al. (2022) pointed out that this connection is due to social presence as being 'real' thereby following Short et al. (1976) who stated that the consequence of social presence is "the salience of the interpersonal relationships", connection is an indicator of interpersonal relationships. We will delve more in depth into what we understand about psychological 'realness' when we arrive at the section Suggestions for improving social presence. For this chapter, it is important to be aware of the different SPTs to rightly interpret the various results that were found in empirical research using a particular SPT. Note that this chapter follows the definition of Kreijns et al. (2022) and uses insights from the comprehensive model of social presence (Kreijns et al., 2024) that is at the basis of the fifth mainstream of social presence theories in Table 1.

In short, the comprehensive model of social presence is very much concerned about the antecedents of social presence and suggests three other theories that augment the space of possible other antecedents beyond media attributes and social contextual factors. The first is Social Information Processing (SIP) Theory (Walther, 1992, 1993, 1996); the second is Construal Level Theory (CLT) (Trope et al., 2007; Trope & Liberman, 2010), and the third is telepresence theory (Steuer, 1992). SIP theory posits that the more remote persons hold individuating impressions of each other, the more the communication becomes personal (i.e., involved persons know each other well and therefore the communication is more informal, casual, and relaxed) rather than impersonal (involved persons are complete strangers and the communication is more formal using appropriate vocabulary and social norms, and avoiding personal topics). The theory further posits that accumulation of messages during multiple communications over time adds to the impression making them more individuating; this process is designated as impression formation. Individuating impressions of remote people make them more 'real' which may contribute to the degree of social presence of these remote people. SIP theory also encompasses the

Table 1 The six mainstreams of social presence theories

	Social presence					
Mainstreams SPTs)	*First* (1976)	*Second* (1995)	*Third* (1999)	*Fourth* (2015)	*Fifth* (2024)	*Sixth* (2005)
Definition emphasizes:	SP as being 'real'	SP as being 'real'	SP as an ability	SP as a critical literacy	SP as being 'real'	SP as a shared social identity
Antecedent:						
Media attributes of the communicating tools	++	+			++	+
Social contextual factors		++	++	++	++	
• Individual factors					+	
• Task factor/topic of communication		+			+	
• Communication style	+	+			+	
SIDE theory (Spears & Lea, 1994)						++
Social information processing theory + hyperpersonal effect (SIP; Walther, 1992, 1993, 1996)					++	
Construal level theory (CLT; Trope et al., 2007; Trope & Liberman, 2010)					+	
Telepresence theory (Steuer, 1992; Waterworth, 2015)					++	
Developed by:	Short et al. (1976)	Gunawardena (1995)	Community of Inquiry (CoI)—Garrison et al. (2000)	Social Presence Model (SPM)—Whiteside & Dickers (2016)	Kreijns et al. (2024)	Rogers and Lea (2005)
Proponents:	Arsenault (2022)	Tu (2000); Zhao et al. (2014)	Garrison and Arbaugh (2007); Saadatmand et al. (2017)			

++ = strongly stresses the antecedent, + = considers the antecedent, □ = does not consider the antecedent process of impression management, whereby a person makes strategic choices about what information they present to others in order to be perceived in the way she or he wants to be perceived. Persons who do so control how they craft their messages and manage their online behaviors. CLT, the second theory, is a general theory that considers the reciprocal relationship between psychological distance and construal. Construals pertain to persons, objects, and events. Psychological distance refers to how close or far away persons, objects, and events are from an individual's direct experience. It is affected by objective distances, which can be temporal (time-related), spatial (space-related), social (interpersonal-related), or hypothetical (likelihood-related). When focusing on people, there are several aspects that make a difference to psychological distance and, thus, to social presence:

- when someone is meeting a person the other day or next year.
- whether this person is living in the same street or lives overseas.
- when someone finds a person more similar in terms of culture, age, hobbies etcetera than when this person is dissimilar.
- when there is ample opportunity to meet the person or that this will never happen.

In these examples, the first implies a small psychological distance whereas the last implies a big psychological distance. As said above, a construal refers to the mental representation or interpretation of persons, objects, and events. The psychological distance to them affects how abstractly or concretely they are construed. If the psychological distance is far, abstract construals will be the result. Abstract construals are generalized, and decontextualized representations; hence they are high level construals. In contrast, if the psychological distance is close, concrete construals will be the result. They are detailed, and context-specific representations; hence they are low level construals. When focusing on people, a construal can be equivalated to the impression of the other person; a concrete construal is the individuating impression, and an abstract construal is related to a stereotypical impression. The third theory, telepresence theory, is about "the experience of presence in an environment by means of communication medium" (Steuer, 1992, p. 6). It is defined as "the psychological phenomenon in which, to a certain extent, in mediated communication one perceives being "present" in another place, which can be mentally constructed, a physical remote place mediated by a computer, or a computer-generated 3D virtual environment" (Kreijns et al., 2024). It is quite possible that the other place is void of people, such as a desert or a planet in the universe. Telepresence can be seen as the counterpart of social presence in that telepresence is the experience of the transportation of the self to there, where 'there' is the other place whereas social presence is the experience of the transportation of other persons to 'here', where 'here' is the place where the self is. It is hypothesized that the two presences are reinforcing each other on the condition that, of course, people are present at the other place. Figure 4 shows a visual representation of the comprehensive model of social presence.

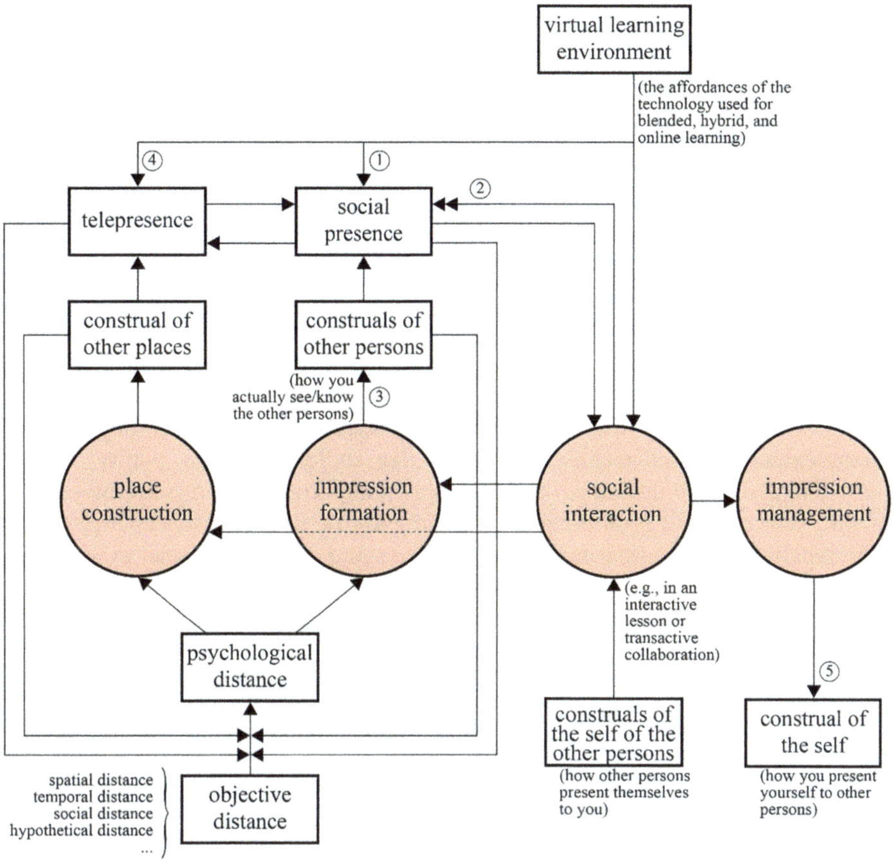

Fig. 4 Visual representation of the comprehensive model of social presence. Numbers in the figure are explained in the section Suggestions for improving social presence. (Figure is taken from Kreijns et al., 2024, and adapted)

5 Suggestions for Improving Social Presence

Interestingly, hybrid learning researchers not knowledgeable about social presence theory (and telepresence theory), did formulate recommendations for increasing engagement and social interaction of remote students with the on-site class and for reducing feelings of disconnections that are fully in line with general recommendations of how to increase the degree of social presence.

Raes (2022) referred to some of these researchers (p. 144). For instance, she pointed to Weitze et al. (2013) who concluded that within hybrid classes the loss of visual and audio cues negatively affects the learning and teaching experience. She, therefore, cited research of Bower et al. (2015) who suggested that remote students should perceive the same audio quality as students who are in-person because the audio component was found to be decisive for success. She also cited research of Irvine et al. (2013) who found that hybrid tools mimicking face-to-face delivery can help students maintain closer connection with peers. Based on their findings, Raes (2022) concluded that audio and video quality is needed when designing a hybrid learning setting. This conclusion, in fact, addressed one factor that affects social presence, namely media attributes (see Table 1). Raes (2022) also cited research of Heilporn et al. (2021) who advised to mitigate for perceived distancing effects that teachers should ask questions throughout the lecture and be attentive to student responses irrespective whether they are in-person or remote.

Yet it should be avoided that remote students will get too much attention in question-and-answer sessions at the cost of in-class students (Szeto & Cheng, 2014). This highlights that fostering social presence in hybrid learning environments extends beyond technical elements like audio and video quality. Teacher behaviors and communication strategies play a important role in reducing feelings of disconnection and promoting a stronger sense of social presence (Fig. 4, path '2'). Apart from this, sharing personal stories and experiences can significantly humanize the virtual classroom. As Aragon (2003) points out, self-disclosure by teachers allows students to perceive them as 'real' individuals, creating a sense of authenticity in their interactions (Fig. 4, path '5'). Similarly, Lowenthal and Snelson (2017; see also Kreijns et al., 2013) argued that live, synchronous video meetings provide opportunities for both teachers and students to feel more connected, not just through structured discussions but also via informal, yet purposeful, off-topic conversations. These conversations, when used strategically, help build rapport and reduce the sense of isolation often experienced in online learning environments. These suggestions are in line with Gunawardena's (1995) guidelines to establish social presence as part of the social contextual factors. Interestingly, in her study aimed at identifying differences between on-site and remote students, which she interpreted as variations in 'presence', Raes (2022) administered a questionnaire designed to measure remote students' sense of presence in terms of 'feeling like being in the classroom;' thus, essentially assessing their sense of telepresence. This approach focused on affective engagement rather than exploring how a sense of presence might influence feelings of physical separation (Huang et al., 2017) or a sense of distance. Raes (2022) found that remote students felt less sense of presence than those who were on-site and this sense of presence was worse for students who only followed lectures through streaming when compared with remote students who, in addition, could use interactive tools. Furthermore, Szeto and Cheng (2014) reported that remote students "perceived that the interactions were indirect and that they were not physically present in the virtual face-to-face environment" (p. 495) even though the use of multiscreen projections showing the instructor's teaching and on-site students admittedly mitigated their low social presence. In conclusion, when looking at the students' and teachers' responses from the study of Raes (2022) and Szeto and Cheng (2014), the degrees of social presence and telepresence and their interaction take center stage.

To grasp the above recommendations and the below suggestions for increasing social presence, it is crucial to understand the concept of psychological 'realness' and how the degree of it can be influenced using the comprehensive model of social presence. For instance, in the case of holographic technology, where a remote person is projected as a three-dimensional, lifelike form, such a projection can evoke a strong sense of the other person's 'realness' and thus of social presence (Fig. 4, path '1'). This perception is particularly strong when the interaction involves direct communication; that is, when the remote person initiates a conversation with someone who is physically present in the same location. The interaction includes several cues—eye contact, body language, and verbal exchange—that reinforce the perception of presence and 'realness'. In the holographic setting, other factors that also influence the perception of social presence are most likely to play a minor role due to the dominance of the purely visual aspect of the holographic projection. The use of video communication, which also emphasizes the visual aspects of the communication, can therefore lead to similar perceptions as holographic projections. Note that while video typically shows only the faces of participants whereas holographic projections show full body representations, this difference suggests that video communication may result in a weaker perception of social presence in comparison. However, the other factors whose influence were suppressed in the holographic projection may become more important in video communication, so a weaker perception of social presence in video communication is not necessarily true. For example, when all communicators are heavily involved in a debate about a controversial issue such as how to reverse climate change. Thus, when the social interaction is highly transactive, i.e., participants build on each other's reasoning, and emotionally involving, communicator will perceive the others as 'real' (Tu & McIsaac, 2002; see also Fortin & Dholakia, 2005). The same processes will take place for audio-only conferencing and text-based communication where the visual aspect is diminished. Experiences of psychological 'realness' may thus occur to the same extent in less visually immersive communication environments including text-based communication and even—to provide an extreme example—in communication using morse codes. These kinds of effects and shifts in the relevant importance of the various individual factors influencing the degree of social presence has been captured by the comprehensive model of social presence. For instance, knowing each other is one such factor: it makes a difference in perceptions of social presence if individuals already are familiar with each other when communicating (Short et al., 1976). In text-based communication, the use of emoticons and emojis, and paralanguage is affecting social presence (Shuqair et al., 2024). Also, factors as technological skills may influence social presence; if one is busier with the getting the audio right in a video-conferencing system than with the communication itself, the degree of social presence of the other persons may be very low (Tu, 2000).

We now continue with suggestions that help to increase social presence in terms of psychological 'realness', focusing on three areas: pedagogical, social, and technological. The pedagogical aspect highlights how teaching strategies and instructional design can foster social presence in hybrid environments. The social aspect explores methods to build stronger connections and a sense of community between remote and in-person learners. Lastly, the technological aspect addresses how positioning and the use of tools can enhance interaction between remote and in-person participants. We use the term 'suggestions' because there is a lack of research providing solid evidence-based guidelines, as extensive studies on hybrid learning have only recently been conducted following the COVID-19 pandemic. Our suggestions, therefore, stem from research in online settings and from research in (online) group learning (as is reflected in the comprehensive model of social presence).

5.1 Suggestions for a Hybrid Learning Pedagogy

In online group learning environments, for example, psychological 'realness' and thus social presence, can emerge through transactive collaborative processes that take place during the performance of the group task. Transactive collaboration, in which students engage with, challenge, and build upon the reasoning of their peers (Teasley, 1997; Weinberger & Fischer, 2006) encourages deep and meaningful intellectual engagement. This type of engagement goes beyond surface-level participation, making both in-person and remote students feel equally involved and valued. Such interactions allow students to build on one another's ideas, creating a more connected and invested learning community. In addition, they experience a collective sense of progress toward a shared goal. This collaborative dynamic fosters a sense of cohesion in which group members feel emotionally and cognitively connected to each other. The sense of connectedness is further enhanced by positive emotions such as enjoyment and satisfaction that result from the experience of a productive collaboration (Pekrun, 2022). These achievement emotions contribute to a positive group atmosphere in which members respect each other's contributions while remaining critical in a constructive way. The combination of these factors—collaborative success, positive emotions and connectedness—reinforces the perception of others as being 'real', even in an online setting where lean communication media are used (Fig. 4, path '2'). Thus, when teachers arrange a group learning situation either in a HVC or RVC setting (Fig. 3a and b), it is important that the group task is invoking transactive collaboration by carefully designing the group task, for example, by using scripts, that prescribe what steps students need to do (see more about scripting: Fischer et al., 2013; Weinberger et al., 2010).

In general, social presence researchers have found that social interaction among students and their teachers plays a significant role in increasing social presence (Tu & McIsaac, 2002; Wut & Xu, 2021) and vice versa (Tu, 2000; Kreijns et al., 2022). Thus, a hybrid learning pedagogy either for HVC or RVC (Figs. 1a, b and 2a, b) should always include active learning components. Teachers should therefore ensure that their lessons are highly interactive, both for in-class and for remote learners, for example, as suggested above, by asking questions, not forgetting to also address remote students, and be attentive to the students' responses (Heilporn et al., 2021) while avoiding to put more attention to the remote students than to the on-site students (Szeto & Cheng, 2014).

In addition, teachers should strengthen their social presence among remote students. Raes (2022) reports that some teachers therefore prefer livestream teaching to desk teaching because students can see the teacher's whole posture rather than just the face, and because they can use a lot of gestures that don't come across as well when teaching behind a screen (p. 154). Hence, a pedagogy for hybrid learning should stress the role of the teacher.

5.2 Suggestions for the Social Aspects

Hybrid learning environments involve distinct dynamics between in-person and remote students, requiring strategies that encourage a sense of connection among all participants. To facilitate interaction and engagement, approaches that enhance teacher presence, support group collaboration, and provide opportunities for informal social exchanges can be implemented. These strategies aim to create a more integrated learning experience, ensuring that both groups of students can actively participate and feel involved in the classroom community.

Active teacher involvement plays a key role in promoting social presence in hybrid settings. Teachers can engage both in-person and remote students by ensuring that all participants are included in discussions. This can be done through strategies such as real-time questioning, which keeps students from both groups involved in the learning process. Encouraging remote students to keep their cameras on can also help reduce the sense of separation and foster a stronger connection between participants, leading to a more cohesive and inclusive experience (Toth et al., 2024). Providing timely and personalized feedback further supports an environment where students feel acknowledged and engaged.

Collaboration between in-person and remote students is another important aspect to consider. Designing group tasks that promote meaningful collaboration is key to ensuring that students work together effectively. Activities should be structured in ways that encourage mutual dependence, allowing students to build on one another's ideas and knowledge (Yoon & Leem, 2021). Technology can facilitate this process, with tools such as video conferencing platforms and collaborative whiteboards enabling smooth communication and interaction across groups. In addition, encouraging transactivity—where students engage with and expand upon each other's contributions—can lead to more meaningful and in-depth discussions (Vogel et al., 2016).

Creating opportunities for informal social interaction is also beneficial for building relationships and a sense of community. Introducing ice-breaking activities at the beginning of sessions can help students become familiar with one another before formal learning begins (Jiang & Zhang, 2020). Additionally, online spaces, such as discussion forums or chat groups, can provide a platform for students to socialize outside of academic activities, helping to bridge the gap between remote and in-person participants and reducing feelings of isolation.

Engagement in open, positive social exchanges contributes significantly to a sense of connection among students. Teachers and students can share personal stories and experiences to make interactions feel more genuine and human, which helps to foster a stronger sense of community (Aragon, 2003). Such exchanges build trust and mutual respect, creating a more welcoming learning environment. Similarly, the use of humor in communication can help reduce social barriers and create a more comfortable and engaging atmosphere.

5.3 Suggestions for the Technological Aspects

In tackling the issue of remote students feeling physically separated from the teacher and in-class students in HVC and RVC settings and, the other way round, teacher and in-class students feel also a distance from the remote students. From the perspective of the remote students, it seems that the challenge is partly due to the absence of telepresence and the perceived lack of the teachers' and peers' social presence. From the perspective of the teacher and the in-class students, it seems that the social presence of the remote students is low.

It is thus questionable whether the positioning of the screens in front or at the back of the classroom is optimal for achieving social presence of remote students and whether the positioning of the cameras and microphones will give rise to feelings of telepresence by remote students (Figs. 1a, b and 2a, b). The usual case is that camera and microphone are packed in one small housing that is fixed on top of the screen. When remote students are speaking, their voices are heard via the standard loudspeaker's setup of the classroom, which may or may not produce high quality sound. In most cases, Teams or Zoom are used for video-conferencing. If remote students want to react or respond, they must 'raise their hand', which is usually unnoticed by the teacher, especially when the screen is in front of the classroom and the teacher's attention is to the in-class students. Succinctly, here we see that positioning of the equipment and media attributes are playing a crucial role in establishing social presence and telepresence (Fig. 4, path '1' and '4').

6 Conclusion

We are now entering an era where hybrid learning is increasingly prevalent. The full range of possibilities, benefits, and drawbacks has yet to be thoroughly explored to develop a robust pedagogy for this approach. In this chapter, we emphasize that an effective pedagogy for hybrid learning must prioritize both telepresence and social presence, as these are crucial for enhancing the learning experience and maintaining the motivation of both in-person and remote students. This is particularly important in group learning contexts, where the social presence of all group members, whether physically present or remote, is essential for productive interaction and achieving positive learning outcomes.

To strengthen hybrid learning environments, several strategies have been outlined in this chapter. For instance, pedagogical strategies such as real-time questioning, personalized feedback, and the design of transactive group tasks that encourage meaningful collaboration are vital. Social strategies like incorporating informal icebreaker activities and fostering online spaces for casual, non-academic exchanges help build a stronger sense of community. Additionally, technological strategies focused on optimizing audio and video quality, along with the thoughtful positioning of screens and microphones, enhance the feeling of telepresence for remote students.

Taken together, these strategies contribute to creating a more cohesive and socially present hybrid learning environment. However, this exploration is far from definitive, and future research should focus on refining these approaches by further investigating how technology, social modes of interaction, and pedagogical principles can better facilitate social presence, enhancing social and learning outcomes in hybrid settings.

Acknowledgements This research has been funded by Finnish National Agency within Erasmus+ Key Action 2, Cooperation partnerships in higher education (No. 2022-1-FI01-KA220-HED-000086605). The research is conducted in the context of the project "Upgrading higher education teachers' and students' hybrid learning competences" (Hyb-IT-up).

References

Algarni, A., & Burd, L. (2015, October). *Perceptions of students and instructors toward the role of CommEasy in tackling communication and interaction barriers in distance-learning classrooms*. In Frontiers in Education Conference (FIE) (pp. 1–7). IEEE.

Aragon, S. R. (2003). Creating social presence in online environments. *New Directions for Adult and Continuing Education, 2003*(100), 57–68.

Arsenault, A. M. (2022). *Understanding media richness and social presence: Exploring the impacts of media channels on individuals' levels of loneliness, well-being, and belonging* [Master's thesis, University of Montana]. ScholarWorks at University of Montana.

Arslan, G. (2021). Loneliness, college belongingness, subjective vitality, and psychological adjustment during coronavirus pandemic: Development of the college belongingness questionnaire. *Journal of Positive School Psychology, 5*(1), 17–31.

Bell, A., Bartimote, K., Dempsey, N., Mercer-Mapstone, L., Moran, G., & Tognolini, J. (2022). Student and educator perspectives on equity and online work integrated learning. *Australasian Journal of Educational Technology, 38*, 185–200. https://doi.org/10.14742/ajet.7524

Bower, M., Dalgarno, B., Kennedy, G. E., Lee, M. J., & Kenney, J. (2015). Design and implementation factors in blended synchronous learning environments: Outcomes from a cross-case analysis. *Computers & Education, 86*, 1–17.

Butz, N. T., & Stupnisky, R. H. (2016). A mixed methods study of graduate students' self-determined motivation in synchronous hybrid learning environments. *The Internet and Higher Education, 28*, 85–95. https://doi.org/10.1016/j.iheduc.2015.10.003

Castelli, F. R., & Sarvary, M. A. (2021). Why students do not turn on their video cameras during online classes and an equitable and inclusive plan to encourage them to do so. *Ecology and Evolution, 11*(8):3565–3576. https://doi.org/10.1002/ece3.7123

Crawford, J., Butler-Henderson, K., Rudolph, J., Malkawi, B., Glowatz, M., Burton, R., et al. (2020). COVID-19: 20 countries' higher education intra-period digital pedagogy responses. *Journal of Applied Learning & Teaching, 3*(1), 1–20. https://doi.org/10.37074/jalt.2020.3.1.7

Cunningham, U. (2014). Teaching the disembodied: Othering and activity systems in a blended synchronous learning situation. *The International Review of Research in Open and Distributed Learning, 15*(6). https://doi.org/10.19173/irrodl.v15i6.1793

Elmer, T., Mepham, K., & Stadtfeld, C. (2020). Students under lockdown: Comparisons of students' social networks and mental health before and during the COVID-19 crisis in Switzerland. *PLoS One, 15*(7), 1–22. https://doi.org/10.1371/journal.pone.0236337

Fabian, K., Smith, S., & Taylor-Smith, E. (2024). Being in two places at the same time: A future for hybrid learning on student preferences. *TechTrends, 68*, 693–704. https://doi.org/10.1007/s11528-024-00974-x

Fischer, F., Kollar, I., Stegmann, K., & Wecker, C. (2013). Toward a script theory of guidance in computer-supported collaborative learning. *Educational Psychologist, 48*(1), 5666. https://doi.org/10.1080/00461520.2012.748005

Fortin, D. R., & Dholakia, R. R. (2005). Interactivity and vividness effects on social presence and involvement with a web-based advertisement. *Journal of Business Research, 58*(3), 387–396.

Garrison, D. R., & Arbaugh, J. B. (2007). Researching the community of inquiry framework: Review, issues, and future directions. *The Internet and Higher Education, 10*(3), 157–172.

Garrison, D. R., Anderson, T., & Archer, W. (2000). Critical inquiry in a text-based environment: computer conferencing in higher education model. *The Internet and Higher Education, 2*(2–3), 87–105.

Garrison, D. R. (2009). Communities of inquiry in online learning. In P. L. Rogers (Ed.), Encyclopedia of distance learning (2nd ed., pp. 352–355). IGI Global.

Gunawardena, C. N. (1995). Social presence theory and implications for interaction and collaborative learning in computer conferences. *International Journal of Educational Telecommunications, 1*(2&3), 147–166. Retrieved from https://www.learntechlib.org/p/15156/.

Hastie, M., Hung, I. C., Chen, N. S., & Kinshuk. (2010). A blended synchronous learning model for educational international collaboration. *Innovations in Education and Teaching International, 47*(1), 9–24. https://doi.org/10.1080/14703290903525812

Heilporn, G., Lakhal, S., & Bélisle, M. (2021). An examination of teachers' strategies to foster student engagement in blended learning in higher education. *International Journal of Educational Technology in Higher Education, 18*(1), 25. https://doi.org/10.1186/s41239-021-00260-3

Huang, Y., Shu, F., Zhao, C., & Huang, J. (2017). *Investigating and analyzing teaching effect of blended synchronous classroom.* In Proceedings of 6th International Conference of Educational Innovation Through Technology (EITT) (pp. 134–135). The Institute of Electrical and Electronics Engineers. https://doi.org/10.1109/EITT.2017.40

Irvine, V., Code, J., & Richards, L. (2013). Realigning higher education for the 21st-century learner through multi-access learning. *MERLOT Journal of Online Learning and Teaching, 9*(2), 1–15.

Jiang, D., & Zhang, L. J. (2020). Collaborating with 'familiar' strangers in mobile-assisted environments: The effect of socializing activities on learning EFL writing. Computers & Education, 150, 103841. https://doi.org/10.1016/j.compedu.2020.103841

Kim, S.-W. (2016). MOOCs in higher education. In D. Cvetkovic (Ed.), *Virtual learning*. Intech Open. https://doi.org/10.5772/66137

Kreijns, K., Kirschner, P. A., & Vermeulen, M. (2013). Social aspects of CSCL Environments: A research framework. *Educational Psychologist. 48*(4), 229–242. https://doi.org/10.1080/00461520.2012.750225

Klunder, S., Saab, N., & Admiraal, W. (2022). A teacher perspective on using a hybrid virtual classroom for students with a chronic illness in mainstream primary and secondary schools. *Technology, Pedagogy and Education, 31*(4), 493–508. https://doi.org/10.1080/1475939X.2022.2033824

Kreijns, K., Weidlich, J., & Kirschner, P. A. (2023). Pitfalls of social interaction in online group learning. In Z. Yan (Ed.), *Cambridge handbook of cyber behavior* (pp. 588–630). Cambridge University Press.

Kreijns, K., Yau, J., Weidlich, J., & Weinberger, A. (2024). Towards a comprehensive framework of social presence for online, hybrid, and blended learning. *Frontiers in Education, 8*, 1286594. https://doi.org/10.3389/feduc.2023.1286594

Kreijns, K., Xu, K., & Weidlich, J. (2022). Social presence: Conceptualization and measurement. *Educational Psychology Review, 34*(1), 139–170. https://doi.org/10.1007/s10648-021-09623-8. Open Access. Retrieved from https://rdcu.be/cm13N.

Lakhal, S., Mukamurera, J., Bédard, M. E., Heilporn, G., & Chauret, M. (2020). Features fostering academic and social integration in blended synchronous courses. *International Journal of Educational Technology in Higher Education, 17*(5), 1–22.

Leinonen, T., & Mäkelä, T. (2022). *Space and time in hybrid teaching and learning environments: Two cases and design principles.* In M. Dascalu, P. Marti, & F. Pozzi, (Eds.) Proceedings of the 7th Conference on Smart Learning Ecosystems and Regional Development: Polyphonic Construction of Smart Learning Ecosystems (pp. 29–46). Springer. https://doi.org/10.1007/978-981-19-5240-1_3

Lowenthal, P., Dunlap, J., & Snelson, C. (2017). Live synchronous web meetings in asynchronous online courses: Reconceptualizing virtual office hours. *Online Learning, 21*(4), 177–194.

Lowenthal, P. R., & Snelson, C. (2017). In search of a better understanding of social presence: an investigation into how researchers define social presence. *Distance Education, 38*(2), 1–19.

Miller, A. N., Sellnow, D. D., & Strawser, M. G. (2021). Pandemic pedagogy challenges and opportunities: Instruction communication in remote, HyFlex, and BlendFlex courses. *Communication Education, 70*(2), 202–204. https://doi.org/10.1080/03634523.2020.1857418

Moore, M., & Kearsley, G. (1996). *Distance education: A systems view.* Wadsworth.

Moore, J. L., Dean, C. D., & Galyen, K. (2011). E-learning, online learning, and distance learning environments: Are they the same? *Journal of Internet and Higher Education, 14*, 129–135.

Nguyen, P. (2022). *The role of social presence and personality traits on student satisfaction in hybrid education during the Covid-19 pandemic.* Unpublished Master thesis. Tilburg University.

Park, E., Martin, F., & Lambert, R. (2019). Examining predictive factors for student success in a hybrid learning course. *The Quarterly Review of Distance Education, 20*(2), 11–27.

Pekrun, R. (2022). Achievement emotions. In K.-A. Allen, M. J. Furlong, D. Vella-Brodrick, & S. M. Suldo (Eds.), *Handbook of positive psychology in schools: Supporting process and practice* (3rd ed., pp. 319–334). Routledge. https://doi.org/10.4324/9781003013778-25

Peterson, A., & Arnold, B. (2015, March 2–6). *Social presence in synchronous hybrid settings: Being there (symposium contribution).* In D. Rutledge, & D. Slykhuis (Eds.), Proceedings of SITE 2015—Society for Information Technology & Teacher Education International Conference (pp. 211–216). Association for the Advancement of Computing in Education (AACE). Retrieved from https://www.learntechlib.org/p/149991.

Rachmawati, N., Supena, A., Yufiarti, Yarmin, G., & Rudi Casmana, A. (2022). Analysis of hybrid learning for students with learning disabilities in primary schools providing inclusive education. *The Qualitative Report, 27*(10), 185–2201. https://doi.org/10.46743/2160-3715/2022.5432

Ramsey, D., Evans, J., & Levy, M. (2016). Preserving the seminar experience. *Journal of Political Science Education, 12*(3), 256–267. https://doi.org/10.1080/15512169.2015.1077713

Raes, A., Detienne, L., Windey, I., & Depaepe, F. (2020). A systematic literature review on synchronous hybrid learning: Gaps identified. *Learning Environments Research, 23*(3), 269–290.

Raes, A. (2022). Exploring student and teacher experiences in hybrid learning environments: Does presence matter? *Postdigital Science and Education, 4*, 138–159. https://doi.org/10.1007/s42438-021-00274-0

Richardson, J. C., Maeda, Y., Lv, J., & Caskurlu, S. (2017). Social presence in relation to students' satisfaction and learning in the online environment: A meta-analysis. *Computers in Human Behavior, 71*, 402–417. https://doi.org/10.1016/j.chb.2017.02.001
Rogers, P., & Lea, M. (2005). Social presence in distributed group environments: The role of social identity. *Behaviour & Information Technology, 24*(2), 151–158.
Saadatmand, M., Uhlin, L., Hedberg, M., Åbjörnsson, L., & Kvarnström, M. (2017). Examining learners' interaction in an open online course through the community of inquiry framework. *European Journal of Open, Distance and E-Learning, 20*(1), 61–79.
Short, J., Williams, E., & Christie, B. (1976). *The social psychology of telecommunications*. Wiley.
Shuqair, S., Pinto, D. C., Herter, M. M., & Mattila, A. (2024). Emojis as heuristic cues: The multifaceted role of emojis in online service interactions. *Journal of Consumer Behaviour, 23*(4), 1929–1941. https://doi.org/10.1002/cb.2310
Spears, R., & Lea, M. (1994). Panacea or panopticon? The hidden power in computer-mediated communication. *Communication Research, 21*(4), 427–459.
Sprecher, S., & Hampton, A. J. (2017). Liking and other reactions after a get-acquainted interaction: A comparison of continuous face-to-face interaction versus interaction that progresses from text messages to face-to-face. *Communication Quarterly, 65*(3), 333–353. https://doi.org/10.1080/01463373.2016.1256334
Steuer, J. (1992). Defining virtual reality: Dimensions determining telepresence. *Journal of Communication, 42*, 73–93. https://doi.org/10.1111/j.1460-2466.1992.tb00812.x
Storck, J., & Sproull, L. (1995). Through a glass darkly: What do people learn in videoconferences? *Human Communication Research, 22*(2), 197–219. https://doi.org/10.1111/j.1468-2958.1995.tb00366.x
Sung, E., & Mayer, R. E. (2012). Five facets of social presence in online distance education. *Computers in Human Behavior, 28*(5), 1738–1747.
Szeto, E., & Cheng, A. Y. N. (2014). Towards a framework of interactions in a blended synchronous learning environment: What effects are there on students' social presence experience? *Interactive Learning Environments, 24*(3), 487–503. https://doi.org/10.1080/10494820.2014.881391
Teasley, S. D. (1997). Talking about reasoning: How important is the peer in peer collaboration? In *Discourse, tools and reasoning: Essays on situated cognition* (pp. 361–384). Springer.
Toth, G., Tomlins, M., James, T., Bond, K., & Kumar, B. (2024). Is there anybody out there? Educator perception of student social presence and engagement in the zoomosphere. *Open Learning: The Journal of Open and Distance Learning*. Advance online publication. https://doi.org/10.1080/02680513.2024.2322510
Trope, Y., Liberman, N., & Wakslak, C. (2007). Construal levels and psychological distance: Effects on representation, prediction, evaluation, and behavior. *Journal of Consumer Psychology, 17*, 83–95. https://doi.org/10.1016/S1057-7408(07)70013-X
Trope, Y., & Liberman, N. (2010). Construal-level theory of psychological distance. *Psychological Review, 117*(2), 440–463. https://doi.org/10.1037/a0018963
Tu, C. H. (2000). On-line learning migration: From social learning theory to social presence theory in a CMC environment. *Journal of Network and Computer Applications, 23*(1), 27–37.
Tu, C. H., & McIsaac, M. (2002). The relationship of social presence and interaction in online classes. *The American Journal of Distance Education, 16*(3), 131–150.
Vogel, F., Kollar, I., Ufer, S., Reichersdorfer, E., Reiss, K., & Fisher, F. (2016). Developing argumentation skills in mathematics through computer-supported collaborative learning: The role of transactivity. *Instructional Science, 44*(5), 477–500. https://doi.org/10.1007/s11251-016-9380-2
Wagner, M., Pishtari, G., & Ley, T. (2023). Here or there? Differences of on-site and remote students' perceptions of usability, social presence, engagement, and learning in synchronous hybrid classrooms. In: O. Viberg, I. Jivet, P. Muñoz-Merino, M. Perifanou, T. Papathoma (Eds.), *Responsive and sustainable educational futures*. EC-TEL 2023. Lecture Notes in Computer Science, vol 14200. Springer. https://doi.org/10.1007/978-3-031-42682-7_30

Walther, J. B. (1992). Interpersonal effects in computer-mediated interaction: A relational perspective. *Communication Research, 19*(1), 52–90. https://doi.org/10.1177/009365092019001003

Walther, J. B. (1993). Impression development in computer-mediated communication. *Western Journal of Communication, 57*(4), 381–398. https://doi.org/10.1080/10570319309374463

Walther, J. B. (1996). Computer-mediated communication: Impersonal, interpersonal, and hyperpersonal interaction. *Communication Research, 23*, 3–43. https://doi.org/10.1177/009365096023001001

Wang, X., Hegde, S., Son, C., Keller, B., Smith, A., & Sasangohar, F. (2020). Investigating mental health of US college students during the COVID-19 pandemic: Cross-sectional survey study. *Journal of Medical Internet Research, 22*(9), e22817. https://doi.org/10.2196/22817

Weinberger, A., & Fischer, F. (2006). A framework to analyze argumentative knowledge construction in computer-supported collaborative learning. *Computers & Education, 46*(1), 71–95.

Weinberger, A., Stegmann, K., & Fischer, F. (2010). Learning to argue online: Scripted groups surpass individuals (unscripted groups do not). *Computers in Human Behavior, 26*(4), 506–515.

Weitze, C. L., Ørngreen, R., & Levinsen, K. (2013). *The global classroom video conferencing model and first evaluations*. In M. Ciussi, & M. Augier (Eds.), Proceedings of the 12th European Conference on E-Learning: SKEMA Business School, Sophia Antipolis France, 30–31 October 2013 (pp. 503–510). Academic Conferences and Publishing International.

Whiteside, A. L., & Garrett Dickers, A. (2016). Leveraging the social presence model: a decade of research on emotion in online and blended learning. In S. Y. Tettegah & M. P. McGreery (Eds.), Emotions, technology, and learning (pp. 225–241). Elsevier.

Wut, Tm., & Xu, J. (2021). Person-to-person interactions in online classroom settings under the impact of COVID-19: a social presence theory perspective. *Asia Pacific Education Review, 22*, 371–383. https://doi.org/10.1007/s12564-021-09673-1

Yoon, P., & Leem, J. (2021). The influence of social presence in online classes using virtual conferencing: Relationships between group cohesion, group efficacy, and academic performance. Sustainability 2021, 13(4), 1988. https://doi.org/10.3390/su13041988

Zhao, H., Sullivan, K. P., & Mellenius, I. (2014). Participation, interaction and social presence: An exploratory study of collaboration in online peer review groups. *British Journal of Educational Technology, 45*(5), 807–819.

Zydney, J. M., McKimm, P., Lindberg, R., & Schmidt, M. (2019). Here or there instruction: Lessons learned in implementing innovative approaches to blended synchronous learning. *TechTrends, 63*(2), 123–132. https://doi.org/10.1007/s11528-018-0344-z

Teacher Educators' Digital Competence for Hybrid Teaching

Margus Pedaste, Äli Leijen, and Katrin Saks

1 The Need for Operationalising Teacher Educators' Digital Competence

In the European context, experts from several countries have developed DigCompEdu framework (Redecker, 2017) that distinguishes educators' professional competences, pedagogical competences, and learners' competences. The first category, professional competences, is elaborated as professional engagement: organisational communication, professional collaboration, reflective practice, and continuous digital professional development. The second category, pedagogical competences, are operationalised through four competence areas: digital resources, teaching and learning, assessment, and empowering learners. Each of these areas is even further specified through 13 competences, e.g., selecting digital resources, guiding the digital learning process, assessment strategies in digital settings, and accessibility and inclusion in empowering learners. The third category, learners' competence, is specified based on DigComp framework (Vuorikari et al., 2022)—how educators should facilitate learners' digital competence in five areas: information and media literacy, communication, content creation, responsible use, and problem solving. Already, the general description of the DigCompEdu framework reveals how complex the framework is, and yet it does not cover all aspects that should be taken into account in guiding educators to become more competent in not only applying but also in adapting the digital technologies and in designing new solutions—in innovating the learning process. That has led different stakeholders in national and international context towards searching the possibilities for re-conceptualisation of digital competence for educators. One of these attempts is presented in the report

M. Pedaste (✉) · Ä. Leijen · K. Saks
Institute of Education, University of Tartu, Tartu, Estonia
e-mail: margus.pedaste@ut.ee

A. Nakata et al. (eds.), *Hyb-IT-up!*,
https://doi.org/10.1007/978-3-031-99743-3_2

that was presented to the Federal Ministry Republic of Austria Education Science and Research to describe how to support teacher educators' digital competence (see Wagner et al., 2022). This report focused on the frameworks used to support teacher educators' digital competence, methods and learning environments employed to support that competence, and supportive measures used for monitoring digital competence. In this chapter, we depart from this broader review and operationalise further teacher educator' digital competence. In our discussion, we also show how this framework could be applied in the context of hybrid learning.

Our rationale to re-conceptualise the existing frameworks will become clearer if we shortly discuss the conditions and aims in relation to the use of educational technologies in contrast to the already mentioned DigCompEdu framework. In our understanding, this framework concentrates on the use of existing technological tools in the context of learning process but does not bring into the focus, for example, technical competence which might be one reason why many of the teachers might avoid using digital technologies. This does not embrace only technical skills but also attitudes and emotions in using digital technologies. For example, educators might be frustrated if the technology does not work and they do not know how to solve unexpected technical problems. Sometimes educators might feel even ashamed if their students are more fluent users of technology and they lose their control in the classroom. However, even more importantly DigCompEdu framework does not pay sufficient emphasis on the question of why digital technologies should have been used, or even more importantly, why and when these should have been avoided. Without the latter technology might be taken into use rather meaninglessly as it is shown in several studies indicating that mostly, teachers tend to use technology as a substitution for their "traditional" teaching (see Pedaste et al., 2023) and they do not augment, modify or redefine (see Puentedura, 2006) their teaching process in accordance with the affordances of technology and goals of the contemporary learning for future citizens. This has resulted in the situation where, according to the OECD PISA study, several researchers question if technology use should be abandoned at all to reduce students' decline in academic learning outcomes (see Hu & Yu, 2021; Navarro-Martinez & Peña-Acuña, 2022; Petko et al., 2017; Vázquez-Cano et al., 2020). Thus, without the competence to innovate technology and its use for teaching and learning educators' digital competence is not sufficiently operationalised.

Innovation in education could be defined as the systematic creation and implementation of novel, effective processes and solutions for learning, teaching, and management at the level of a system, organization, and class or group (see Maldonado-Mariscal & Alijew, 2023). In the context of educators, it is very important to mention that innovation should be responsible, and research-based. Therefore, it is relevant to apply the framework for responsible research and innovation in analysing the completeness of the frameworks of educators' digital competence. According to a systematic literature review by Burget et al. (2017), responsible research and innovation could be operationalised through six dimensions: inclusion, anticipation, responsiveness, reflexivity, sustainability, and care. According to our interpretation, DigCompEdu mentions inclusion, responsiveness, and reflexivity, but it is not visible how it pays attention to anticipation, sustainability, and care. A digitally competent educator should be able to anticipate what happens if…, or how sustainable technology use is in the long term at personal, societal, and environmental levels. However, most importantly, a competent educator should take a stance towards using or not using technology through the angle of care—when, why and how technology should be used while we care about our environment and limited resources, including energy. At the student level, we should care about our students' mental health in a learning process where their activities are ubiquitously logged and solutions based on learning analytics limit their agency. What is responsible but also ethical use of technology, and how should existing technologies be creatively adapted or new technologies or methodologies designed to empower the learners? A review of the *Handbook of Research on Educational Communications and Technology* showed that the focus in research on using digital technologies has been often mainly on learning subject knowledge and skills but only in a few cases on students' well-being (see Pedaste & Leijen, 2018). If educators cannot consider these aspects in designing a technology-enhanced learning process, then they might not be able to transform the learning process from a traditional technology consumption approach to an innovation that is needed to empower learners and enable their agency. This question is especially relevant in innovating the learning process to design hybrid learning and teaching (see Raes et al., 2020).

Based on the analysis of the leading European framework of educators' digital competence we found that there is some room for improvement in operationalising teacher educators' digital competence for hybrid teaching. Even if the digital competence could be similarly elaborated in several other contexts, this article is guided by the question in the context of hybrid teaching and learning situations. We decided to conduct a literature review to understand the broader view of digital competence frameworks to ensure through reconceptualization of the framework that it would cover not only the pedagogical but also more generic digital competences as well as more advanced sustainable innovation-related competences. More specifically, the guiding research question for our review was "what frameworks have been used to support teacher educators' digital competence, and how could these be used to synthesize a new framework to guide the design of interventions and assessment of educators' digital competence for hybrid teaching?".

2 Procedure of Search, Selection, and Analysis of the Sources

Our guiding research question was approached using a thematic literature review that allows researchers to systematically search and analyse research on one topic to conceptualize it by identifying semantic and latent themes (Braun & Clarke, 2006). Therefore, it is an appropriate method for re-conceptualizing digital competence for educators. We applied the widely used PRISMA guidelines (Moher et al., 2009) to ensure high quality in validity and reliability in the study. We used Google Scholar as a search engine instead of more limited databases indexing high-quality research papers (e.g., EBSCO, Web of Science, ERIC) to increase the chance of finding reports and unpublished analyses (grey literature) that are potentially relevant in re-conceptualisation because the frameworks are often operationalised as policy documents not as research papers. By this approach, we tried to avoid publication bias that has been seen as one of the limitations of review studies. Indeed, a Google Scholar search might reveal too many responses and some of them might have a low quality. Therefore, we carefully checked the quality of all the found materials and included in the analysis only the first 30 materials meeting the quality check and inclusion criteria.

The set of keywords used in the search was developed based on an analysis of the first 30 sources found in the initial search. The final search query included three elements with relevant synonyms or close terms: (1) framework OR standards OR guidelines OR roadmap OR model*, (2) teacher educator OR teaching staff OR university teacher*, (3) digital competence OR information and communication technolog* OR digital literacy OR media literacy OR IT literacy OR information literacy OR technological literacy OR visual literacy OR digital skills.

The search was conducted on January 16, 2022, and it resulted in 20,600 materials. Two inclusion criteria were used in selecting the materials for further analysis: (1) the focus of the study is on teacher educators or the ones focusing otherwise on adult learners; (2) the article is relevant because it introduces a framework(s) to support teacher educators' digital competence or digital competence in general so that the description is applicable in defining digital competence for educators.

The search results were analysed one by one in the sequence they appeared in the Google Scholar search based on relevance. In each case, first the title was assessed against inclusion and exclusion criteria. If it was not possible to make a decision, then the abstract was analysed, and if this was not sufficient, then the full text was analysed (this included the analysis of quality). With this approach, we analysed 88 articles until it was possible to select 30 relevant and high-quality materials for the final analysis. Many of the materials were based on literature reviews, and the studies cited in these were also analysed in the case of relevance.

The selected materials were critically reviewed by the first author of the chapter to extract all semantic themes and discussed with the second author of the chapter to define the latent themes and make notes that would be relevant to achieving the goals of the study. Further, the notes were connected in the discussions of all authors to develop the re-conceptualized framework of digital competence for educators.

3 Frameworks to Describe Teacher Educators' Digital Competence

The systematic search conducted in this study revealed a few literature reviews focusing on the concept of digital competence. For example, Gallardo-Echenique et al. (2015) conducted a review that was not focused on teacher educators or any other specific target group; however, the findings of this study were indeed considered to be applicable for framing the digital competence of teacher educators. For example, the authors discussed, based on Martin (2009), that digital competence might have been seen only as a precursor of digital literacy.

Gallardo-Echenique et al. (2015) also identified several other concepts used to describe digital competence in a way that is relevant for figuring out the digital competence framework of teacher educators. The analysis revealed a number of terms that are overlapping in describing digital competence: Computer literacy (Hawkins & Paris, 1997; National Research Council (NRC), 1999), Computer fluency (National Research Council (NRC), 1999), ICT Literacy (International ICT Literacy Panel, 2002), Information literacy (Bundy, 2004; Jackman & Jones, 2002), Media literacy (Aufderheide & Firestone, 1993), Media and information literacy (Wilson et al., 2011), 21st century literacy (New Media Consortium (NMC), 2005), e-literacy (Martin, 2003), e-skills (European e-Skills Forum, 2010), Digital literacy (Eshet-Alkalai, 2004, 2009; Gilster, 1997; Jones-Kavalier & Flannigan, 2006; Martin & Grudziecki, 2006). Finally, several studies also used the concept of digital competence (Calvani et al., 2008; Calvani et al., 2010; Ferrari, 2012; European Parliament, and Council of the European Union, 2006). However, it appeared that digital literacy and digital competence were by far the most often used terms to define the concept of our interest. Ferrari et al. (2012) saw that there were two main approaches to these concepts—one is the digital literacy and digital competence as a sum of various literacies mentioned earlier, and the other one sees digital competence as a new literacy that goes beyond the sum of different literacies. In their conclusion Gallardo-Echenique et al. (2015) found that digital competence and literacy were closely related and often synonymous concepts but not identical. The unclarity of difference between these two concepts has been reported in more recent studies as well. For example, in the literature review conducted by Spante et al. (2018). They also concluded that the use of these terms might depend on traditions in different regions—in the US and the UK, digital literacy has been more often used, while in other parts of Europe, digital competence seems to be more dominant. In the context of our study, the difference is not so relevant and all studies focusing on either digital competence or digital literacy, or other related literacies seem to be valuable in achieving the goal to re-conceptualise the framework of teacher educators' digital competence.

Interestingly, the more recent studies have not broadened the scope of the concept. The literature review made by Spante et al. (2018) in the context of higher education studies provided us with a very similar result as in the review of Gallardo-Echenique et al. (2015). Only one term could be added to the pool of terms to define the dimensions for a framework of digital competence—this is "values" in addition to knowledge and skills (as abilities) and attitudes (OECD, 2005). In their review, Ilomäki et al. (2016) concluded that in addition to abilities, technical competence and motivation could describe how one participates and commits in the digital culture; however, technical competence could be seen as an ability to use technologies, and motivation could be seen as a construct closely linked to attitudes and values revealed in the review made by Gallardo-Echenique et al. (2015). An earlier review by Ilomäki et al. (2011) did not add new dimensions for defining the concept in our study.

By analysing the definitions of the concepts identified in three reviews conducted by Gallardo-Echenique et al. (2015), Spante et al. (2018), and Ilomäki et al. (2016), we saw some more general and many more specific terms to describe dimensions of digital competence for teacher educators. Exclusively, all definitions pointed to different abilities or skills needed in a digital society. In addition, awareness (Calvani et al., 2008; Ferrari, 2012; Martin, 2003; Martin & Grudziecki, 2006), understanding (Aufderheide & Firestone, 1993; Bundy, 2004; Martin, 2003), attitudes and values (Ferrari, 2012; Martin & Grudziecki, 2006; OECD, 2005), motivation (Ilomäki et al., 2016), confidence (Martin, 2003), socio-emotional aspects (Eshet-Alkalai, 2004; Ferrari, 2012; Martin & Grudziecki, 2006), evaluation (International ICT Literacy Panel, 2002; Martin, 2003), reflection on one's own competence (Ferrari, 2012; Jackman & Jones, 2002; Martin, 2003; Martin & Grudziecki, 2006), socialisation (Eshet-Alkalai, 2004; Ferrari, 2012; Martin & Grudziecki, 2006; European Parliament, and Council of the European Union, 2006), adaptation to professional context (Martin, 2003; New Media Consortium (NMC), 2005), ethics (Calvani et al., 2010; Ferrari, 2012) and responsible use of technology (Calvani et al., 2008; Ferrari, 2012) were mentioned. According to our understanding, these elements might be relevant in every domain. In contrast, Hall et al. (2014) also specified some aspects of digital competence (or, in their work digital literacy) that are specific to the teacher educators. Their definition was "Digital Literacy refers to the skills, attitudes and knowledge required by educators to support learning in a digitally rich world. To be digitally literate, educators must be able to utilise technology to enhance and transform classroom practices, and to enrich their own professional development and identity. The digitally literate educator will be able to think critically about why, how and when technology supplements learning and teaching" (Hall et al., 2014, p. 47).

One of the very few frameworks focusing on educators, according to our literature review, was the DigCompEdu framework (Redecker, 2017) that has been developed and widely used in the European context. This framework was already analysed as the starting point for our study (see the introductory section). In short, it is mainly focusing on pedagogical competences and professional engagement in the context of educators' work (see Fig. 1). However, it does not include generic or transformative competence, for example, on the questions of what technical abilities or attitudes educators need to have to be digitally competent or how to use critical approach on choosing when and for what to use or not to use educational technologies so that these would increase equity and inclusion.

Another framework focusing specifically on educators' digital competence has been proposed by Krumsvik (2011), who claimed that for teachers and teacher educators, the pedagogical framework of digital competence should be more complex than in the context of everyday use of digital tools. He specified four dimensions of competency—adoption, adaptation, appropriation, and innovation—and presented these with gradual complexity (see Fig. 2). The more complex dimensions will be in focus through better self-awareness, and their application leads towards higher

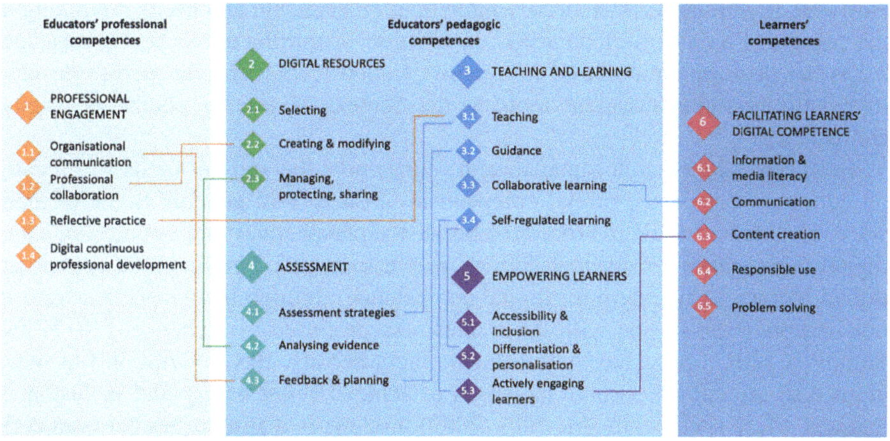

Fig. 1 The DigCompEdu framework (Redecker, 2017)

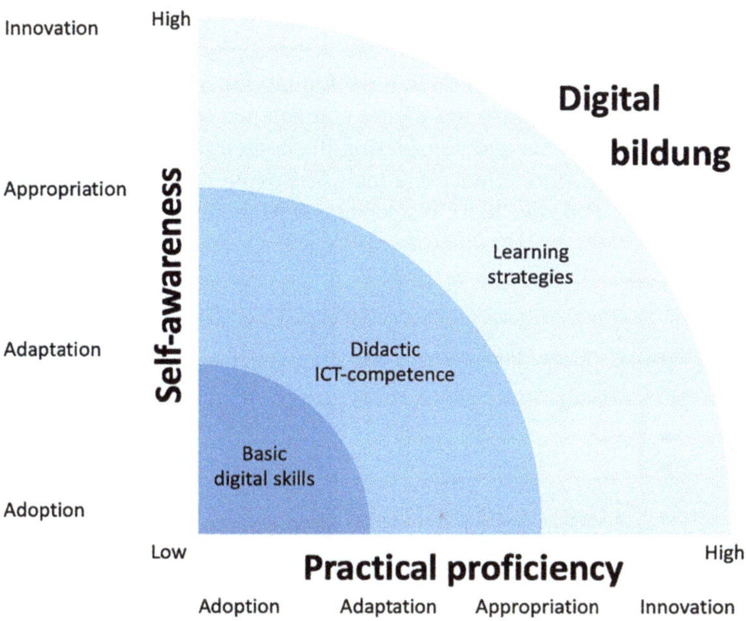

Fig. 2 Model of digital competence for teachers and teacher educators (Krumsvik, 2011, p. 45)

practical proficiency. At the lowest level, the focus is on basic digital skills and adoption or adaptation. Appropriation is related to didactic competence (how to apply digital tools in the context of a specific subject), and innovation is related to learning strategies (how to innovate learning using digital tools) that leads to "digital Bildung" (how digitalization of society influences identity development in the digital era) as the fourth core component of digital competence of educators.

However, this framework is already more than 10 years old and needs rethinking in the context of today's societal needs. In addition, according to our best knowledge, it has not been operationalised in a more detailed level that is needed to develop interventions and assessment tools in the context of teacher educators' digital competence.

In addition, our search found several frameworks that did not focus specifically on educators but on the digital competence of citizens in general. Some of them were valuable to discuss in order to elaborate the perspectives for re-conceptualising digital competence for teacher educators. For example, Martin (2009) described digital literacy (a synonym for digital competence) through five levels that were in our interpretation in line with the frameworks proposed by Redecker (2017) and Krumsvik (2011) but gave some valuable input because this description was more aligned to the contemporary challenges to achieve better equity and inclusion of learners. More specifically, Martin's (2009) framework distinguishes between digital competence as the generic level, digital usage as the contextual competence, and digital transformation as the highest level of digital competence. The latter means creative innovation in the application of technologies and modifying existing practices or even designing new ones (Fig. 3).

In conclusion, it is evident that there are a few digital competence frameworks focusing on educators, and even these have limitations in some aspects; therefore, we decided to re-conceptualise the digital competence of teacher educators based on the existing frameworks and considering the contemporary societal challenges; for example, how to support equity and inclusion using new technology and digital worlds (see Nelis & Pedaste, 2020; Warschauer & Matuchniak, 2010 for overviews).

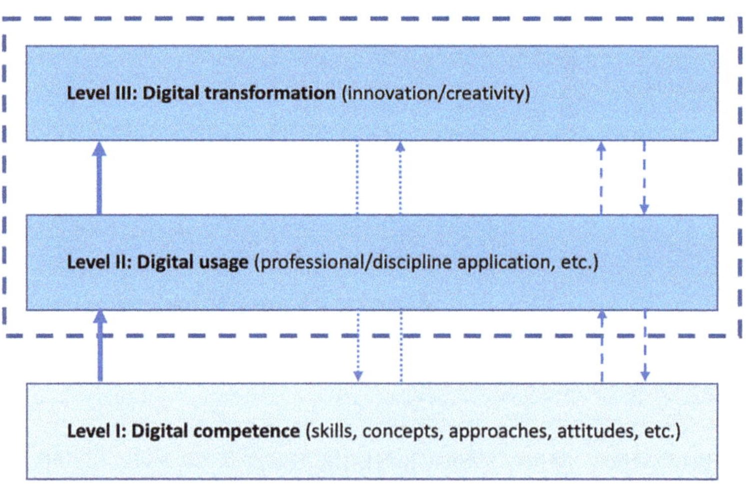

Fig. 3 Levels of Digital literacy (Martin, 2009, p. 8.)

4 New Framework of Teacher Educators' Digital Competence

The iterative analysis of the selected articles led us to design a framework that consists in accordance with the framework presented by Krumsvik (2011) of three levels of digital competence: generic competence, contextual competence, and transformative competence (see also Wagner et al., 2022 for the initial analysis of the findings). However, these levels were further described considering all materials selected in the literature review. Generic competence is not specific to a professional context but describes abilities, knowledge, beliefs, values, emotions, and motivation in using digital technologies in general. Contextual competence describes the competence needed to adapt digital competence in an educational context individually or in collaboration with other educators through self-regulation or co-regulation. Transformative competence describes an even higher level of digital competence—innovation by creative adaptation of digital technologies in an ethical and responsible way (see Fig. 4).

More specifically, we specified how eight different competence areas could describe teacher educators' digital competence within the three levels:

(A) Generic competence

A1. Abilities: (1) what is the teacher educators' proficiency in using digital technologies needed in the learning process?, (2) what is the teacher educators' proficiency in using digital technologies for assessment?

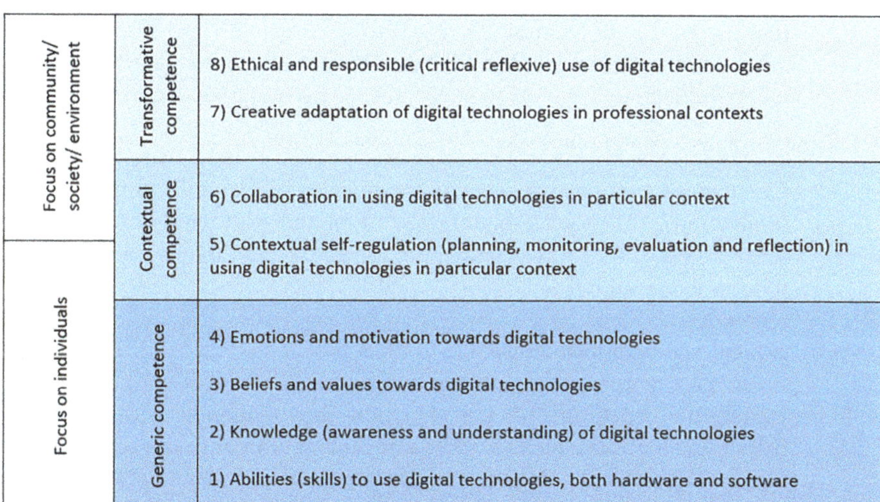

Fig. 4 Framework for teacher educators' digital competence

A2. Knowledge: (1) how well do the teacher educators know how to use digital technologies to promote learning?
A3. Beliefs and values: (1) what is the teacher educators' self-efficacy in using digital technologies?, (2) how confident are the teacher educators in creating digital learning environments?, (3) how do the teacher educators value digital technologies for learning?, (4) what are teacher educators' attitudes toward the use of digital technologies (ease of use, usefulness, and compatibility of technologies) in learning and teaching?
A4. Emotions and motivation: (1) what emotions do teacher educators associate with use of digital technologies?, (2) how motivated are teacher educators to use digital technologies?

(B) Contextual competence

B1. Self-regulation: (1) what is the teacher educators' vision in using digital technologies for learning and teaching?, (2) to what extent (how often and with what quality) do the teacher educators support learners' use of digital technologies?, (3) to what extent (how often and with what quality) do the teacher educators support implementing effective instructional strategies for using digital technologies in learning?, (4) to what extent (how often) do the teacher educators express supportive pedagogical beliefs about the use of digital technologies?
B2. Collaboration: (1) to what extent (how often and with what quality) do the teacher educators learn from each other and mentor others in the contextual use of digital technologies?, (2) to what extent (how often and with what quality) do the teacher educators collaborate with others in contextual use of digital technologies?, (3) to what extent (how often and with what quality) do the teacher educators reflect on contextual use of digital technologies?

(C) Transformative competence

C1. Creative adaptation: (1) what is the teacher educators' competence for innovation?, (2) to what extent (how often and with what quality) do the teacher educators express and apply innovative and inquiry-oriented attitude in using digital technologies and are, therefore also role models for learners?
C2. Ethical and responsible use: (1) to what extent are teacher educators role models for learners in the ethical and responsible use of digital technologies in their teaching?, (2) to what extent (how often and with what quality) do the teacher educators raise ethical and critical issues related to the use of digital technologies and learning environments (e.g., in using social media)?

The most innovative of the identified focus areas is, in our view, the ethical and responsible use under the transformative competence. This is a dimension that highlights the need for a more critical view of the decisions to use or not to use and how to use technology in the teaching and learning process. Among other aspects, there should also be considered how the technology use would empower the teachers in achieving their short-term or, even more importantly, long-term goals, e.g., equity and inclusion. For example, the use of hybrid learning could increase equity and inclusion for some learners but decrease it for others. Therefore, educators need to be aware of how technology could enable learners to learn and experience more equity and inclusion, but there is also a need to understand the challenges some learners might face in the new unfamiliar contexts that might cause significant uncertainty.

In operationalising the re-conceptualised framework in the context of hybrid teaching and learning, we can say that the possibility to benefit from hybrid learning starts from the abilities of both teachers and students. They have to know how to prepare the equipment and software, e.g., video, audio, online shared learning environments, MS Teams or Zoom, to have a good learning experience. They should also have knowledge of solving common technical problems that might appear in the learning process. In addition, they should have positive beliefs and values for taking the risks that are always there in using technologies. However, they should also have the ability to regulate their emotions and motivation which might change fast in the hybrid learning contexts that often cause uncertainty. At the level of contextual competence, the teachers should be able to formulate their vision for applying hybrid learning. This should be based on the understanding of how different pedagogical methods and strategies might have an effect on the quality of the learning process and outcomes, both in the case of onsite and online learners who have to work in collaborative learning communities. In collaboration with other teachers they should be able to share those visions in order to build a shared vision, a common understanding that could be applied consistently in different classes. Finally, at the level of transformative competence, teachers should be able to adapt the existing methods to new conditions and need to keep in mind different aspects of ethical and responsible use of technology to ensure alignment with shared long-term goals, e.g., sustainability-related ones. For example, it might not be reasonable to record every hybrid learning session or to turn off cameras if these are not needed to ensure better engagement.

5 Conclusions

Our study re-conceptualized digital competence for educators by highlighting transformative competence in addition to generic competence and contextual competence. Conceptualizing transformative competence is significant because it describes how educators have a key role not only in teaching learners how to use technologies but also in how to innovate creatively in adapting technologies to the needs of the learners. However, even more important is that we described the focus area of ethical and responsible use of technology. This should lead educators towards increased equity and inclusion in the classroom. Indeed, further studies should focus on analysing how educators' practices are in line with the framework and how to assess these practices for identifying needs for improvement and for designing relevant professional development programs.

References

Aufderheide, P., & Firestone, C. M. (1993). *Media literacy: A report of the national leadership conference on media literacy*. Aspen Institute.
Braun, V., & Clarke, V. (2006). Using thematic analysis in psychology. *Qualitative Research in Psychology, 3*(2), 77–101.
Bundy, A. (2004). *Australian and New Zealand information literacy framework: Principles, standards and practice* (2nd ed.). Australian and New Zealand Institute for Information Literacy (ANZIIL).
Burget, M., Bardone, E., & Pedaste, M. (2017). Definitions and conceptual dimensions of responsible research and innovation: A literature review. *Science and Engineering Ethics, 23*, 1–19.
Calvani, A., Cartelli, A., Fini, A., & Ranieri, M. (2008). Models and instruments for assessing digital competence at school. *Journal of E-Learning and Knowledge Society, 4*(3), 183–193.
Calvani, A., Fini, A., & Ranieri, M. (2010). Digital competence in K-12: Theoretical models, assessment tools and empirical research. *Anàlisi, 40*, 157–171.
Eshet-Alkalai, Y. (2004). Digital literacy: A conceptual framework for survival skills in the digital era. *Journal of Educational Multimedia and Hypermedia, 13*(1), 93–106.
Eshet-Alkalai, Y. (2009). Real-time thinking in the digital era. In M. Khosrow-Pour (Ed.), *Encyclopedia of information science and technology* (2nd ed., pp. 3219–3223). Information Resources Management Association. https://doi.org/10.4018/978-1-60566-026-4.ch514
European e-Skills Forum. (2010). E-skills for Europe: Towards 2010 and beyond (Synthesis report). European Commission.
European Parliament, & Council of the European Union. (2006). Recommendation of the European Parliament and of the Council of 18 December 2006 on key competences for lifelong learning (2006/962/EC). *Official Journal of the European Union, L394*, 10–18.
Ferrari, A. (2012). *Digital competence in practice: An analysis of frameworks*. Publications Office of the European Union. https://doi.org/10.2791/82116
Ferrari, A., Punie, Y., & Redecker, C. (2012). *Understanding digital competence in the 21st century: An analysis of current frameworks*. In A. Ravenscroft, S. Lindstaedt, C. Delgado Kloos, & D. Hernández-Leo (Eds.), Proceedings 7th European Conference on Technology Enhanced Learning, EC-TEL2012 (pp. 79–92). Springer.
Gallardo-Echenique, E. E., de Oliveira, J. M., Marqués-Molias, L., Esteve-Mon, F., Wang, Y., & Baker, R. (2015). Digital competence in the knowledge society. *MERLOT Journal of Online Learning and Teaching, 11*(1), 1–16.
Gilster, P. (1997). *Digital literacy*. Wiley.
Hall, R., Atkins, L., & Fraser, J. (2014). Defining a self-evaluation digital literacy framework for secondary educators: The DigiLit Leicester project.
Hawkins, R., & Paris, A. E. (1997). Computer literacy and computer use among college students: Differences in Black and White. *The Journal of Negro Education, 66*(2), 147–158.
Hu, J., & Yu, R. (2021). The effects of ICT-based social media on adolescents' digital reading performance: A longitudinal study of PISA 2009, PISA 2012, PISA 2015 and PISA 2018. *Computers & Education, 175*, 104342.
Ilomäki, L., Kantosalo, A., & Lakkala, M. (2011). What is digital competence?. Linked portal.
Ilomäki, L., Paavola, S., Lakkala, M., & Kantosalo, A. (2016). Digital competence—An emergent boundary concept for policy and educational research. *Education and Information Technologies, 21*(3), 655–679.

International ICT Literacy Panel. (2002). *Digital transformation: A framework for ICT literacy.* A report of the international ICT literacy panel. Educational testing (p. 42). Educational Testing Service.

Jackman, L. W., & Jones, L. D. (2002). Information literacy, information communications technologies (ICT) and the nongovernmental organization (NGO)/non profit world: As practitioner's perspective. In *Information literacy meeting of experts.* UNESCO, the U.S National Commission on Libraries and Information Science, and the National Forum on Information Literacy.

Jones-Kavalier, B. B. R., & Flannigan, S. L. (2006). Connecting the digital dots: Literacy of the 21st century. *Educase Quartely, 2*, 8–10.

Krumsvik, R. J. (2011). Digital competence in the Norwegian teacher education and schools. *Högre utbildning, 1*(1), 39–51.

Maldonado-Mariscal, K., & Alijew, I. (2023). Social innovation and educational innovation: A qualitative review of innovation's evolution. *Innovation: The European Journal of Social Science Research, 36*(3), 381–406.

Martin, A. (2003). Essential E-literacy. *Connected, 9*, 22–24.

Martin, A. (2009). Digital literacy for the third age: Sustaining identity in an uncertain world. *eLearning Papers, 12*, 1–15.

Martin, A., & Grudziecki, J. (2006). DigEuLit: Concepts and tools for digital literacy development. *ITALICS, Innovation in Teaching and Learning in Information and Computer Sciences, 5*(4), 249–267.

Moher, D., Liberati, A., Tetzlaff, J., Altman, D. G., & PRISMA Group. (2009). Preferred reporting items for systematic reviews and meta-analyses: The PRISMA statement. *Annals of Internal Medicine, 151*(4), 264–269.

National Research Council (NRC). (1999). *Being fluent with information technology.* National Academy Press.

Navarro-Martinez, O., & Peña-Acuña, B. (2022). Technology usage and academic performance in the Pisa 2018 report. *Journal of New Approaches in Educational Research, 11*(1), 130–145.

Nelis, P., & Pedaste, M. (2020). A model of inclusive education in the context of Estonian preschool education: A systematic literature review. *Eesti Haridusteaduste Ajakiri. Estonian Journal of Education, 8*(2), 138–163.

New Media Consortium (NMC). (2005). *A global imperative: The report of the 21st century literacy summit.* NMC.

OECD (2005). Definition and selection of key competencies. Executive Summary (online resource). OECD Publishing.

Pedaste, M., & Leijen, Ä. (2018, July). *How can advanced technologies support the contemporary learning approach?* In 2018 IEEE 18th International Conference on Advanced Learning Technologies (ICALT) (pp. 21–23). IEEE.

Pedaste, M., Raave, D. K., & Baucal, A. (2023). Digitaalsete õppematerjalide kasutamise efekt õpilaste õpitulemustele. DigiEfekti projekti lõppraport. Tartu Ülikool.

Petko, D., Cantieni, A., & Prasse, D. (2017). Perceived quality of educational technology matters: A secondary analysis of students' ICT use, ICT-related attitudes, and PISA 2012 test scores. *Journal of Educational Computing Research, 54*(8), 1070–1091.

Puentedura, R. (2006). *Transformation, technology, and education.* Retrieved from http://hippasus.com/resources/tte/puentedura_tte.pdf.

Raes, A., Detienne, L., Windey, I., & Depaepe, F. (2020). A systematic literature review on synchronous hybrid learning: Gaps identified. *Learning Environments Research, 23*(3), 269–290. https://doi.org/10.1007/s10984-019-09303-z

Redecker, C. (2017). *European framework for the digital competence of educators.* Publications Office of the European Union. https://doi.org/10.2760/159770

Spante, M., Hashemi, S. S., Lundin, M., & Algers, A. (2018). Digital competence and digital literacy in higher education research: Systematic review of concept use. *Cogent Education, 5*(1), 1519143.

Vázquez-Cano, E., Gómez-Galán, J., Infante-Moro, A., & López-Meneses, E. (2020). Incidence of a non-sustainability use of technology on students' reading performance in Pisa. *Sustainability, 12*(2), 749.

Vuorikari, R., Kluzer, S., & Punie, Y. (2022). *DigComp 2.2: The digital competence framework for citizens, EUR 31006 EN*. Publications Office of the European Union. isbn:978-92-76-48882-8. https://doi.org/10.2760/115376, JRC128415. Retrieved from https://data.europa.eu/doi/10.2760/115376.

Wagner, M., Kammerer, L., Ley, T., Helm, C., McGarr, O., Pedaste, M., Leijen, Ä., Rillo, K., & Veskimägi, D. (2022). International good practices on digital skills development of teacher educators. *Report for Deliverable 3*. Federal Ministry Republic of Austria Education, Science and Research.

Warschauer, M., & Matuchniak, T. (2010). New technology and digital worlds: Analyzing evidence of equity in access, use, and outcomes. *Review of Research in Education, 34*(1), 179–225.

Wilson, C., Grizzle, A., Tuazon, R., Akyempong, K., & Cheung, C.-K. (2011). *Media and information literacy curriculum for teachers*. UNESCO.

Regulation of Learning: Cognition, Motivation and Emotion

Sara Ahola, Azusa Nakata, and Hanna Järvenoja

1 Introduction

Self-regulated learning—or SRL—has become the hallmark for skillful learning in the twenty-first century. The necessity of being able to regulate one's own learning processes is underlined by the emerging era of intelligent technologies and hybrid learning and working scenarios which make learning and studying, especially in higher education, more diverse. Moreover, it is not only the individual learner that remains at the center of current learning experiences across various arenas, but more profoundly the interactive dynamic that is the people around us. The need to work together to tackle local and global challenges without definitive answers has brought forward the need to figure out how people learn, adapt, and solve problems together. Thus, skillful learning in the twenty-first century is also characterized by the skill to regulate learning collaboratively and in harmony with others.

This chapter highlights the role of SRL skills in hybrid learning. Grounded in SRL theories, the chapter begins by defining the theoretical foundations for the different types of regulation—self-regulation, co-regulation, and socially shared regulation—emphasizing their significance in managing learning across physical, social, and virtual settings from both cognitive and motivational-emotional perspectives. It then moves on to discuss the importance of SRL in digital landscapes and pose a challenge to consider how different hybrid settings shape the need for regulated learning. Practical examples are provided to illustrate the relevance of regulation from the cognitive, motivational and emotional perspectives in hybrid scenarios with different types of demands they place on the learner. The chapter concludes with implications for teaching by providing insights into optimizing regulated

S. Ahola (✉) · A. Nakata · H. Järvenoja
Learning and Educational Technology Research Lab (LET), Faculty of Education and Psychology, University of Oulu, Oulu, Finland
e-mail: sara.ahola@oulu.fi

A. Nakata et al. (eds.), *Hyb-IT-up!*,
https://doi.org/10.1007/978-3-031-99743-3_3

learning strategies for hybrid learning situations. By doing so, it emphasises the importance of adapting SRL strategies to the specific challenges and opportunities presented by hybrid learning, suggesting that effective regulation is key to navigating and succeeding in diverse learning environments.

2 Theoretical Foundations of Regulation of Learning

SRL refers to the strategic management of one's own learning process, calling for active agency, awareness, and adaptation (Hadwin et al., 2018). This means that while self-regulated learners engage in tasks and activities in face-to-face and online settings, they take an active role and responsibility for their learning process, constantly monitoring their progress towards their goals and making strategic adjustments when necessary. The cyclical model of SRL recognizes that there are specific stages to which this regulation activity is attuned; strategic learning involves setting goals and subgoals for learning, planning how to achieve these goals, and then executing appropriate strategies (Panadero, 2017). However, as learning does not always progress as planned, SRL involves constant monitoring of the learning process and readiness to react, modify and adapt the learning strategies used according to situational needs and challenges. Self-regulated learners are also strategic in evaluating and reflecting on their performance to inform and adjust their future approaches (Zimmerman, 2000). Just as learning situations are complex and dynamic, regulation of learning often does not follow a straightforward, predetermined order. Instead, SRL provides learners with a way to exercise metacognitive level control over their learning as a vigilant skill that enables learners to optimize their learning goal attainment, regardless of the nature of their tasks or academic settings.

2.1 Fueling SRL: Cognitive, Motivational and Emotional Processes

In essence, SRL is a multifaceted theoretical framework that provides insight into strategic learning behaviour across the cognitive, motivational, and emotional dimensions of the learning process (Panadero, 2017). While different models present SRL as a cyclical goal-directed process, SRL also includes the ability to react adaptively to unexpected circumstances that may arise during learning and call for adaptation of goals, strategies, and behaviours. That is, while SRL is inherently a strategic and planned activity, it also includes contextually evolving activities that aim to optimize learning within existing circumstances and conditions (Järvenoja et al., 2015). SRL skills enable students to attune their cognitive, motivational, and emotional processes to these situational factors influencing learning.

Cognitive Processes

Cognitive processes refer to the mental mechanisms through which individuals process information. These mechanisms include processes such as searching, comprehending, predicting, and encoding and retrieving information from memory (Winne, 2017). These cognitive processes are an integral part of learning as they enable knowledge acquisition through the creation of new connections between prior knowledge and new knowledge. Cognitive processes also include intentional strategies and tactics through which learners aim to enhance the achievement of their learning goals, such as highlighting or paraphrasing important parts of a text (Winne, 2013). Self-regulated learners can keep track of how well they understand a task and choose the right strategies to help them learn better. This ability to think about their own thinking is called metacognitive monitoring and controlling; it allows learners to take control of their learning, including their content understanding and related cognitive processing, motivation, and emotions (Järvelä & Hadwin, 2024).

Motivational Processes

Motivational processes play an important role in initiating, directing, and sustaining goal-directed actions in learning (Dörnyei, 2000), being crucial for overcoming difficulties in achieving desired progress and managing the constant distractions competing for our attention. While we all have a general idea of what motivation is, in reality, it is a complex and multifaceted phenomenon, consisting of various concepts that aim to capture the versatility of the processes influencing our goals, decisions, and actions. From an educational standpoint, perhaps the most important motivational processes have to do with how we maintain our motivation during learning, especially in the face of obstacles or unexpected incidents. Self-regulated learners, in particular, have the necessary means to understand and strengthen their motivational basis for the task at hand (Wolters, 2003). These premises include one's self-efficacy beliefs, interests, and personal values, which influence how learners perceive and approach the task at hand (Bandura, 1997; Pintrich, 2000). For example, if a learner is not confident in their ability to execute the task, does not find it engaging, or fails to see its relevance for themselves, this could seriously undermine the learner's willingness to engage in the activity in the first place. However, by strategically modifying these motivational processes, self-regulated learners can persist in their activities, even if the task is cognitively challenging or lacks immediate appeal to the learner.

Emotional Processes

Emotions are individuals' dynamic reactions to the surrounding learning context and events (Gross, 2014). They inform learners about meaningful aspects of learning, being indicative of how an individual's goals are being met. Emotional processes are crucial for both our learning and well-being: "… judging from the general functions of emotions for human agency, it may be assumed that emotions influence students' cognitive processes and performance, as well as their psychological and physical health" (Pekrun et al., 2002, p. 92). It is important to note that emotional processes are inherently social in nature, meaning that they are situated in and shaped by interactions with the learning environment as well as other people (Fischer et al., 2011; Op't Eynde et al., 2007). This means that emotional processes are very sensitive to situational variations in the task context. Emotional expressions and socio-emotional interactions among learners have an important role in building and maintaining a beneficial emotional atmosphere for learning (Bakhtiar et al., 2018). Self-regulated learners are able to influence the intensity of their emotional experiences and reactions, modifying them into more constructive forms to enable and benefit goal attainment both individually and in groups.

2.2 Sharing the Responsibility of Regulated Learning: Co-Regulation (CoRL) and Socially Shared Regulation of Learning (SSRL) Between Collaborative Group Members

As the importance of collaboration in our future becomes increasingly evident, understanding how to navigate the challenges of effective teamwork calls for developing strong social learning skills. While the key processes of regulation, the cognitive, motivational, and emotional, are occurring inside individual minds, novel problems require finding solutions together with others. This requires shared awareness of learning processes among members of the group. While engaged in learning activities, there are moments when regulatory support is needed, or the collective learning process of the group needs to be re-coordinated. In those moments, skillful learners engage in co-regulation and socially shared regulation of learning (Järvelä et al., 2018).

Co-regulation refers to a one-way form of regulation support, such as making sure that another group member is aware of the task instructions or feels reassured in their capabilities. Socially shared regulation refers to a more joint process where multiple group members come together to regulate their shared learning progress as a collective, such as negotiating the optimal course of action after experiencing difficulties in proceeding or encouraging positive determination towards the task. Whereas CoRL is closer to prompting or scaffolding regulation of other individuals ("you"), SSRL is more about negotiation and joint decision-making as a group ("we"; Miller & Hadwin, 2015). What is important is that all modes of regulation—SRL, CoRL, and SSRL—are about promoting the attainment of learning goals through monitoring and strategically adjusting cognitive, motivational and emotional learning processes (Järvelä & Hadwin, 2024). In order to succeed in groups, learners need to become aware of each other's learning processes to enhance the learning and progress of the whole group. This can happen either through social interaction or be mediated by technological tools, such as dashboards or group awareness tools (Miller & Hadwin, 2015). Either way, regulation is a skill that does not develop on its own: it relies on the support and guidance of teachers and educators alike.

3 Perspectives on Regulation of Learning as a Profound Skill in Advancing Digital Landscapes

In the age of societal digitalization, digital learning, and advanced technologies, the role of regulation becomes apparent. Hybrid learning scenarios, along with both synchronous and asynchronous online and distance learning place greater demands on the organization of learning environments as well as on learner autonomy. Understanding hybrid learning from the learners' perspectives requires us to investigate how they navigate challenges with their cognition, motivation, and emotions; hybrid learning requires new levels of vigilance.

Skills that enhance human adaptability amid changing societal demands have remained in high demand ever since the pandemic. From the learning perspective, adaptive and personalized paths towards acquiring knowledge and skills are sought after features in contemporary online and blended learning contexts. In these settings, SRL has been deemed effective in terms of academic performance and competence (Vanslambrouck et al., 2019; Xu et al., 2023). Barnard et al. (2009) state that the increased autonomy in online learning settings makes SRL a critical factor for success. It is also demonstrated that one's SRL skills are associated with learners' well-being as good self-regulated learners tend to experience lower levels of stress and burnout (Heikkilä et al., 2012). Some studies even suggest that students characterized by high levels of SRL have higher work quality in online learning than in traditional teaching methods, which might be explained by more autonomy and greater control over the pace of learning (Lin, 2022, see also Deci & Ryan, 2000). In other words, learners cannot take advantage of the flexibility of online and hybrid learning without good SRL competencies (see Azevedo, 2008).

SRL strategies have been linked to positive learning outcomes in e-learning contexts (Lai & Hwang, 2023), yet such digital environments require different SRL strategies from conventional in-person classrooms. For instance, online learning might require placing special attention on time management, critical thinking and effort regulation to make those strategies effective outside the more traditional learning settings (Broadbent & Poon, 2015). Learning with hypermedia, for example, requires learner's decision-making on what to learn and how to learn as well as how to allocate time and access learning materials (Azevedo, 2008). Ali and Hanna (2022) found in their study that students can promote their learning achievement in hybrid learning settings with strategies such as finding a comfortable place to study, pausing to check comprehension, asking course members for clarification, and sharing ideas and consulting classmates to solve problems. Ultimately, the affordances and constraints of the hybrid mode require heightened adaptability from learners. This emphasizes the importance of meaningfully designing hybrid learning environments to support the development and use of SRL (Broadbent & Poon, 2015).

Understanding how to promote SRL in hybrid settings is a daunting yet worthwhile endeavour. It would be safe to assume that given the importance of SRL skills in learning in traditional classroom settings, the rise of hybrid and online learning, as well as advanced technologies, would emphasize this importance even more (Barnard et al., 2009). Some contemporary research on SRL has started to underline the relevance of these skills as an important human capability in the era of artificial intelligence (Molenaar, 2022). Within these new learning contexts, there is a need to reconsider how students' learning is supported (Edisherashvili et al., 2022). In the next section, we attempt to outline the role of SRL in hybrid settings and suggest a set of SRL supports particularly important in this context to inform the development of practice.

4 Translating Theory into Practice: Supporting Regulation Processes in Hybrid Learning Settings

While learners in hybrid settings engage in their tasks and learning activities, they interact with various aspects influencing the regulated learning process, such as subject materials, technologies and social factors —making learning a process constantly shaped by the surrounding situation and context. In such complex scenarios, what are the crucial elements for regulating one's learning and securing progress towards one's goals? This section provides a case example and pedagogical suggestions to support the emergence of regulation and the development of students' and teachers' ability to optimizecognitive, motivational, and emotional learning processes in hybrid and online learning settings.

4.1 Example Case: A Hybrid Lesson on Global Education

We will now look at a fictional example of Harper (See Fig. 1), who is a higher education student participating in a hybrid lesson. Harper is joining the collaborative group task of preparing a sustainable development plan. Their group consists of four students: three students participating in the classroom, including Harper, and one student joining them remotely. For Harper, things aren't going particularly well.

To begin their task, the group gathers around the table. Harper is asked to open a Teams call on his laptop so the remote student can join. He struggles to find the right contact, as he doesn't know the online participant well. Meanwhile, one of the

Fig. 1 Hybrid lesson

onsite group members opens a Word document and asks, "What should we write?" Harper quickly responds, "I don't know, I didn't really understand the task" (cognitive challenge). A silence lingers, as no one takes the initiative.

After some delay, the remote participant joins the call but faces technical difficulties. As the group continues their discussion, the online participant's questions are distorted due to poor connection (technical challenge). Harper struggles to understand her and grows frustrated. "I'll try to fix it," the online participant says, before leaving to resolve the issue.

The group begins to argue about the format of the sustainable development plan. Harper, feeling unsure and unmotivated, thinks, "Global education isn't my strong suit, and this task won't be graded or implemented, so why put in the effort?" (motivational challenge). The hybrid setup complicates things, and Harper has always preferred working alone. He disengages from the conversation.

The online participant fixes her audio but remains mostly silent, communicating through emojis that only Harper sees. The onsite group drifts off-topic. No one has shared the Word document with the online participant, and Harper, feeling socially awkward, doesn't know how to better involve her (social challenge). He also doesn't feel confident in managing the group dynamic, especially with an online member who remains disconnected.

More than half the time has passed, and Harper begins to feel anxious about their lack of progress. The group has been off-task for most of the session, and there's little agreement on the direction of their plan. Only James has contributed to the document, which barely makes sense to anyone else. Harper's frustration builds, and he sighs and utters, "We'll never finish in time!" (emotional challenge).

James finally signals the teacher for help, and the teacher approaches the group. The online participant mentions in the chat that she has prepared a PowerPoint, but Harper, distracted and unmotivated, misses the message. Instead, he scrolls through social media, disengaging from the task completely. "Maybe James will take care of the presentation," Harper thinks, avoiding responsibility (lack of accountability).

4.2 Designing Pedagogical Supports for Regulation in Hybrid Learning

Harper's case represents a common hybrid learning situation where the complexity of navigating both onsite and online collaboration becomes problematic. Looking at the case, a lot can be learned about the need to support regulation processes. Harper's group struggled with task understanding and failed to revisit instructions or discuss perspectives. Technical difficulties also hindered the online student's participation, resulting in poor integration. Harper's lack of perceived value in the task and his frustration as time ran out led to disengagement and avoidance of accountability. This case raises a key question: how can teachers support students' regulatory processes?

To support SRL, teachers should aim to create a learning environment that is both supportive and motivating (Kong & Lin, 2023). This involves designing a hybrid learning setting that encourages collaboration, SRL, and active participation. Students should be able to engage with their learning materials, reflect on their learning, and seek support when needed. This is important in hybrid and online settings as research has indicated that learners with low SRL skills might find increased autonomy to be a challenge to their progress (Barnard et al., 2009; Lin, 2022). Research has also indicated that technological supports, such as dashboards, intelligent agents and AI applications can be useful in enhancing SRL (Alvarez et al., 2022; Chen, 2009; Edisherashvili et al., 2022; Jin et al., 2023). A recent review by Edisherashvili et al. (2022) investigated interventions to support regulation of cognition, motivation, and emotions, and their results highlight the benefit of meaningfully combining different interventions, such as prompts and feedback, and incorporating personalized and adaptive features, to support SRL in distance learning contexts (see Edisherashvili et al., 2022). Thus, teachers need to actively develop their knowledge on orchestrating hybrid teaching as the available technology advances. The focus should always be on developing pedagogically meaningful supports that can be properly implemented into teaching.

We believe that teachers can create a functional hybrid environment by balancing structured guidance with opportunities for SRL. A pedagogical design for supporting regulated learning in hybrid learning requires a multifaceted approach and strong digital pedagogical skills of teachers as the methods for supporting SRL would need to cater to both onsite and online participants. The following chapter outlines specific strategies that can be used to enhance SRL in hybrid settings, such as the case of Harper, to overcome common challenges and foster effective learning (see Table 1 for summary).

Supporting Task Understanding and Planning

Harper's case highlights how confusion and cognitive challenges can arise quickly in hybrid settings. Teachers should prepare clear instructions before group work begins to ensure every student is on the same page with the task. Supporting cognitive processes also involves activating prior content knowledge and helping to select appropriate learning strategies (Jin et al., 2023). Teachers should encourage

Table 1 Pedagogical supports for fostering SRL

Challenge	SRL support	Teacher activities
Cognitive	Supporting task understanding and planning	**Before**: Prepare clear instructions, activate prior knowledge, provide planning tools **During:** Clarify tasks, guide cognitive learning strategies **After:** Reflect on individual and group learning and performance
Motivational	Fostering task value, self-efficacy and interest	**Before**: Communicate task relevance, add personalization **During:** Motivation check-ins, set small goals **After:** Review achievement of goals, provide feedback
Emotional	Creating a supportive socio-emotional atmosphere	**Before**: Foster a supportive environment **During**: Acknowledge emotions, foster positive interactions **After**: Reflect on emotional challenges
Technical	Providing digital pedagogical support	**Before**: Ensure access to digital platforms, provide technical consultation **During:** Troubleshoot issues, ensure digital collaboration **After:** Reflect on digital competence
Social	Facilitating group communication and collaboration	**Before**: Assign roles, create collaborative scripts **During:** Rotate roles, facilitate discussions, increase social presence **After**: Reflect on group collaboration and participation
Lack of accountability	Encouraging active participation	**Before:** Provide tools for self-reflection **During:** Facilitate reflection, encourage peer feedback **After:** Encourage ongoing reflection via learning journal, foster help-seeking culture

students to think about their current understanding of the topic and promote cognitive learning strategies, such as highlighting key points and summarizing information. Teachers should also support learners' metacognitive processes of setting goals, making plans, and monitoring progress by utilizing technological tools, such as interactive whiteboards for shared notes, planning tools and quizzes (Jin et al., 2023).

Fostering Task Value, Self-Efficacy and Interest

In all learning environments, teachers should be aware of what motivates their students (Kong & Lin, 2023). Learning motivation can be fostered by emphasizing the value and relevance of the task (Vanslambrouck et al., 2018; Wolters, 2003) and providing meaningful feedback (Usher & Pajares, 2008). Teachers should encourage students to reflect on the importance of the task for their learning, future endeavours or career. Teachers should also create possibilities for learners to stimulate their interest by offering options for personalization, such as the possibility to choose tasks, topics, and tools. Finally, teachers should encourage students to set small, achievable goals to maintain momentum and help them recognize effort and progress (Constantine et al., 2019).

Facilitating Group Communication and Collaboration

Functional collaboration is crucial for hybrid learning, and teachers must guide students in developing productive social interaction and communication (Webb, 2009). To structure group work in the beginning, students can be encouraged to take on specific roles within the group, such as discussion starter, explainer, or timekeeper (Gu et al., 2015; Kollar et al., 2006). This helps distribute responsibility and ensure all group members' active contribution. Collaborative scripts could further be utilized to prompt students to regularly discuss their progress and strategies (Kollar et al., 2006). Furthermore, students should be taught how to increase their social presence in hybrid settings to make interaction between online and onsite participants smoother and more engaging (Kreijns et al., 2024).

Creating a Supportive Socio-Emotional Atmosphere

Regulating one's emotions is important in hybrid environments where some students may feel disconnected and isolated from others. Teachers can help students develop skills for regulating emotions by creating a supportive environment where emotional challenges can be expressed and acknowledged. By fostering a positive socio-emotional climate, teachers can build trust and strengthen group cohesion, which leads to a more supportive, engaging and productive learning environment for students (Bakhtiar et al., 2018; Lobczowski et al., 2020). At best, expressing and acknowledging negative emotions can invite co-regulation of emotions among peers (Järvenoja & Järvelä, 2013). The teacher should be there to create possibilities for groups to reflect on their emotions and step in to offer guidance and solve conflicts when needed.

Providing Digital Pedagogical Support

Technical challenges are common in hybrid learning environments, and to ensure fair and efficient teaching, teachers need to make sure that students have access to and can navigate digital tools effectively. By planning ahead, anticipating bottlenecks, and guiding students in using the appropriate platforms and software, teachers can reduce the likelihood of technical issues hindering learning. Students can also be encouraged to take initiative in resolving technical problems themselves, such as troubleshooting issues with connection, to develop their digital competences and problem-solving abilities in hybrid contexts. However, teachers should also be able to provide technical support "on the fly" and create opportunities for students to try out and practice with the necessary tools to ensure they can utilize the technology productively.

Encouraging Active Participation

Active participation is essential for student engagement in hybrid learning environments where students might feel less connected to their peers and to the teacher. Teachers can encourage students to take an active role in their learning by structuring tasks and activities that promote agency and self-reflection (Sierens et al., 2010; Fabriz et al., 2014). For instance, students can be asked to regularly reflect on their progress, identify areas for improvement, and set goals for future learning. It is also important that the teacher implements clear protocols and channels for help-seeking. Finally, formative assessments, such as peer feedback or reflective journals, can provide opportunities for students to critically evaluate their work and make necessary adjustments, further developing their sense of agency and autonomy.

5 Conclusion

This chapter aimed to showcase how we as educators can enhance students' learning by supporting the regulation of cognitive, motivational, emotional, and collaborative processes in various hybrid learning settings. Like other chapters of the book point out (see part "Conceptual Pillars of Hybrid Teaching and Learning in Higher Education"), hybrid learning requires continuous effort from the teacher, but it can also challenge students' learning skills and commitment in multiple ways. This invites the teacher to design hybrid learning scenarios that facilitate students' SRL processes in addition to knowledge construction processes.

While teachers must be ready to hand in some responsibility to their students and stimulate their autonomy in learning, creating a successful hybrid learning experience is still very dependent on teachers' digital competence combined with pedagogical understanding of regulated learning. By considering the hybrid learning design and implementation also from an SRL perspective, teachers can decrease the orchestration load of hybrid teaching by sharing responsibility for learning with agentic, self-regulated learners.

In the end, we wish to reiterate that despite novel technological advancements to enable learning support, one important question remains as posed by Howard-Rose and Winne already in 1993: *how detailed must instruction be?* When and how to support regulation of learning is more complex than an occasional situational prompt, as the need for regulation depends on the affordances and constraints of the learning environment as well as the current skill level of students. It would also be important to make sure that supports and technologies do not merely offload SRL from learners, but foster it instead (Molenaar, 2022). To us, this emphasizes one key path of development for hybrid education: teachers need not only support their students' regulation skills, but to do so appropriately and effectively, they must also develop those skills for themselves (Kramarski, 2017).

To conclude, SRL is pivotal in hybrid learning environments, empowering students to take ownership of their learning across both physical and virtual spaces. For teachers, fostering SRL skills is not just about enhancing academic outcomes but about equipping students with the tools to navigate the complexities of hybrid learning effectively. By deliberately designing instruction that supports SRL, teachers can help students develop the cognitive, emotional, and motivational strategies needed to thrive in diverse and dynamic learning settings. In doing so, teachers play a crucial role in bridging the gap between in-person and online learning experiences, ultimately preparing students for lifelong learning in an increasingly digital world.

References

Ali, A. D., & Hanna, W. K. (2022). Predicting students' achievement in a hybrid environment through self-regulated learning, log data, and course engagement: A data mining approach. *Journal of Educational Computing Research, 60*(4), 960–985. https://doi.org/10.1177/07356331211056178

Alvarez, R. P., Jivet, I., Pérez-Sanagustin, M., Scheffel, M., & Verbert, K. (2022). Tools designed to support self-regulated learning in online learning environments: A systematic review. *IEEE Transactions on Learning Technologies, 15*(4), 508–522. https://doi.org/10.1109/TLT.2022.3193271

Azevedo, R. (2008). The role of self-regulated learning about science with hypermedia. In D. H. Robinson & G. Schraw (Eds.), *Recent innovations in educational technology that facilitate student learning* (pp. 127–156). Information Age Publishing.

Bakhtiar, A., Webster, E. A., & Hadwin, A. F. (2018). Regulation and socio-emotional interactions in a positive and a negative group climate. *Metacognition and Learning, 13*(1), 57–90. https://doi.org/10.1007/s11409-017-9178-x

Bandura, A. (1997). *Self-efficacy: The exercise of control.* W. H. Freeman and Company.

Barnard, L., Lan, W. Y., To, Y. M., Paton, V. O., & Lai, S. L. (2009). Measuring self-regulation in online and blended learning environments. *The Internet and Higher Education, 12*(1), 1–6. https://doi.org/10.1016/j.iheduc.2008.10.005

Broadbent, J., & Poon, W. L. (2015). Self-regulated learning strategies & academic achievement in online higher education learning environments: A systematic review. *The Internet and Higher Education, 27*, 1–13. https://doi.org/10.1016/j.iheduc.2015.04.007

Chen, C. M. (2009). Personalized E-learning system with self-regulated learning assisted mechanisms for promoting learning performance. *Expert Systems with Applications, 36*(5), 8816–8829. https://doi.org/10.1016/j.eswa.2008.11.026

Constantine, J., Fernald, J., Robinson, J., & Courtney, M. B. (2019). *Best practices guidebook: Supporting students' self-efficacy.* Online Submission. Retrieved from https://files.eric.ed.gov/fulltext/ED592850.pdf.

Deci, E. L., & Ryan, R. M. (2000). The "what" and "why" of goal pursuits: Human needs and the self-determination of behavior. *Psychological Inquiry, 11*(4), 227–268. https://doi.org/10.1207/S15327965PLI1104_01

Dörnyei, Z. (2000). Motivation in action: Towards a process-oriented conceptualisation of student motivation. *British Journal of Educational Psychology, 70*(4), 519–538. https://doi.org/10.1348/000709900158281

Edisherashvili, N., Saks, K., Pedaste, M., & Leijen, Ä. (2022). Supporting self-regulated learning in distance learning contexts at higher education level: Systematic literature review. *Frontiers in Psychology, 12*, 792422. https://doi.org/10.3389/fpsyg.2021.792422

Fabriz, S., Dignath-van Ewijk, C., Poarch, G., & Büttner, G. (2014). Fostering self-monitoring of university students by means of a standardized learning journal—A longitudinal study with process analyses. *European Journal of Psychology of Education, 29*(2), 239–255. https://doi.org/10.1007/s10212-013-0196-z

Fischer, A. H., Manstead, A. S., & Zaalberg, R. (2011). Social influences on the emotion process. *European Review of Social Psychology, 14*(1), 171–201. https://doi.org/10.1080/10463280340000054

Gross, J. J. (2014). Emotion regulation: Conceptual and empirical foundations. In J. J. Gross (Ed.), *Handbook of emotion regulation* (pp. 3–20). The Guilford Press.

Gu, X., Shao, Y., Guo, X., & Lim, C. P. (2015). Designing a role structure to engage students in computer-supported collaborative learning. *The Internet and Higher Education, 24*, 13–20. https://doi.org/10.1016/j.iheduc.2014.09.002

Hadwin, A., Järvelä, S., & Miller, M. (2018). Self-regulation, co-regulation, and shared regulation in collaborative learning environments. In D. Schunk & A. J. Greene (Eds.), *Handbook of self-regulation of learning and performance* (pp. 83–106). Routledge.

Heikkilä, A., Lonka, K., Nieminen, J., & Niemivirta, M. (2012). Relations between teacher students' approaches to learning, cognitive and attributional strategies, well-being, and study success. *Higher Education, 64*, 455–471. https://doi.org/10.1007/s10734-012-9504-9

Howard-Rose, D., & Winne, P. H. (1993). Measuring component and sets of cognitive processes in self-regulated learning. *Journal of Educational Psychology, 85*(4), 591–604. https://doi.org/10.1037/0022-0663.85.4.591

Järvelä, S., & Hadwin, A. (2024). Triggers for self-regulated learning: A conceptual framework for advancing multimodal research about SRL. *Learning and Individual Differences, 115*, 102526. https://doi.org/10.1016/j.lindif.2024.102526

Järvelä, S., Hadwin, A., Malmberg, J., & Miller, M. (2018). Contemporary perspectives of regulated learning in collaboration. In F. Fischer, C. E. Hmelo-Silver, S. R. Goldman, & P. Reimann (Eds.), *International handbook of the learning sciences* (pp. 127–136). Routledge.

Järvenoja, H., & Järvelä, S. (2013). Regulating emotions together for motivated collaboration. In M. Baker, J. Andriessen, & S. Järvelä (Eds.), *Affective learning together* (pp. 162–181). Routledge.
Järvenoja, H., Järvelä, S., & Malmberg, J. (2015). Understanding regulated learning in situative and contextual frameworks. *Educational Psychologist, 50*(3), 204–219. https://doi.org/10.1080/00461520.2015.1075400
Jin, S. H., Im, K., Yoo, M., Roll, I., & Seo, K. (2023). Supporting students' self-regulated learning in online learning using artificial intelligence applications. *International Journal of Educational Technology in Higher Education, 20*(1), 37. https://doi.org/10.1186/s41239-023-00406-5
Kollar, I., Fischer, F., & Hesse, F. W. (2006). Collaboration scripts—a conceptual analysis. *Educational Psychology Review, 18*, 159–185. https://doi.org/10.1007/s10648-006-9007-2
Kong, S. C., & Lin, T. (2023). Developing self-regulated learning as a pedagogy in higher education: An institutional survey and case study in Hong Kong. *Heliyon, 9*(11), e22115. https://doi.org/10.1016/j.heliyon.2023.e22115
Kramarski, B. (2017). Teachers as agents in promoting students' SRL and performance: Applications for teachers' dual-role training program. In D. H. Schunk & J. A. Greene (Eds.), *Handbook of self-regulation of learning and performance* (pp. 223–239). Routledge.
Kreijns, K., Yau, J., Weidlich, J., & Weinberger, A. (2024). Towards a comprehensive framework of social presence for online, hybrid, and blended learning. *Frontiers in Education, 8*, 1286594. https://doi.org/10.3389/feduc.2023.1286594
Lai, C. L., & Hwang, G. J. (2023). Strategies for enhancing self-regulation in e-learning: A review of selected journal publications from 2010 to 2020. *Interactive Learning Environments, 31*(6), 3757–3779. https://doi.org/10.1080/10494820.2021.1943455
Lin, J. W. (2022). Hybrid online learning for a software practice course and how it affects students with different self-regulated learning levels. *Australasian Journal of Educational Technology, 38*(5), 77–89. https://doi.org/10.14742/ajet.7678
Lobczowski, N. G., Allen, E. M., Firetto, C. M., Greene, J. A., & Murphy, P. K. (2020). An exploration of social regulation of learning during scientific argumentation discourse. *Contemporary Educational Psychology, 63*, 101925. https://doi.org/10.1016/j.cedpsych.2020.101925
Miller, M., & Hadwin, A. (2015). Scripting and awareness tools for regulating collaborative learning: Changing the landscape of support in CSCL. *Computers in Human Behavior, 52*, 573–588. https://doi.org/10.1016/j.chb.2015.01.050
Molenaar, I. (2022). The concept of hybrid human-AI regulation: Exemplifying how to support young learners' self-regulated learning. *Computers and Education: Artificial Intelligence, 3*, 100070. https://doi.org/10.1016/j.caeai.2022.100070
Op't Eynde, P., De Corte, E., & Verschaffel, L. (2007). Students' emotions: A key component of self-regulated learning? In P. A. Schutz & R. Pekrun (Eds.), *Emotion in education* (pp. 185–204). Academic.
Panadero, E. (2017). A review of self-regulated learning: Six models and four directions for research. *Frontiers in Psychology, 8*, 422. https://doi.org/10.3389/fpsyg.2017.00422
Pekrun, R., Goetz, T., Titz, W., & Perry, R. P. (2002). Academic emotions in students' self-regulated learning and achievement: A program of qualitative and quantitative research. *Educational Psychologist, 37*(2), 91–105. https://doi.org/10.1207/S15326985EP3702_4
Pintrich, P. R. (2000). The role of goal orientation in self-regulated learning. In M. Boekaerts, P. R. Pintrich, & M. Zeidner (Eds.), *Handbook of self-regulation* (pp. 451–502). Academic. https://doi.org/10.1016/B978-012109890-2/50043-3
Sierens, E., Vansteenkiste, M., Goossens, L., Soenens, B., & Dochy, F. (2010). The synergistic relationship of perceived autonomy support and structure in the prediction of self-regulated learning. *British Journal of Educational Psychology, 79*(1), 57–68. https://doi.org/10.1348/000709908X304398
Usher, E. L., & Pajares, F. (2008). Sources of self-efficacy in school: Critical review of the literature and future directions. *Review of Educational Research, 78*(4), 751–796. https://doi.org/10.3102/0034654308321456

Vanslambrouck, S., Zhu, C., Lombaerts, K., Philipsen, B., & Tondeur, J. (2018). Students' motivation and subjective task value of participating in online and blended learning environments. *The Internet and Higher Education, 36*, 33–40. https://doi.org/10.1016/j.iheduc.2017.09.002

Vanslambrouck, S., Zhu, C., Pynoo, B., Thomas, V., Lombaerts, K., & Tondeur, J. (2019). An in-depth analysis of adult students in blended environments: Do they regulate their learning in an 'old school' way? *Computers & Education, 128*, 75–87. https://doi.org/10.1016/j.compedu.2018.09.008

Webb, N. (2009). The teacher's role in promoting collaborative dialogue in the classroom. *British Journal of Educational Psychology, 79*(1), 1–28. https://doi.org/10.1348/000709908X380772

Winne, P. H. (2013). Learning strategies, study skills, and self-regulated learning in postsecondary education. In M. B. Paulsen (Ed.), *Higher education: Handbook of theory and research* (pp. 377–403). Springer.

Winne, P. H. (2017). Cognition and metacognition within self-regulated learning. In D. H. Schunk & J. A. Greene (Eds.), *Handbook of self-regulation of learning and performance* (pp. 36–48). Routledge.

Wolters, C. A. (2003). Regulation of motivation: Evaluating an underemphasized aspect of self-regulated learning. *Educational Psychologist, 38*(4), 189–205. https://doi.org/10.1207/S15326985EP3804_1

Xu, Z., Zhao, Y., Liew, J., Zhou, X., & Kogut, A. (2023). Synthesizing research evidence on self-regulated learning and academic achievement in online and blended learning environments: A scoping review. *Educational Research Review, 39*, 100510. https://doi.org/10.1016/j.edurev.2023.100510

Zimmerman, B. J. (2000). Attaining self-regulation: A social cognitive perspective. In M. Boekaerts, P. R. Pintrich, & M. Zeidner (Eds.), *Handbook of self-regulation* (pp. 13–40). Academic. https://doi.org/10.1016/b978-012109890-2/50031-7

Orchestration Load of Hybrid Teaching

Ishari Amarasinghe, Alejandro Ortega-Arranz, Lubna Hakami, Davinia Hernández-Leo, Yannis Dimitriadis, and Alejandra Martínez Monés

1 Introduction

Teachers' role in managing everyday teaching and learning situations is indispensable. Rather than being a *guide on the side*, teachers actively engage in effectively regulating learning that occurs at different social levels: individual, group, and whole-class (Dillenbourg & Jermann, 2010). Such regulation of learning situations demands teachers to divide their attention among individual students and multiple groups to cater to their unique needs, as well as adapting the learning design in real-time while considering extrinsic constraints, such as available time (Van Leeuwen et al., 2019). The notion of orchestration aims to capture how an active teacher manages integrated learning scenarios in real-time in a highly constrained environment (Prieto et al., 2018).

Given that orchestration is a demanding task, it often adds to the workload of the teachers. The notion of orchestration load is a "fuzzy" concept (Prieto et al., 2015), and it broadly aims to capture the attentive yet essential workload teachers encounter when managing classroom learning situations in real-time. It is worth noting that several previous studies have aimed to define orchestration load, while others have

I. Amarasinghe (✉)
National Education Lab AI (NOLAI), Radboud University, Nijmegen, the Netherlands

Universitat Pompeu Fabra, Barcelona, Spain
e-mail: ishari.amarasinghe@upf.edu

A. Ortega-Arranz · Y. Dimitriadis · A. M. Monés
School of Computer Engineering, Universidad de Valladolid, Valladolid, Spain
e-mail: alex@infor.uva.es; yannis@tel.uva.es; amartine@infor.uva.es

L. Hakami · D. Hernández-Leo
Department of Engineering, Universitat Pompeu Fabra, Barcelona, Spain
e-mail: lubna.hakami01@estudiant.upf.edu; davinia.hernandez@upf.edu

A. Nakata et al. (eds.), *Hyb-IT-up!*,
https://doi.org/10.1007/978-3-031-99743-3_4

referred to it as a 'black box' without exploring it in detail (Amarasinghe et al., 2022). However, defining this notion and its related facets, requires a further exploration on the factors that influence the orchestration load. A comprehensive understanding of these factors, along with methods to measure their influence on orchestration load, can lead to the proposal of strategies for lowering teachers' burden.

Specifically, with the recent COVID-19 pandemic, hybrid learning models have gained popularity among researchers and practitioners (Eyal & Gil, 2022). One such model is the *synchronous hybrid model*, that merges onsite (e.g., in the physical classroom) and online (e.g., out of the physical classroom) students at the same time (Raes et al., 2020). Synchronous hybrid models have been adopted by many higher education institutions given its flexibility for online participation (Badiozaman et al., 2023). While these models have been acute during COVID-19 pandemic, they remain highly relevant even at present as they promote accessibility and equity among students (Badiozaman et al., 2023). These learning models have altered teaching and learning and have created a need to adapt and do things differently for teachers and students. Specifically, in complex learning situations such as Computer-Supported Collaborative Learning (CSCL), attending to students' needs and fostering positive group interactions among students located at different locations can become challenging for teachers. Yet, limited research has explored the role of teachers in hybrid CSCL situations (Ortega-Arranz et al., 2024) and how such shifts in teaching practices influence teachers' workload remains unclear. Existing studies have mostly focused on the impact of hybrid teaching on students and their perceptions (Raes et al., 2020). However, the design requirements of orchestration systems that facilitate the regulation of learning activities in hybrid teaching situations specifically, in complex learning situations such as CSCL are not well understood (Ortega-Arranz et al., 2024).

Therefore, in this chapter first, we aim to provide a conceptual understanding of the notion of orchestration load, its facets and the instruments that can be used to estimate this notion within the context of CSCL. Second, we provide details of several cases that were implemented in onsite, online and synchronous hybrid CSCL situations. Instead of focusing only on the orchestration load in hybrid teaching, we aimed to compare it with onsite and online teaching models. This helped us to explain: (1) which are the factors influencing orchestration load in different teaching modalities and (2) what are the unique factors that influence orchestration load specifically in synchronous hybrid settings.

2 What is Orchestration Load? What Are Its Facets? How Can It Be Measured?

Orchestration of learning situations is demanding, given that teachers need to intervene and handle multiple tasks simultaneously in real-time. Such orchestration is even more aggravated in CSCL situations where multiple groups engage in learning activities. For instance, consider the deployment of the pattern-based Pyramid script (Hernández-Leo et al., 2019). The script aims to provide a structure for collaboration and to facilitate students to reach a consensus on a given problem within several phases that occur one after the other following a Pyramid structure (i.e., from individual to small and large group phases). Within this structured group learning process, the pedagogical aim is to provide opportunities for all learners to express and discuss their ideas with peers (Hernández-Leo et al., 2019).

Although scripts provide a structure for collaboration, their implementation in practice often presents challenges for teachers (Dillenbourg & Tchounikine, 2007). For instance, teachers need to handle individual students' problems, (e.g., answer questions), and at the group level they need to divide their attention to diagnose collaboration. Moreover, without expert monitoring, there are also chances that students may reach a potentially misleading consensus. At the class level, teachers need to track the activity progress while considering other constraints such as the limited time available to complete tasks. These challenges illustrate just a few scenarios that can impede achieving positive learning outcomes in CSCL situations. In these cases, teachers need to intervene at individual, group, and class level providing further guidance and additional scaffolding (Rodríguez-Triana et al., 2015). In other words, managing collaboration in real-time requires teachers to constantly monitor the current state of the interactions against the desired outcomes in order to detect any discrepancies (Soller et al., 2005). They also need to divide their attention across multiple social levels, i.e., individual, group, and class level to detect deviations, decide on the next best course of actions, and implement those actions in real-time. This adds to the orchestration load of teachers.

Based on what was learned from implementing CSCL situations in multiple authentic onsite learning situations, previous studies have attempted to analyze different facets of orchestration load. For instance, previous work has deconstructed this notion into three different facets including *situation evaluation, goal formation,* and *action-taking* (Amarasinghe et al., 2021). *Situation evaluation* refers to the sense-making process of teachers with supporting tools (e.g., mirroring dashboards) to diagnose the state of a given learning situation. *Goal formation* involves deciding the next best action in order to reduce the gap between the ideal state and the current state (Soller et al., 2005). *Action-taking* refers to the implementation of the best action such as revising the learning design in real-time to accommodate the emerging needs of the learning situation. *Situation evaluation* and *goal formation* refer to unobservable cognitive processing of teachers that involves decision making whereas *action taking* is physical and observable. In a broader sense, as described in Dillenbourg (2015), orchestration load constitutes two aspects including physical load (or the energy that teachers need to put in to monitor a learning situation, to perform adaptations, etc.) and cognitive load (the amount of cognitive resource required to process information, to think, and to make decisions).

It is clear that orchestration load is multifaceted as outlined above. In order to estimate orchestration load measurements are needed. Measuring orchestration load is often overlooked given the ill-defined nature of this construct. Traditional ways of measuring orchestration load include the use of questionnaires (e.g., using the

NASA-TLX questionnaire Hart, 2006). However, the use of questionnaires is not reliable as it depends on teachers' memory of events. Asking teachers to answer a questionnaire several times throughout a learning activity can disrupt the learning activity. Therefore, recent studies have emphasized the use of mixed-methods that triangulate multimodal data (e.g., subjective data (self-reported), and objective data (physiological data) collected from physiological sensors) as an alternative approach to estimate orchestration load (Hakami et al., 2024). For instance, in Hakami et al. (2024) heart rate variability (HRV) which refers to the variation in the time intervals between consecutive heartbeats (Shaffer & Ginsberg, 2017) was triangulated with self-reported data to estimate orchestration load. These approaches proved to be particularly effective in estimating teacher orchestration load in CSCL situations.

Despite the growing research on teacher orchestration load, there remains a lack of analysis and case-based reflections about teacher orchestration load considering different teaching modalities. Many studies have focused only on onsite or online learning situations. However, hybrid learning situations have received far less attention (Ortega-Arranz et al., 2024). This gap highlights the need for further exploration into how hybrid learning impacts teacher orchestration load, considering the unique challenges and complexities these settings pose for teachers.

3 Case Studies

In the following, we provide details of three case studies where teachers reported their practical experiences in regulating CSCL situations, each differing in the modality of the learning activities, i.e., an onsite CSCL activity, an online CSCL activity, and a synchronous hybrid CSCL activity.

3.1 Orchestrating Onsite CSCL Situations

Five teachers (2 females and 3 males) from a Spanish public university, conducted Pyramid script-based CSCL activities onsite using a tool called PyramidApp (Manathunga & Hernández-Leo, 2018). Each session lasted around 10–35 min. Thirty-two sessions involving five teachers were considered for further analysis.

Both subjective and objective measures were collected from the participating teachers. Objective data included (a) physiological data (i.e., HRV measured using Cosinuss° sensor; (b) log data captured teachers' use of the CSCL tool; (c) observation notes taken by the researchers during the CSCL activities to capture relevant details about teachers' behavior. Subjective data were collected employing self-reported post-activity questionnaires that capture teachers' perceptions of the activity. Visual inspection methods were used to analyze physiological signals (Price et al., 2015). Mixed methods to triangulate subjective and objective measurements were adopted.

The results of the analysis identified several stressful moments that added to teachers' orchestration load. One stressful moment happened when students faced issues accessing Google Forms provided by the teacher after the activity. However, this issue was not directly related to the scripted activity itself. Another stressful moment was during the activity, as teachers struggled to identify which student-proposed options required further discussion. In other words, evaluating the content of students' work demanded significant cognitive effort. Additionally, technological disruption such as the teacher's laptop was running low on power and was required to find a power source while simultaneously managing the flow of the session. Personal distractions, such as cleaning spectacles and dealing with a problem with a bag clipper while monitoring the activity, were also reported as key moments that added to the cognitive load of the teacher. In addition to these specific moments that were self-reported, objective measures indicated that the physical movement around the classroom have elevated physiological stress indicators, such as Root Mean Square of Successive Differences (RMSSD). Further details of this case are presented in (Hakami et al., 2024).

3.2 *Orchestrating Online CSCL Situations*

A female teacher from a Spanish university deploy PyramidApp based CSCL activities. University students joined the activities online due to COVID-19 restrictions. Each session lasted approximately 9–18 minutes. Six sessions were considered for further analysis.

Both subjective and objective measures were collected from the participating teachers. Objective data collected included (a) physiological data (i.e., ElectroDermal Activity (EDA) data that provided information on skin conductivity and hand movement); (b) log data that captured teachers' use of CSCL tool; (c) screen recordings from the dashboard of the CSCL tool; (d) video recordings collected by the researchers during the CSCL activities to capture relevant details about the teachers' behavior and reactions to the activities. Self-reported post-activity questionnaire captured teachers' subjective perception of the activity.

Responses from the post-activity questionnaire were analyzed to identify the situations that added to the orchestration load of the teacher. Both the dashboard screen recordings and video footage of each activity were reviewed to pinpoint the exact moments. Line charts were used to plot EDA data for each activity, followed by a visual inspection—an established method for skin conductance analysis (Gersak, 2020).

Across all activities, teachers reported many situations that added to their workload. For instance, running out of time in the class forced teachers to reduce the time allocated for the CSCL activity. Moreover, at the beginning of the activity, the teacher noted that the CSCL activity was not deployed, and therefore it was not ready for the students to participate. Once deployed somehow, the teacher shared a wrong activity link to the students that created problems for students to join the activity. During the activity, teachers faced issues with PyramidApp such as students having difficulties in editing their options. Apart from the students' side, the teacher facing the dashboard was also not responsive at a specific moment when she tried to add time to the activity but the dashboard did not respond as expected. The teacher also mentioned that she was surprised when the activity changed levels, as she was focused on reading the students' output. Finally, before debriefing, the teacher noticed that the virtual classroom software stopped working and she needed to restart her browser. The teacher explained this moment was more stressful than the others. Further details of this case are presented in (Crespi et al., 2022).

3.3 Orchestrating Hybrid CSCL Situations

Two teachers (a male and a female) from another Spanish university used Engageli[1] software to deploy a Jigsaw-scripted CSCL activity (Hernández-Leo et al., 2019) in a synchronous hybrid mode. The activity involved three phases which approximately lasted 2 h each. The two phases requiring group work (i.e., the expert and Jigsaw phases) were considered for further analysis regarding teacher orchestration load. While the expert phase involved a homogeneous grouping strategy (all students of each group were either onsite or online), the Jigsaw phase involved a heterogeneous grouping strategy (all groups were formed by both onsite and online students).

Teachers' post-interviews, questionnaire responses as well as observations (through recordings and researcher observations taken during the CSCL activities) were used to capture all teachers' behavior and reactions to the collaborative activities. Teachers also completed the NASA-TLX questionnaire (Hart, 2006) to measure their perceived workload of carrying out the collaborative hybrid session. Unlike in the aforementioned two cases, in this case, objective data through sensors was not collected.

The teachers' observable behaviors (captured through recordings and researcher observations) during the four sessions (two per teacher) were independently coded by two authors. Epistemic Network Analysis (ENA) (Shaffer et al., 2016) was utilized to investigate potential differences in the teachers' orchestration actions, targeting at specific moments either exclusively onsite students (onsite actions), exclusively online students (online actions), or both groups (hybrid actions). The coded recordings and observations served as inputs for the ENA. After the completion of the CSCL activity, both teachers were jointly interviewed to obtain a more detailed understanding of their experiences and to clarify certain responses from their questionnaires.

Both teachers reported a medium-to-high workload in scripting and orchestrating the sessions. Considering specifically the hybridity of the learning situation

[1] Engageli: https://www.engageli.com/. Accessed October 2024.

teachers mentioned they faced difficulties with the CSCL software listening modes (i.e., who can listen to who); how to address multiple questions simultaneously from both onsite and online students; how to reassign students to different groups considering different modalities; and the need of wearing headphones and microphone to keep track of online students which is different from teachers' everyday classroom practice. Moreover, teachers found it difficult to know which students were connected and actively contributing within the groups (due to absence of physical presence). ENA indicated that solving technical issues becomes important when synchronous online students are involved in collaboration. Guiding students to use collaboration technology appropriately and solving technical problems in real-time was identified as a factor influencing teachers' orchestration load. The NASA-RTLX dimensions that contributed least to their orchestration load were the "physical demand" (one teacher stayed seated during the orchestration of the activities) and "performance" (one teacher perceived as successful the orchestration of both sessions). Further details of this case are presented in (Ortega-Arranz et al., 2024).

4 Cross-Case Analysis and Discussion

A thematic analysis was performed to summarize specific factors that influence orchestration load in different teaching modalities, i.e., onsite, online, and hybrid teaching. Researchers went through the case studies reported above and grouped the factors influencing orchestration load under eight main themes. In the following, we provide details of these themes and explain which of these themes are common across the three different teaching modalities, and which of them are distinct, in order to shed light on the specific factors that influence orchestration load in hybrid teaching situations.

4.1 Content Load

This factor refers to the epistemic aspect of the learning activity. From a cognitive load theory perspective, information processing can be dichotomous (Sweller, 1994). *Controlled processing* happens when information requires conscious attention. For instance, teachers reading and processing the content of students' answers requires controlled processing. On the other hand, *automatic processing* refers to processing information without conscious effort (Sweller, 1994). Perhaps, if a specific learning task was conducted by a teacher in several consecutive years, they may be aware of the type of content students usually produce for a specific task. This reduction in the need to devote extensive attention allows for the processing of information to become automatic and less reliant on conscious effort, freeing up cognitive resources for other activities.

In the cases analyzed, teachers reported high content load in both onsite and online modes but not in the hybrid teaching. This can be understood by referring to the contextual aspects of the learning situations. For instance, in both onsite and online modes the teacher was using the PyramidApp tool that provided real-time monitoring of the activity via a teacher-facing dashboard. The script progresses in changing group structures fairly rapidly and each phase produces fairly new content/improved answers in multiple groups. This requires a teacher's conscious effort *(controlled processing)*. On the other hand, in the hybrid teaching situation, although the activities are scripted (Jigsaw script) the script was designed in a way that each phase of the activity (expert and Jigsaw phases) took around two hours and occurred in two different sessions with relatively small number of groups (Ortega-Arranz et al., 2024). Although the content processing may have required conscious effort, this was not rapid (much longer activities) when compared to the Pyramid activities that were conducted in onsite and online situations. Therefore, content load can be identified as a factor that influenced orchestration load in onsite and online modes, but it should be noted that this has been influenced by distinctive learning designs.

4.2 Physical Load

Based on the findings from the case studies it was noted that physical load was high (as indicated in physiological measurements) in onsite teaching situations although it was not explicitly mentioned by the teachers. It is not surprising that teachers in onsite learning situations visit students and often attempt to diagnose learning activities. In online situations this is not obviously the case as the teacher was sitting in front of a computer and monitoring collaboration while in the hybrid learning situation teachers moved partially. Although our case studies do not provide fine-grained teachers' positioning data to understand the patterns of teachers' movements, recent research has shown that positioning data may inform the process of designing learning spaces to explain the impact of the space characteristics on the activity itself (Martinez-Maldonado et al., 2020). A further exploration on these aspects will help teachers to gain insights to their practice and understand how different spaces and movements influence their orchestration load.

4.3 Time-Management

Allowing sufficient time to interact with peers is essential for collaboration. Previous literature has identified time as an extrinsic constraint (Dillenbourg et al., 2018) that has been underexplored in the learning sciences and has been often referred to as "classroom logistics" (Nussbaum & Diaz, 2013). Our findings indicate that teachers struggle to determine how much extra time students need to complete their learning activities during online learning situations. This is perhaps due to the lack of *teacher noticing* (ability to observe the classroom) (König et al., 2022) and *cues* available in online teaching. For instance, in onsite learning situations, *teacher noticing*, that involves predicting students' needs and acting accordingly (e.g., providing extra time) is possible. However, in online situations, unless the teacher supporting tools provide explicit support (e.g., alerting mechanism in teacher-facing dashboards) (Amarasinghe et al., 2021), noticing as well as reasoning on the current state of the learning activities becomes difficult and may add to the orchestration load of the teachers. Specifically, in the scripted CSCL situations, increasing time for a specific phase has a cascading effect and can result in an overall longer activity than anticipated. Moreover, in online settings, if teachers are not provided with means for activity monitoring, students may wait until the last minute to request such changes and teachers need to act quickly because otherwise students will move to the next script level (e.g., from small groups to large groups in Pyramid script). Overall making sense of the status of the learning situation and acting rapidly can add to the orchestration load of the teachers. In hybrid teaching situations, even though some students participate online, teachers may base their logistical estimate such as adjusting the duration of activities on the cues available in the in-person classroom.

4.4 Problems with CSCL Technology

Within the context of CSCL, technological tools are aimed at providing computer support to peer interactions and serve to realize the benefits of collaboration. However, it was noted that in the cases described above teachers reported issues with CSCL tools in online and hybrid teaching situations that are much oriented to technology use as opposed to onsite teaching in which interactions occur physically. Malfunctioning of the CSCL tools was highlighted as a factor affecting teachers' orchestration load in online situations. In the hybrid teaching, teachers reported issues related to CSCL software listening modes (i.e., who can listen to who), as well as guiding students to use collaboration technology appropriately and solving technical problems in real-time as factors that added to their orchestration load. As explained in previous research, as it is important for these tools to be learner-centric to support learning, they also need to be teacher-centric to be used effectively in formal education (Dillenbourg et al., 2018). It should be noted that both onsite and online CSCL activities were conducted using the same tool, PyramidApp. Teachers may not have reported problems with CSCL technology affecting orchestration load in onsite learning situations. While issues may have arisen, they likely resolved them using other strategies, such as directly communicating with students about those problems.

4.5 Other Technical Issues

Apart from the CSCL tools themselves, teachers also noted moments that added to their orchestration load due to other technical issues. For instance, in the onsite teaching students reported having technical issues related to other technologies such as Google Forms that are not directly related to the CSCL tools, yet required teachers' attention to successfully finish the activity itself. In online settings, issues with virtual classroom software can create a huge cognitive demand for the teacher given that delivering the entire lesson (in which CSCL is part of) depends on the technical infrastructure. As mentioned above these technical issues can also be referred to as classroom logistics (Nussbaum & Diaz, 2013) that are critical to carry out learning activities effectively.

4.6 Diagnosing Group Performance

Diagnosing the status of learning activity requires effort from the teacher and can be outlined as a factor that influences orchestration load. Recent research has shown that the incorporation of teacher-facing dashboards with relevant learning analytics indicators can be useful in diagnosing group performance (Van Leeuwen et al., 2019). We found that teachers reported diagnosing group performance became difficult in hybrid teaching situations. Specifically, they found it difficult to diagnose whether students are connected and actively contributing to the activity. Teachers also struggled to respond to both onsite and online groups at the same time because of the distributed nature of the setting. Therefore, diagnosing group performance in hybrid settings is cognitively demanding and adds to the orchestration load of the teachers. It should be noted that in the onsite and online modalities teachers had access to a dashboard that visualizes group performance. Perhaps this may have helped to reduce their burden on group monitoring and diagnosing.

4.7 Group Formation

Group formation in CSCL concerns the adequate selection and allocation of students into groups using different grouping criteria, e.g., based on students' personality traits (Sánchez et al., 2021), learning styles (Battur et al., 2016). Based on the findings of the case studies we noted that teachers find it difficult to reassign students to different groups considering different modalities in hybrid teaching situations. Implementing algorithms to provide automatic group recommendations would reduce the burden on the teachers. Moreover, using intelligent mechanisms (e.g., conversational agents as group partners in case students are absent in original groups) may help to share orchestration load among multiple actors (Sharples, 2013).

4.8 Personal Distractions

Apart from the aforementioned technical aspects, personal distractions were also seen to impact teachers' orchestration load in real-time. In onsite teaching situations these included for instance, teachers' running out of laptop battery power. Such incidents can take teachers' attention away from students and learning activity regulation. In hybrid teaching situations, wearing headphones and microphone to keep track of online students, which is different from teachers' everyday classroom practice, was also seen as a factor that influenced teacher's orchestration load. Although it was not explicitly mentioned in the case studies it can be assumed that similar personal distractions can occur even in online settings (e.g., running out of battery power) yet may not be a crucial factor for orchestration load, given that teachers are not directly interacting with students.

Figure 1 presents a summary of the findings. Based on the findings it becomes clear that factors which are unique to each teaching modality are somehow characterizing the nature of the teaching modality itself. For instance, when compared to other teaching modalities physical load is has a high presence in onsite teaching. Given the lack of *teacher noticing* and *cues*, time management is difficult in online teaching. Finally, diagnosing group performance and group formation becomes challenging in hybrid teaching given the distributed nature of the students across onsite and online spaces.

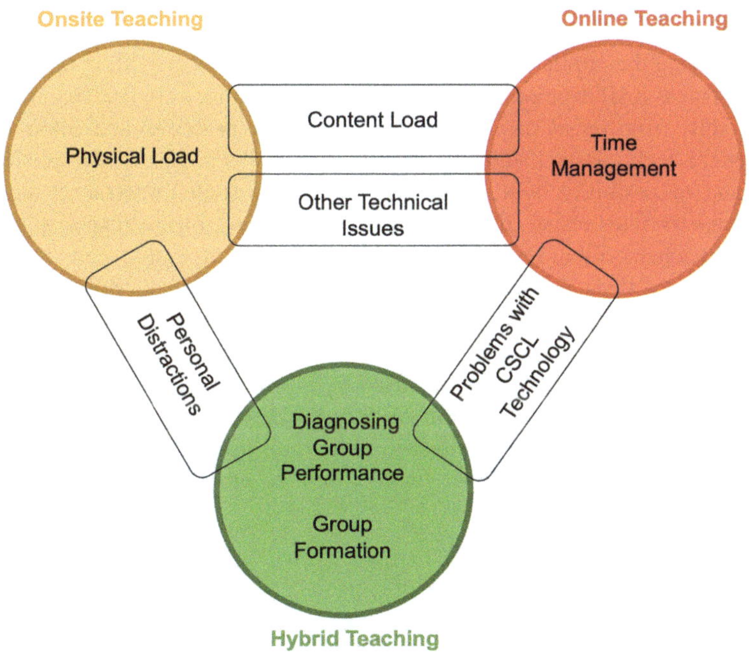

Fig. 1 Factors Influencing Orchestration Load in Different Teaching Modalities

5 Conclusions and Future Work

Educational institutions are in different phases of hybrid teaching implementations and as Gil et al. (2022) outlined "hybridity is here to stay". While some have conducted several pilot studies and are exploring the possibilities, others have already set up the hybrid teaching and learning infrastructure and are looking to scale up (Raes et al., 2020). Despite the scale of implementation, understanding the factors that influence the workload of the teachers is critical for successful implementation of hybrid teaching (Huang et al., 2017). In particular, we found that in hybrid teaching environments, elements such as diagnosing group performance and group formation impact teachers' orchestration load. The nature of synchronous hybrid teaching, blur the boundaries between online and onsite learning and demands teachers to split their attention between onsite and online students (Gil et al., 2022).

Further research is required to develop tools that enhance teachers' situational awareness of hybrid learning situations as well as to examine the process of how teachers interpret and take actions based on analytics (Mor et al., 2022). In terms of *teacher noticing,* further research is required to understand the types of interpretational aids teachers require in hybrid teaching situations. It should be noted that although the presented case studies shed light on the factors influencing orchestration load in different teaching modalities, the differences in study contexts may have influenced teachers' real-time regulation of learning activities and therefore factors influencing orchestration load. Further research is needed to develop a standardized measurement framework to estimate orchestration load across different teaching modalities and further research studies to enable more accurate comparisons.

Considering the implications for practice, it is clear that providing targeted training and professional development to teachers is important as hybrid teaching represents a shift from usual onsite classroom teaching practices and often involves pedagogical, technological and space challenges (Gil et al., 2022). Despite the flexibility and accessibility hybrid teaching entails for students (Raes et al., 2020), many teachers may resist changing their conventional onsite teaching practices. Enabling teachers to share how the shift to hybrid modality influenced their existing pedagogical practices and workload may encourage them to adopt hybrid teaching mode. Understanding what works and not with existing educational technologies and assessing whether new hybrid teaching infrastructures are needed or whether existing tools can be customized and used in hybrid settings is essential. Not only the development and customization of new tools to deploy hybrid teaching but establishing ways to connect teachers to share their practical experiences and continuous technical and institutional support may be essential to adopt and sustain hybrid teaching (Mor et al., 2022).

References

Amarasinghe, I., Hernández-Leo, D., & Ulrich Hoppe, H. (2021). Deconstructing orchestration load: comparing teacher support through mirroring and guiding. *International Journal of Computer-Supported Collaborative Learning, 16*(3), 307–338.

Amarasinghe, I., van Leeuwen, A., Dimitriadis, Y., Martínez-Monés, A., Hernández-Leo, D., Hoppe, U., Wiley, K., & Martinez-Maldonado, R. (2022). Teacher orchestration load: What is it and how can we lower the burden? In *Rapid community reports—Digital promise and the international society of the learning sciences* (pp. 1–13).

Badiozaman, I. F., Ng, A., & Mung Ling, V. (2023). "Here we go again": Unfolding HE students' hybrid experience and resilience during post-covid times. *Asia Pacific Journal of Education, 45*(3), 920–941.

Battur, S., Patil, M.S., Desai, P., Vijayalakshmi, M., Raikar, M.M., Hegde, P., & Joshi, G.H. (2016). *Enhancing the students project with team based learning approach: A case study.* In IEEE 4th International Conference on MOOCs, Innovation and Technology in Education (pp. 275–280).

Crespi, F., Amarasinghe, I., Vujovic, M., & Hernández-Leo, D. (2022). *Estimating orchestration load in CSCL situations using EDA.* In 2022 International Conference on Advanced Learning Technologies (pp. 128–132).

Dillenbourg, P. (2015). *Orchestration graphs: Modelling scalable education* (1st ed.). EPFL Press.

Dillenbourg, P., & Jermann, P. (2010). Technology for classroom orchestration. In *New science of learning* (pp. 525–552).

Dillenbourg, P., Prieto, L. P., & Olsen, J. K. (2018). Classroom orchestration. In *International handbook of the learning sciences* (pp. 180–190).

Dillenbourg, P., & Tchounikine, P. (2007). Flexibility in macro-scripts for computer-supported collaborative learning. *Journal of Computer Assisted Learning, 23*(1), 1–13.

Eyal, L., & Gil, E. (2022). Hybrid learning spaces—A three-fold evolving perspective. In *Hybrid learning spaces* (pp. 11–23).

Gersak, G. (2020). Electrodermal activity: A beginner's guide. *Electrotechnical Review, 87*(4), 175–182.

Gil, E., Mor, Y., Dimitriadis, Y., & Köppe, C. (Eds.). (2022). *Hybrid learning spaces*. Springer.

Hakami, L., Hernández-Leo, D., Amarasinghe, I., & Sayis, B. (2024). Investigating teacher orchestration load in scripted CSCL: A multimodal data analysis perspective. *British Journal of Educational Technology, 55*(5), 1926–1949.

Hakami, L., Sayis, B., Amarasinghe, I., & Hernandez-Leo, D. (2024). *Exploring teacher orchestration load in scripted CSCL: The role of heart rate variability.* In 17th International Conference on Computer-Supported Collaborative Learning (pp. 163–170).

Hart, S. G. (2006). *NASA-task load index (NASA-TLX); 20 years later.* In Human Factors and Ergonomics Society Annual Meeting (pp. 904–908).

Hernández-Leo, D., Asensio-Pérez, J. I., Dimitriadis, Y., & Villasclaras, E. D. (2019). *Generating CSCL scripts: From a conceptual model of pattern languages to the design of real scripts.* In Technology-enhanced learning, design patterns and pattern languages (pp. 49–64).

Huang, Y., Zhao, C., Shu, F., & Huang, J. (2017). *Investigating and analyzing teaching effect of blended synchronous classroom.* In 2017 International conference of educational innovation through technology (pp. 134–135).

König, J., Santagata, R., Scheiner, T., Adleff, A. K., Yang, X., & Kaiser, G. (2022). Teacher noticing: A systematic literature review of conceptualizations, research designs, and findings on learning to notice. *Educational Research Review, 36*, 100453.

Manathunga, K., & Hernández-Leo, D. (2018). Authoring and enactment of mobile pyramid-based collaborative learning activities. *British Journal of Educational Technology, 49*(2), 262–275.

Martinez-Maldonado, R., Schulte, J., Echeverria, V., Gopalan, Y., & Shum, S. B. (2020). Where is the teacher? Digital analytics for classroom proxemics. *Journal of Computer Assisted Learning, 36*(5), 741–762.

Mor, Y., Gil, E., Dimitriadis, Y., & Köppe, C. (2022). Forward looking: Predictions for the future of hybrid learning spaces. In *Hybrid learning spaces* (pp. 311–333). Springer International Publishing.

Nussbaum, M., & Diaz, A. (2013). Classroom logistics: Integrating digital and non-digital resources. *Computers & Education, 69*, 493–495.

Ortega-Arranz, A., Amarasinghe, I., Martínez-Monés, A., Asensio-Pérez, J. I., Dimitriadis, Y., Corrales-Astorgano, M., & Hernández-Leo, D. (2024). Collaborative activities in hybrid learning environments: Exploring teacher orchestration load and students' perceptions. *Computers & Education, 219*, 105105.

Price, P. C., Jhangiani, R., & Chiang, I. C. A. (2015). *Research methods in psychology* (5th ed.). McGraw-Hill.

Prieto, L. P., Sharma, K., & Dillenbourg, P. (2015). *Studying teacher orchestration load in technology enhanced classrooms.* In Design for teaching and learning in a networked world (pp. 268–281).

Prieto, L. P., Sharma, K., Kidzinski, Ł., & Dillenbourg, P. (2018). Orchestration load indicators and patterns: In-the-wild studies using mobile eye-tracking. *IEEE Transactions on Learning Technologies, 11*(2), 216–229.

Raes, A., Detienne, L., Windey, I., & Depaepe, F. (2020). A systematic literature review on synchronous hybrid learning: gaps identified. *Learning Environments Research, 23*, 269–290.

Rodríguez-Triana, M. J., Martínez-Monés, A., Asensio-Pérez, J. I., & Dimitriadis, Y. (2015). Scripting and monitoring meet each other: Aligning learning analytics and learning design to support teachers in orchestrating CSCL situations. *British Journal of Educational Technology, 46*(2), 330–343.

Sánchez, O. R., Ordonez, C. A. C., Duque, M. A. R., & Pinto, I. I. B. S. (2021). Homogeneous group formation in collaborative learning scenarios: An approach based on personality traits and genetic algorithms. *IEEE Transactions on Learning Technologies, 14*(4), 486–499.

Shaffer, D. W., Collier, W., & Ruis, A. R. (2016). A tutorial on epistemic network analysis: Analyzing the structure of connections in cognitive, social, and interaction data. *Journal of Learning Analytics, 3*, 9–45.

Shaffer, F., & Ginsberg, J. P. (2017). An overview of heart rate variability metrics and norms. *Frontiers in Public Health, 5*, 258.

Sharples, M. (2013). Shared orchestration within and beyond the classroom. *Computers and Education, 69*, 504–506.

Soller, A., Martínez, A., Jermann, P., & Muehlenbrock, M. (2005). From mirroring to guiding: A review of state of the art technology for supporting collaborative learning. *International Journal of Artificial Intelligence in Education, 15*(4), 261–290.

Sweller, J. (1994). Cognitive load theory, learning difficulty, and instructional design. *Learning and Instruction, 4*(4), 295–312.

Van Leeuwen, A., Rummel, N., & Van Gog, T. (2019). What information should CSCL teacher dashboards provide to help teachers interpret CSCL situations? *International Journal of Computer-Supported Collaborative Learning, 14*, 261–289.

Unlocking the Potential of Hybrid Teaching and Learning in Higher Education Through Co-design

Constructing a Hybrid Learning Design Framework: A Group Concept Mapping Study

Slavi Stoyanov, Olga Firssova, and Karel Kreijns

1 Framing the Narrative

The development of hybrid learning has been inextricably linked to the COVID-19 pandemic, although some ideas about this educational model have been known earlier (Bower et al., 2015; Cohen et al., 2020; Kreijns et al., 2024; Singh et al., 2021). The pandemic could be considered a 'critical incident method' for hybrid learning, representing a large-scale educational and social experiment. The range of hybrid learning definitions includes relatively narrow to relatively broad considerations. Most authors favor a definition that emphasizes the design of learning through the simultaneous integration of face-to-face and online delivery modes (Hafni & Fithriani, 2021; Ibrahim & Suhaimi, 2022; Raes et al., 2020). Others introduce the concept of 'hybrid learning spaces', which extends beyond merely integrating online and onsite environments or blending synchronous and asynchronous learning. The emergence of hybrid learning spaces requires reimagining time, space, and structures, freeing them from the conventional constraints of traditional dichotomies such as digital versus physical, formal versus informal, and individual versus collective (Cohen et al., 2020; Eyal & Gil, 2022).

Whatever definition is adopted, hybrid learning seems to offer numerous benefits to students, educators, and institutions, while also presenting distinct challenges that must be addressed to ensure effectiveness. One primary advantage is its inherent flexibility, which allows students to choose between attending classes in person or remotely, thereby accommodating diverse needs, including those with work or family commitments. This flexibility promotes inclusivity by broadening access to education for a wider range of students, irrespective of their geographical location. Furthermore, hybrid learning can enhance learning experiences by integrating

S. Stoyanov (✉) · O. Firssova · K. Kreijns
Open University of the Netherlands, Heerleen, the Netherlands
e-mail: slavi.stoyanov@ou.nl; olga.firssova@ou.nl; karel.kreijns@ou.nl

A. Nakata et al. (eds.), *Hyb-IT-up!*,
https://doi.org/10.1007/978-3-031-99743-3_5

external expertise and facilitating diverse perspectives within the classroom. Additionally, hybrid environments foster student autonomy, enabling learners to cultivate essential time management and technological skills necessary for their future professional pursuits. Institutions can also offer a broader array of specialized courses that may otherwise be restricted to certain campuses, thus enriching the educational offerings available to students. Socially, hybrid learning fosters a sense of community among students, including those in remote locations, by facilitating connections with peers and educational institutions. From an institutional perspective, hybrid learning can lead to significant operational efficiencies, allowing educational institutions to accommodate more students with fewer resources by reducing the need for physical space and associated costs. It also contributes to environmental sustainability by minimizing commuting (Bülow, 2022; Cohen et al., 2020; Raes et al., 2020).

However, hybrid learning also presents notable challenges that must be effectively managed. The implementation of hybrid learning requires substantial adjustments in both technology and pedagogy. Educators must become proficient in new technologies and rethink their instructional approaches to maintain educational standards across various learning environments. This adaptation process can be time-consuming and necessitates ongoing professional development to ensure that educators can effectively manage both in-person and remote students. Coordinating activities across multiple locations and managing the operational aspects of the learning platform adds to the cognitive load on educators (Ortega-Arranz et al., 2024). Ensuring equitable engagement for both in-person and remote students presents a significant challenge in hybrid learning. The lack of non-verbal cues and the potential for technical issues exacerbate this sense of exclusion, making it imperative for educators to design activities that actively engage all students, regardless of their physical location. Thus, although hybrid learning can foster a sense of community among students, it is not guaranteed. Furthermore, remote students often feel a psychological distance between them and the students in the classroom (Raes, 2022). Hybrid learning environments require students, particularly those learning remotely, to exhibit a higher level of self-discipline and motivation. The reliance on technology in hybrid learning introduces several challenges as well, including the need for high-quality audio and video setups to ensure that remote students have an experience comparable to those in the physical classroom. Technical issues, such as poor internet connections or outdated software, can disrupt the learning process and frustrate students and teachers (Bülow, 2022; Raes et al., 2020).

Neither narrow nor broad definitions of hybrid learning offer operationalizations that can effectively guide the design of learning and instruction to address the challenges inherent in hybrid learning. The design of hybrid learning is arguably the most underdeveloped aspect of the hybrid learning paradigm, both in theory and practice. Some general statements assert that hybrid pedagogy redefines the concept of location by integrating physical and virtual learning environments into a cohesive educational experience. Others propose that hybrid learning affords the flexibility to combine various instructional methods, media, and learning environments, thereby providing a more personalized learning experience (Musdariah et al., 2021).

It is suggested that the design for hybrid learning is not fundamentally different from that for on-campus or online learning, emphasizing the integration of diverse learning and instructional approaches, such as direct teaching, individual practice, and collaborative discovery. Design patterns, the Here or There approach (HOT), the Virtual Flipped Classroom, the Community of Inquiry (CoI) model, and the Activity-Centered Analysis and Design (ACAD) framework, as well as collaborative work orchestration, are mentioned as potential solutions. More concrete methods include the implementation of polls, quizzes, and questions throughout lessons, alongside discussion forums, virtual chat rooms, and breakout sessions (Bülow, 2022; Cornell Center for Teaching and Innovation, 2024, Goodyear, 2020; Goodyear et al., 2021; Ortega-Arranz et al., 2024; Zydney et al., 2019; Warburton & Mor, 2015).

However, these methods emerge from isolated efforts with no underlying structure and lack a conceptual foundation to guide hybrid learning and instruction. Most theoretical frameworks are based upon assumptions not directly related to hybrid learning and have been devised by researchers in different learning and instruction contexts. Like any other learning design approach, hybrid learning requires a theoretically grounded and evidence-informed framework comprising concrete guidelines. This chapter discusses the development of such a hybrid learning design framework that is not imposed a priori. Instead, it emerges from empirical data through the collaborative efforts of designers in the field of hybrid learning and instruction. The principal challenge is: What are the guidelines for the hybrid learning design framework, and how are they interrelated?

To address this challenge, we conducted a Group Concept Mapping Study (GCM) as part of a European research and development project Hyb-it-up involving five universities (https://Hyb-it.up.org). This project is presented elsewhere in the book.

2 Mapping Collective Intelligence

Group Concept Mapping (GCM) is a consensus-driven approach that combines qualitative data collection with quantitative analysis. This study applied it to help learning designers identify and visually represent an emerging conceptual structure, such as a hybrid learning design framework. The data collection in GCM involves idea generation, organizing the ideas into thematic groups (sorting), and evaluating the ideas on specific criteria such as importance and feasibility (rating) by the participants. Subsequently, multivariate statistical techniques, including multidimensional scaling (MDS) and hierarchical cluster analysis (HCA), are employed to aggregate the individual contributions made by participants during the idea generation, sorting, and rating phases to depict and visualize the group's collective perspective on the issue at hand (the hybrid learning design framework) through graphical representations, such as conceptual maps and ladder graphs, known as pattern matches (Kane & Trochim, 2007; Kane & Rosas, 2018; Trochim & McLinden, 2017).

2.1 Crafting Research: Participants, Procedure and Analysis

We invited representatives from the project's institutions to participate in the study and provided them with a secure link to access the web-based application (The Concept System® Groupwisdom™, 2022). Informed consent was requested upon their first use of the application, and participation was anonymous. Eighteen project members participated in idea generation, nine in sorting, eight in rating, and nine in interpreting the results.

GCM comprised the following stages: preparation, idea generation, idea synthesis, structuring the ideas through sorting and rating, data analysis, and interpretation of the outcomes.

The preparation involved the following steps: introduction of GCM to representatives of the project's institutions; a discussion for reaching an agreement on the trigger statement (focus prompt) for the idea generation; and designing and testing the online environment for data collection and analysis built upon Groupwisdom™ (2022), a platform that supports the entire GCM workflow, including the introduction to the project, the informed consent, the instructions for the idea generation, sorting and rating, and data analysis (The Concept System® Groupwisdom™, 2022).

A literature review on bibliographic databases and generative AI tools for literature search compiled the initial list of ideas (short phrases) in the idea generation. The process was guided by the following trigger statement (focus prompt): "A specific guideline that informs the design of a hybrid learning session is…" The participants were then asked to add ideas to the list, completing the focus prompt. They were given 1 week for this activity.

After the idea generation phase, all generated ideas underwent editing while preserving the overall integrity of the set. The final randomized list of ideas was sent to participants for anonymous sorting and rating.

For the sorting activity, participants were asked to individually and independently group the provided statements into categories in any way they saw fit and label the categories using their own descriptive names. They were instructed not to create categories based on priority or value, to avoid using categories like 'Miscellaneous' or "Other" for unrelated statements, and to place unrelated statements in their own category. After sorting, the participants were asked to rate each statement individually on a five-point Likert scale on two values: importance, where 1 = relatively unimportant and 5 = extremely important, and feasibility, where 1 = least feasible and 5 = most feasible. They had 2 weeks to complete the sorting and rating.

Multidimensional scaling was applied to the raw participant groupings of the statements to identify each idea's position relative to others in a two-dimensional space (a point map). Two additional measures were generated to help the interpretation of the results: a goodness-of-fit index and a bridging value. The goodness-of-fit index is routinely generated by MDS (Kruskal & Wish, 1978) to indicate how closely the participants' raw sorting as input aligns with the final MDS configuration in the concept map (the point map). The bridging value ranges from 0 to 1 and indicates the frequency with which a statement has been grouped with others. A lower bridging value indicates that a statement was sorted with nearby statements on the map, while a higher bridging value suggests that it was sorted with statements that were further apart.

An agglomerative hierarchical cluster analysis (HCA) was conducted on the two-dimensional coordinates of the statements in the point map to identify broader thematic categories (a cluster map). The number of clusters was initially determined by two researchers using a well-established procedure (Kane & Trochim, 2007), and the results were further discussed in an interpretation session with representatives of the partner organizations.

In addition, average rating values were calculated for importance and feasibility for each cluster. A graphical representation called pattern match was created to compare the rating values of clusters on the two dimensions and to indicate the strength of the relationship between the two data sets.

The Welch's t-test for unequal variance was used to check if there was a significant difference between the two rating values within and between clusters.

3 From Data to Findings

This section presents the GCM's outcomes on hybrid learning design based on the sorting and rating data analyses.

3.1 Idea Generation

The data collection process involved extracting short phrases from a literature search using the organization's bibliographic databases on hybrid learning design guidelines. In addition, several AI-based searching tools were utilized that offer advantages over traditional search engines. These AI tools not only provide access to a vast amount of bibliographic sources but also facilitate conversation with researchers and stimulate asking specific questions about hybrid learning design guidelines. The AI search was not restricted to peer-reviewed papers only but extended the search to include web resources as well, involving a larger expert community and professional networks virtually. The following AI search tools were used: Perplexity, Consensus, Scispace, Ask iAi, Keymate, Groq, Scite, Andisearch, OpenRead, and Scholar GPT.

The idea generation process resulted in 109 statements. After idea synthesis, 87 statements were selected for sorting and rating.

3.2 Sorting Data Analysis

The point map in Fig. 1 is a mathematical model generated by MDS on the raw sorting data. The closer the statements are to each other on the map, the closer they are in meaning. Numbers are unique identifiers of the statements randomly assigned by Groupwisdom™. The stress value statistic of 0.29 was within the accepted range (Rosas & Kane, 2012), indicating that the point map accurately represented the data set.

Figure 2 displays the final thematic clusters after the interpretation session. Each cluster is described in detail, accompanied by exemplary ideas and their unique identifiers.

The cluster *Implementing hybrid learning and teaching methods* contains some generic ideas such as "Design learning activities according to the principles of active learning, student-centeredness, and differentiation" (84), and "Challenge students by encouraging them to participate in activities that require critical thinking, problem-solving, and decision-making to keep them engaged and stimulated" (41). These generic guidelines are combined with some more concrete suggestions: "Write pedagogical and technical scripts that take into consideration the learning contents, delivery of teaching, and different modes of participation" (57) and "Combine different teaching activities and modes of learning (individual, peer-to-peer, or group), such as lecturing style, small group discussion, brainstorming" (69). There are also ideas promoting specific hybrid learning models, such as Flex Hybrid

Fig. 1 Relationships between the statements (a point map)

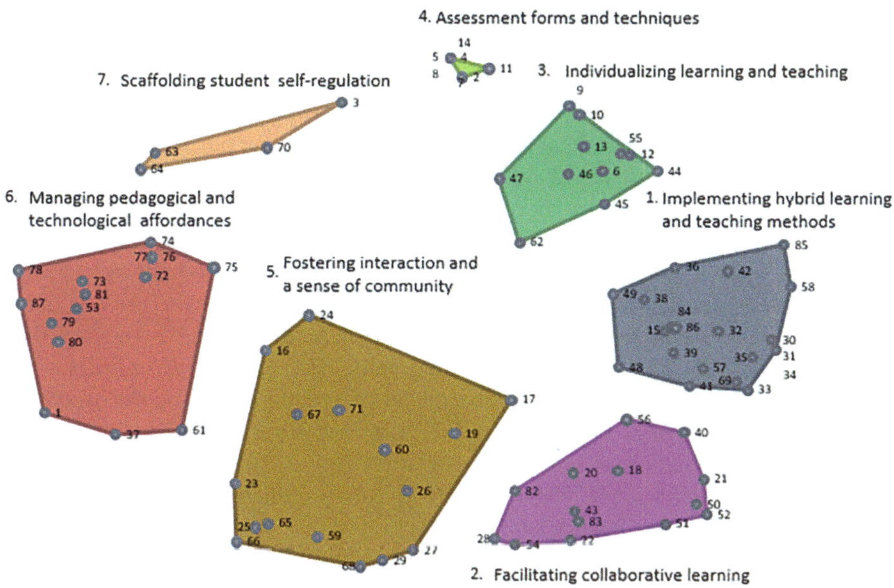

Fig. 2 Thematic areas (a cluster map)

Learning and Rotation Hybrid Learning. Flipped Classroom approach is also included (statements 30, 31, and 34, respectively).

A common theme throughout the cluster is designing in multiple modalities and across spaces: "Develop hybrid learning solutions along the dimensions of the learning process (individual collaborative), settings (classroom, extra-classroom), and the learning space (onsite, online)" (32), and "Strive to strike a balance between in-person and virtual instruction" (86).

Some examples of statements that support collaborative learning in the cluster *Facilitating collaborative learning* are: "Facilitate collaboration by creating online forums, discussion boards, or group projects" (20); "Assign collaborative projects that can be completed both in-person and online"(21); and "Encourage collaboration and teamwork by assigning group projects that require students to work together, sharing ideas, and problem-solving" (22). The cluster also contains some statements about facilitating group cohesion and dynamics: "Use icebreakers to build rapport, trust, and motivation among learners" (43) and "Foster group cohesion by joint activities, e.g., by playing get-to-know-each-other games across online and face-to-face sites" (54). One of the pedagogical and technological benefits of hybrid learning is the possibility of involving external experts in the learning process, as indicated in the statement, "Motivate students to interact with researchers or outstanding professionals to deepen their knowledge and share their "savoir and savoir-faire" with all the class" (28).

Individualizing learning and teaching is a thematic cluster with guidelines on providing individual feedback to students, assessing the specific needs of students, and providing additional support for struggling and advanced students (e.g., statements 9, 12, 45, 46). The statement "Utilize online analytics to tailor instruction to meet individual student needs, ensuring adaptability and personalized learning experiences" (6) highlights specific learning technology designed to address the need for individualization. Notably, the statements about supporting peer feedback and self-directed learning are also part of this cluster (13, 62).

The cluster *Assessment forms and techniques* includes guidelines that refer to specific methods for evaluating knowledge and skills (e.g., "Apply performance-based assessment strategies like presentations, videos, and podcasting", 2) and some concrete practical suggestions (e.g., "Use a comment feature to provide qualitative feedback about student performance when assessing and reviewing their work", 7). With the lowest average bridging value (BV = 0.03), this cluster is the most coherent one, suggesting the highest level of agreement among the experts.

The cluster *Fostering interaction and sense of community* highlights the need to facilitate communication and interaction between face-to-face and remote students. Examples of statements are: "Establish effective communication channels for feedback and support" (19), "Facilitate the interaction of face-to-face students and those participating mainly online to create critical friend groups" (27), "Facilitate student interactions among face-to-face groups, online groups, and between face-to-face and online to increase the feeling of belonging to the classroom" (29), "Consider teaching presence, cognitive presence and social presence in designing hybrid learning solutions" (59), and "Foster students' sense of belonging, trust, and respect" (65).

The *Managing pedagogical and technological affordances* cluster contains statements emphasizing the significant role of technologies in hybrid learning environments. Examples of statements are: "Integrate digital tools like educational apps, online simulations, and multimedia content to create an immersive and interactive learning environment" (76), "Set up a big screen and a good meeting camera with a high-quality audio system to support interaction and social presence of students in different spaces" (72), and "Ensure that all students have equal access to resources and technology" (74). Some statements highlight the importance of teachers' and students' competencies in using digital tools and platforms: "Implementing a successful hybrid learning model requires educators to be proficient in using various educational technologies and platforms" (79), and "Ensure that all students are proficient in using various educational technologies and platforms for their learning" (80). Most of the statements in this cluster have relatively low bridging values, except three, which, in contrast, have one of the highest. These statements are: "Consider that students in hybrid learning environments may struggle to balance their academic commitments with other responsibilities, such as work or family" (1, BV = 0.93), "Adapting to hybrid teaching methods can be challenging, especially for educators who are accustomed to traditional teaching methods" (37, BV = 0.86), and "Professional development and training are essential to ensure that educators can effectively deliver content in both settings" (61, BV = 0.79).

Semantically, the ideas in the cluster *Scaffolding student self-regulation* can be divided into two parts: two ideas on organizational and pedagogical support of self-regulated learning, such as "Ensure that students can manage their time effectively" (63) and "Encourage students to take ownership of their learning by setting goals, managing their time and seeking additional resources" (64), and two ideas on the use of technological support tools like dashboards, completions badges and leaderboards, for that purpose (e.g., "Assign a dashboard for every student", 70). Statement 64 has the highest bridging value among all the statements (BV = 1), and statement 63 has one of the highest (BV = 0.85). These two statements contribute to this cluster's highest average bridging value (BV = 0.71).

3.3 *Rating Data Analysis*

Although secondary for GCM research, the rating data analysis shed additional light on the findings. The ladder graph in Fig. 3, known as pattern match, compares the clusters' average means on the two rating values of importance and feasibility. In general, there was no big difference between the two rating values in most of the clusters, with an overall moderate association ($r = 0.54$). A notable exception was *Individualizing learning and teaching,* which scored relatively high on importance and relatively low on feasibility ($M_{importance} = 3.77$, $SD = 0.11$; $F_{easibility} = 2.84$, $SD = 0.18$). The Welch's t-test for unequal variance indicated a significant difference in this cluster's mean value of importance and feasibility: $t(20) = 5.69$, $p < 0.001$. This was the only significance detected between the rating values on a cluster level.

The cluster *Scaffolding student self-regulation* scored relatively low on both ratings, as the relationship was visualized with a strength line. It is important to note

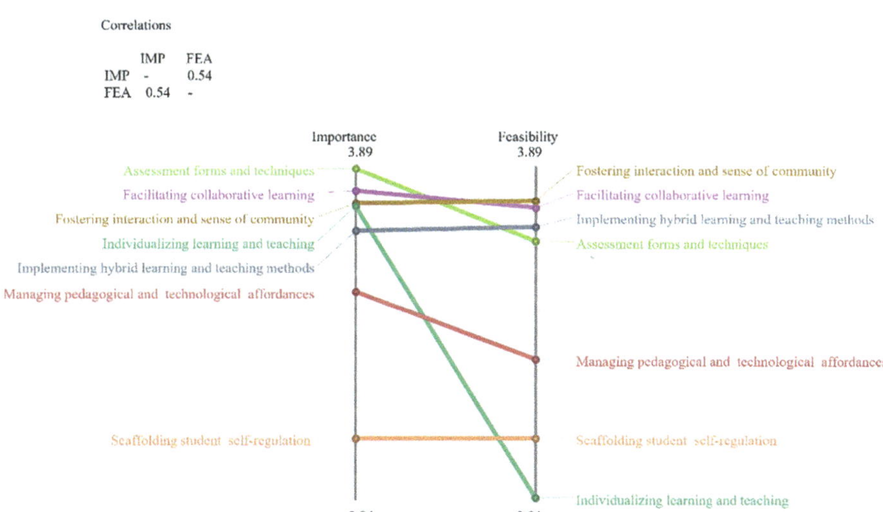

Fig. 3 Comparing clusters on importance and feasibility

that the scores on the importance of statements 63 and 64 on self-regulation "Ensuring that students can manage their time effectively is essential for their success in hybrid learning" (M = 3.25, SD = 0.94) and "Encourage students to take ownership of their learning by setting goals, managing their time, and seeking additional resources" (M = 4.38, SD = 0.23) were much higher than those referring to technology (3, 70): "Use completion badges and leaderboards" (M = 2.38; SD = 0.48), and "Assign a dashboard for every student" (M = 2.13; SD = 0.36).

4 From Findings to Insights

The hybrid learning framework that has emerged from the study's empirical findings implies that learning and instructional designers should consider the following groups of guidelines: (1) *Implementing hybrid teaching methods*, (2) *Facilitating collaborative learning*, (3) *Individualizing learning and teaching*, (4) *Assessment forms and techniques*, (5) *Fostering interaction and a sense of community*, (6) *Managing pedagogical and technological affordances*, and (7) *Scaffolding student self-regulation*. The statements in each cluster can be seen as operationalizations of the overarching categories. Although these statements may not comprehensively cover all thematic areas of the framework, they provide valuable directions for further elaboration.

The current study proposes a cohesive structure that can seamlessly integrate hybrid learning methods and techniques, including those not initially included in the set of guidelines. The clusters can serve as foundational components for a hybrid learning design blueprint.

The positions of the clusters *Implementing hybrid learning and teaching methods*, *Facilitating collaborative learning*, *Individualizing learning and teaching*, and *Assessment forms and techniques*, which are all located in the 'Eastern' section of the framework map, indicate their interrelatedness by contributing to the design of the hybrid learning constructive alignment of learning objectives, learning and instruction methods, and assessment. The findings support the inclusive relationship between narrow and broad definitions of hybrid learning by proposing solutions that integrate online and offline spaces, blend synchronous and asynchronous learning, and accommodate both individual and group activities.

Notably, the clusters *Facilitating collaborative learning* and *Individualizing learning and teaching* are identified as independent thematic areas rather than subsets of the cluster *Implementing hybrid learning and teaching methods*, an outcome that may be in contrast to what is expected. The finding emphasizes the importance of focusing on individualization and collaboration and putting more design effort into them. However, it is essential to recognize that the cluster *Implementing hybrid learning and teaching methods* bridges *Facilitating collaborative learning* and *Individualizing learning and teaching*, indicating a strong relationship between these clusters.

A similar rationale applies to the close association between the clusters *Facilitating collaborative learning* and *Fostering interaction and a sense of community*. While one might anticipate a straightforward fusion of these two clusters, the designation of *Fostering interaction and a sense of community* as an independent cluster underscores the importance of managing interactions between on-site and off-site students—one of the primary concerns in hybrid learning design. Learning designers must ensure equitable learning experiences for both in-person and remote students, fostering a sense of belonging and community.

Statements with high cross-sectional values warrant particular attention in the design of a hybrid learning environment. These statements are frequently associated with those from both their current cluster and other clusters, bridging distinct thematic areas. Such statements should be interpreted in the context of their respective clusters, as defined by HCA, while also considering their connections to other thematic areas. Most high-bridging value statements are found within the clusters *Managing pedagogical and technological affordances* and *Scaffolding student self-regulation*. The statements with high bridging values in the cluster *Managing pedagogical and technological affordances* are closely interrelated yet also linked to statements in other clusters, most notably the cluster *Implementing hybrid learning and teaching methods*. This implies that teachers must adapt their instructional strategies to cater to both in-person and online learners simultaneously, necessitating careful planning and flexibility. Furthermore, they must effectively utilize various digital tools and platforms, which can be overwhelming. This finding highlights the critical need for comprehensive training and support in both pedagogical and technological dimensions. Hybrid learning environments necessitate the adaptation of pedagogical approaches to suit hybrid learning technologies. Technologies transform the execution of learning and teaching tasks and influence the perception of those tasks.

The statement "Consider that students in hybrid learning environments may struggle to balance their academic commitments with other responsibilities, such as work or family" (1) has been frequently associated with the two statements regarding self-regulation in the cluster *Scaffolding student self-regulation*. While defined in the study as a challenge, this statement can also be perceived as an opportunity. One potential method for transforming this challenge into a benefit is by enhancing learners' ownership of their education and promoting self-regulated learning, with a particular focus on time management training.

Unsurprisingly, the statements concerning self-regulation within the cluster *Scaffolding student self-regulation* are strongly linked to the statement, "Support self-directed learning by providing students with clear expectations, guiding them through the learning process, and encouraging them to reflect on their progress" (62) in the cluster *Individualizing learning and teaching*.

4.1 Caveats

The GCM study was not initially planned, and due to the project's tight schedule, it needed to be completed in a relatively short timeframe. This may have compromised the participation and commitment of the project members.

Eighteen individuals were involved in the idea generation phase, which represents a small sample. However, we believe that the literature review, which synthesized various methods and tools, adequately covered the domain of hybrid learning design.

We undertook a swift yet comprehensive literature search using bibliographic databases and AI search tools. However, we did not document the steps and outcomes of this process, which would have facilitated a systematic description (e.g., PRISMA statement).

The level of participation in the rating process was low, indicating that caution should be exercised in drawing strong conclusions. It is important to note that in the GCM, the rating supplements the sorting activity. We employed Welch's t-test for measuring significance, which is suitable for our data. This test compares two datasets with unequal variances, particularly when the samples are small. Welch's t-test is more conservative regarding Type I error rates than the Mann-Whitney U test in situations involving small samples, rendering it a reliable choice in practical applications. Although Welch's test is sensitive to the assumption of normal distribution, it demonstrates consistent performance even in real-life scenarios involving moderately skewed data distributions.

The sorting sample also appears to be small. However, it is essential to acknowledge that sorting is distinct from rating, as it relies on a different logical operation—classification. The statistical methods applied in these two activities differ accordingly. One approach to assess the reliability and validity of the sorting data analysis is to compare it with similar methodologies. A well-regarded method for this purpose is Cohen's Kappa, which measures inter-rater reliability when two evaluators categorize items. In our study, nine participants sorted statements anonymously and independently of one another. The MDS technique subsequently aggregated their input to calculate the level of agreement. The internal validity, as measured by the stress value, was within an acceptable range.

To avoid overstretching this study's implications for research and practice in hybrid learning, we prefer to designate the hybrid learning framework as the Hyb-IT-Up Hybrid Learning Design Framework, thus limiting the findings to this particular project only.

5 Key Takeaways

The study empirically identifies the constituent elements of a hybrid learning framework designed to facilitate hybrid learning sessions. This framework can serve as both a design blueprint and a foundation for creating templates that support hybrid learning and instruction.

In this framework, individualization and collaborative learning, traditionally regarded as distinct approaches, are recognized as separate yet interrelated entities. This suggests that both elements require careful consideration when designing a hybrid learning environment. While individualization is critical for fostering an effective hybrid learning experience, it is also the most challenging aspect.

The guidelines that promote interaction and a sense of community form a distinct group that is closely associated with collaborative learning. However, they are not integrated into a single cluster, as one might expect. This finding underscores the necessity of arrangements that support group dynamics and foster a sense of community among learners. In this regard, it may be necessary to also pay more attention to increasing the social presence of remote students and reducing the feelings of psychological distance (see this book: chapter A social presence perspective on hybrid learning).

Ideas for high-level interactivity should be carefully evaluated. This indicates that designing hybrid learning requires adapting teaching methods to the specific nature of the hybrid environment, seamlessly integrating technological tools with pedagogical approaches, ensuring professional training in this area, and facilitating self-regulated learning.

Acknowledgments This research has been funded by the Finnish National Agency within Erasmus+ Key Action 2, Cooperation partnerships in higher education (No. 2022-1-FI01-KA220-HED-000086605). It is conducted in the context of the project "Upgrading higher education teachers' and students' hybrid learning competences" (Hyb-IT-up).

References

Bower, M., Dalgarno, B., Kennedy, G. E., Lee, M. J. W., & Kenney, J. (2015). Design and implementation factors in blended synchronous learning environments: Outcomes from a cross-case analysis. *Computers & Education, 86*, 1–17. https://doi.org/10.1016/j.compedu.2015.03.006

Bülow, M. W. (2022). Designing synchronous hybrid learning spaces: Challenges and opportunities. In E. Gil, Y. Mor, Y. Dimitriadis, & C. Köppe (Eds.), *Hybrid learning spaces* (pp. 135–163). Springer. https://doi.org/10.1007/978-3-030-88520-5

Center for Teaching and Innovation. (2024). *Getting started with designing a hybrid learning course*. Cornell University. Retrieved from https://teaching.cornell.edu/resource/getting-started-designing-hybrid-learning-course.

Cohen, A., Nørgård, R. T., & Mor, Y. (2020). Hybrid learning spaces. Design, data, didactics. *British Journal of Educational Technology, 51*(4), 1039–1044. https://doi.org/10.1111/bjet.12964

Eyal, L., & Gil, E. (2022). Hybrid learning spaces—A three-fold evolving perspective. In E. Gil, Y. Mor, Y. Dimitriadis, & C. Köppe (Eds.), *Hybrid learning spaces* (pp. 11–23). Springer. https://doi.org/10.1007/978-3-030-88520-5

Goodyear, P. (2020). Design and co-configuration for hybrid learning: Theorising the practices of learning space design. *British Journal of Educational Technology, 51*(4), 1045–1060. https://doi.org/10.1111/bjet.12925

Goodyear, P., Carvalho, L., & Yeoman, P. (2021). Activity-centred analysis and design (ACAD): Core purposes, distinctive qualities and current developments. *Educational Technology Research and Development, 69*, 445–464. https://doi.org/10.1007/s11423-020-09926-7

Hafni, A., & Fithriani, R. (2021). Integrating wiki in hybrid EFL writing class: Exploring Indonesian students' perceptions of its benefits and challenges. *Journal of Community Research and Service, 5*(1), 27–41. https://doi.org/10.24114/jcrs.v5i1.27186

Ibrahim, E., & Suhaimi, A. (2022). Preliminary investigation of undergraduate learner's satisfaction towards hybrid learning. *International Journal of Academic Research in Progressive Education and Development, 11*(3), 1727–1739. https://doi.org/10.6007/ijarped/v11-i3/15496

Kane, M., & Rosas, S. (2018). *Conversations about group concept mapping: Applications, examples and enhancements*. Sage.

Kane, M., & Trochim, B. (2007). *Concept mapping for planning and evaluation*. Sage.

Kreijns, K., Yau, J., Weidlich, J., & Weinberger, A. (2024). Towards a comprehensive framework of social presence for online, hybrid, and blended learning. *Frontiers in Education, 8*, 286594. https://doi.org/10.3389/feduc.2023.1286594

Kruskal, J. B., & Wish, M. (1978). *Multidimensional scaling*. Sage.

Musdariah, A., Basri, M., & Jabu, B. (2021). The impact of hybrid learning in teaching English for business communication in vocational higher education of Indonesia. *International Journal of Humanities and Innovation (IJHI), 4*(3), 104–110. https://doi.org/10.33750/ijhi.v4i3.124

Ortega-Arranz, A., Amarasinghe, I., Martínez-Monés, A., Asensio-Pérez, J., Dimitriadis, Y., Corrales-Astorgano, M., & Davinia Hernández-Leo, D. (2024). Collaborative activities in hybrid learning environments: Exploring teacher orchestration load and students' perceptions. *Computers & Education, 219*, 105105. https://doi.org/10.1016/j.compedu.2024.105105

Raes, A. (2022). Exploring student and teacher experiences in hybrid learning environments: Does presence matter? *Postdigital Science and Education, 4*, 138–159. https://doi.org/10.1007/s42438-021-00274-0

Raes, A., Detienne, L., Winder, I., & Depaepe, F. (2020). A systematic literature review on synchronous hybrid learning: Gaps identified. *Learning Environments Research, 23*, 269–290. https://doi.org/10.1007/s10984-019-09303-z

Rosas S.R., & Kane, M. (2012). Quality and rigor of the concept mapping methodology: a pooled study analysis. Evaluation and Program Planning, 35(2),236–345. https://doi.org/10.1016/j.evalprogplan.2011.10.003.

Singh, J., Steele, K., & Singh, L. (2021). Combining the best of online and face-to-face learning: Hybrid and blended learning approach for COVID-19, post-vaccine, & post-pandemic world. *Journal of Educational Technology Systems, 50*(2), 140–171. https://doi.org/10.1177/00472395211047865

The Concept System® Groupwisdom™ (Build 2022.30.10) [Web-based Platform]. (2022). Retrieved from https://www.groupwisdom.tech.

Trochim, W. M., & McLinden, D. (2017). Introduction to a special issue on concept mapping. *Evaluation and Program Planning, 60*, 166–175. https://doi.org/10.1016/j.evalprogplan.2016.10.006

Warburton, S., & Mor, Y. (2015). Double loop design: Configuring narratives, patterns and scenarios in the design of technology-enhanced learning. In Y. Mor, M. Maina, & B. Craft (Eds.), *The art and science of learning design* (pp. 93–104). Sense.

Zydney, J. M., McKimmy, P., Lindberg, R., & Schmidt, M. (2019). Here or there instruction: Lessons learned in implementing innovative approaches to blended synchronous learning. *TechTrends, 63*(2), 123–132. https://doi.org/10.1007/s11528-018-0344-z

Competence-Driven Guidelines for Hybrid Teaching

António Moreira, Marta Fortunato, Cecília Guerra, Maria João Loureiro, and Rita Tavares

1 Introduction

To our knowledge, hybrid teaching and learning has been a research concern since 2018. The COVID-19 confinement and the future return to a novel normality made hybrid teaching come up with new teaching and learning scenarios that persist considering some basilar aspects that could determine the success of education systems: resilience, sustainability, adaptability and future approaches related to hybrid teaching and learning. These approaches foresee learning environments supported by an information and communication technologies (ICT) infrastructure, including both in-person and virtual learners, meaning that some learners are physically present, and others are participating remotely synchronously. Lázár et al. (2021) define hybrid teaching and learning as three different combinations of face-to-face and online delivery modes:

> (1) the teacher and some learners in the same physical space plus other learners connecting remotely; (2) all the learners in the same physical space with the teacher connecting remotely; (3) some learners in the same physical space plus the teacher and other learners connecting online (p. 23).

Recently, many studies have disclosed that hybrid teaching and learning approaches can present some advantages in comparison with traditional classrooms, namely: (1) flexibility for learners, enabling them to engage with the learning process and materials according to their individual preferences, path and schedules; (2) fewer infrastructures, allowing more learners to participate in a course, a discipline or even a specific class; (3) technology integration, benefitting from several kinds of technological advances, for instance, live-streamed lectures, interactive multimedia

A. Moreira (✉) · M. Fortunato · C. Guerra · M. J. Loureiro · R. Tavares
CIDTFF (Centro de Investigação em Didática e Tecnologia na Formação de Formadores), University of Aveiro, Aveiro, Portugal
e-mail: moreira@ua.pt

A. Nakata et al. (eds.), *Hyb-IT-up!*,
https://doi.org/10.1007/978-3-031-99743-3_6

resources, polls, virtual and augmented reality; (4) collaboration through online discussions, shared projects, and other forms of virtual teamwork; and (5) effectiveness, allowing learners to easily engage with the teachers, peers, and the learning process, due to the aspects mentioned above (Gao et al., 2021; Scaringella et al., 2022; Usmani, 2021). To sum up, hybrid teaching and learning is a model that is the result of combining face-to-face and online classes simultaneously, with a focus on student-centred teaching, in which the teacher plans, designs and delivers classes adapted to both formats, using ICT infrastructures to integrate all those involved. The design and organization of lessons can range in both scope and form, i.e. they can result in online lectures and respective face-to-face discussions; and/or they can incorporate multiple online content materials as a complement to face-to-face lessons (Gao et al., 2021; Scaringella et al., 2022; Usmani, 2021).

To design and implement these approaches, there are few practical frameworks established in the literature (related to the education and social sciences scope). Hartono et al. (2018) introduced the Smart Hybrid Learning Method, integrating case-based learning, technology, MOOCs, and social media, including online materials, forum discussions, peer learning, videos and exercises. Mlotshwa et al. (2020), based on the constructivist framework proposed by Hirumi, developed a study where learning was promoted through: instruction; human interaction, as well as interaction with digital learning resources; and self-learning, valuing past experiences, individual needs, active participation, critical thinking and continuous learning, to promote interaction with teachers, peers and technology. Kentel (2022) introduced a Hybrid Teaching of Drawing Framework, combining face-to-face and online teaching, that promotes active learning, consistency in course planning and activities, and uses various communication channels to support the pedagogy of care, with 6 weeks of face-to-face teaching and 6 weeks online, using synchronous and asynchronous methods. On the other hand, UNESCO (2023) created the HELA framework, focusing on infrastructure, technology, accessible digital resources, pedagogy, continuous assessment, learning-teaching supports, collaboration, and flexible hybrid education.

From the examples presented above, it becomes clear that there is a gap in practical frameworks for hybrid teaching and learning approaches in the literature. They all seem to focus on the student and the curriculum. In response to that, and within the scope of the Hyb-IT-up Project, a comprehensive hybrid teaching framework focused on how teachers can design and implement hybrid approaches was defined, aiming to outline a set of guidelines in line with the three key competences to thrive in this emergent educational landscape: generic competences, contextual competences, and transformative competences.

The research design was divided into two phases: (1) a systematic literature review to understand the current landscape regarding hybrid teaching and learning guidelines put forth by various researchers as descriptors of a framework; and (2) a workshop to co-design scenarios of hybrid teaching and learning based on the guidelines gathered in the systematic literature review to highlight the guidelines deemed important for the framework.

2 Methodology

2.1 Systematic Literature Review

A systematic literature review must follow specific methodological procedures to ensure replicability. This kind of review differs from traditional or narrative reviews in that it is expected to be rigorous, transparent, replicable, and updatable (Zawacki-Richter et al., 2020). These include formulating clear research questions, selecting appropriate databases, defining selection criteria, searching the databases, applying the selection criteria, and presenting results and conclusions (adapted from Sampaio & Mancini, 2007). The systematic literature review adhered to the PRISMA guidelines and presented the results through its flowchart (Page et al., 2021). The search focused on peer-reviewed articles to ensure quality, aiming to identify guidelines for designing hybrid teaching and learning environments. The empirical corpus consisted of articles from education journals indexed in Scopus, Web of Science, and ERIC, chosen for their relevance and filtering capabilities in the educational field. The search was restricted to open-access scientific articles published between 2014 and 2023, in English. Two keywords/expressions were used: "hybrid learning" AND "higher education" and "hybrid teaching" AND "higher education," combined with the Boolean operator AND, and quotation marks to limit results. Only empirical studies that discussed guidelines for developing hybrid teaching/learning activities were considered. Excluded from the analysis were literature reviews, theses, and dissertations.

The search yielded 175 texts (47 from Scopus, 82 from ERIC, 46 from Web of Science), that were uploaded to Mendeley to remove duplicates, identifying 28. Screening revealed 102 texts unrelated to hybrid teaching guidelines, 33 not open access, one systematic review, and one bibliographical review. Ultimately, 10 articles were selected for analysis, as shown in the flowchart (Fig. 1).

The corpus was read and analysed. Data collection was supported by filling in a table (shared on Google Drive), organised by authors and year of publication, and guidelines for hybrid teaching and learning were collected. The reading and analysis were based on the content analysis technique and aprioristic categories (Bardin, 2016), presented in Table 1.

The application of these three categories was considered for its relevance in the effective integration of digital technologies into teaching and learning practices (Wagner et al., 2022).

2.2 Co-Design Workshop

Co-design is a process that requires the collaboration between designers and potential users in the design process from the problem clarification to the design of a solution (Sanders & Stappers, 2008). The users have a fundamental role in the

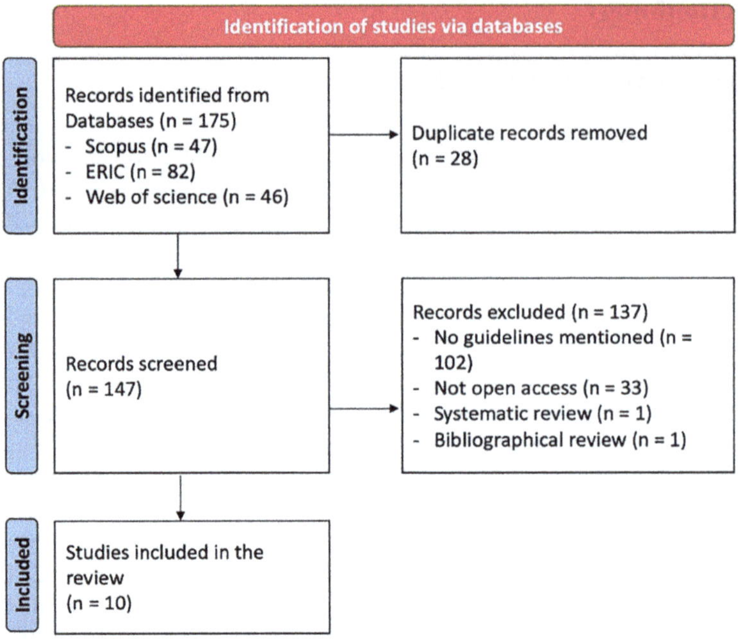

Fig. 1 Flowchart of the results

Table 1 Categories of analysis

Categories	Description
Generic competence	Competence involves: (1) pedagogical skills; (2) knowledge; (3) beliefs and values; and (4) emotions in the use of technology in the teaching and learning process
Contextual competence	Competence related to self-regulation and co-regulation
Transformative competence	Competence covers creativity and the ethical and responsible use of technology

process and contribute as specialists in their own practices, enabling a user-centred approach (Sanders & Stappers, 2008; Sandström et al., 2022). Each co-design process is planned in relation to the participants and context, and users are invited to talk about their practices and visions, as well as design prototypes related to the research problem (Bøjer & Brøns, 2022).

In this text, such an approach has been used to design technology-enhanced learning scenarios (Barbera et al., 2017), as well as hybrid teaching and learning scenarios (Bøjer & Brøns, 2022; Sandström et al., 2022; Zeivots & Shalavin, 2021). To our knowledge, this participatory design technique has not been explored to design/upgrade a guidelines' framework (emerged from a systematic literature review) that should guide the design of hybrid teaching and learning scenarios. This was the main goal of one of the Hyb_IT_up project initiatives, a workshop entitled

"Co-design of a framework for implementing hybrid teaching and learning strategies". As explained below, at the beginning of the workshop several resources were shared to build a common understanding among the participants (activities 1 and 2), followed by a creative development process using different tools to prototype hybrid teaching and learning scenarios considering the competence framework (activities 3–6).

The workshop was promoted at the University of Aveiro and the University of Porto. There were 16 participants, who were teachers/researchers in Education. The time allocated to the workshops was three and a half hours. Participants had to: (1) design a hybrid teaching and learning scenario; (2) discuss the solutions found for different scenarios; and (3) discuss the adequacy and relevance of the guidelines included in the resulting framework.

The workshop encompassed several activities described in the following paragraphs.

1. Presentation of the workshop objectives, the activities, and the main theoretical background, namely hybrid teaching, the pedagogical approach underlying the development of the guidelines' framework for the use of digital technologies in hybrid teaching and different hybrid teaching and learning scenarios.
2. Organisation of the groups and analysis of the proposed competence framework. Each group should first think of two guidelines, analyse the proposed framework, mark identical guidelines and add a post-it if no identical guidelines were found. The groups were also required to signal the three most relevant guidelines and the three least relevant.
3. Design a teaching and learning scenario, considering a common code and representing it in the upper left corner of the working sheet (Fig. 2).
4. Definition of the elements related to the teaching and learning activity to be developed in the created scenario: pedagogical objective(s); competences; tasks (format, interaction, materials & tools); dynamics of learning and assessment (including feedback for continuous improvement); and fill in the working sheet.
5. Identify valid guidelines to operationalize the designed activity from the point of view of the teacher, considering the competences (groups should identify two to three guidelines for each type) and prepare a three-minute pitch.
6. Presentation and discussion of the activities and evaluation of the workshop.

3 Results and Discussion

Based on the analysis of the corpus, 45 guidelines were identified: 19 generic competences, 20 contextual competences, and six transformative competences (Tables 2, 3, and 4). As mentioned above, during the workshop, the participants had to brainstorm and discuss guidelines, before the analysis of the designed framework (group guidelines) and, after its exploration, indicating which were the most

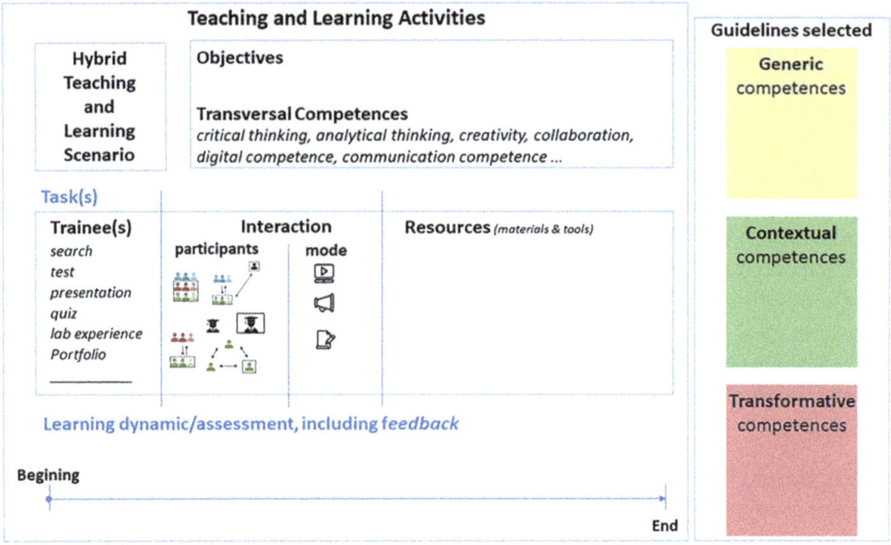

Fig. 2 Workshops' worksheet

important guidelines. After the scenarios design, they had to state the competences under consideration during the process.

In the first task, participants had to come up with more specific guidelines than the ones presented in the framework. For instance, participants indicated several transversal competences, like collaboration or reflection, that are related to the competence "develop transversal competences leveraging the potential of ICT" already foreseen. Another example is the mention of the need of preparedness and clarity, included in the competence "create a plan and materials that last beyond the course".

The results are all presented in a single table for each group of competences (Tables 2, 3, and 4) to facilitate the analysis by crosschecking the results. In addition, we highlighted with different shades of grey the competences chosen before the design of the hybrid activities (light grey), those selected only after this activity (grey) and the competences considered before and after (dark grey). Terms between brackets or highlighted (in bold) are concepts that allow to underline the competence areas that emerge from the guidelines' intersection.

From the analysis of Table 2, it can be inferred that out of the 19 generic competences of the framework, 10 were either selected during the first activity or valued during its design. Those that seem more significant concerning the creation of sustainable plans and materials (Guerra & Costa, 2021) were the promotion of live discussion, teacher/peer feedback, hands-on activities, and inclusiveness. Scenario design also led participants to value competences related to the preparation of introductory activities, such as acquainting the students with the activity plan and with each other (ice-breaking). Competences aimed at developing group work and preparing video materials were also selected at this stage.

Table 2 Generic competences

Generic competences	References	Groups' guidelines	Most relevant	Valid ones
Familiarisation (program & tools) ice-breaking team building (interaction)	Taimur et al. (2022) Unger et al. (2022)			X
Create a plan and materials that last beyond the course (sustainability)	Kauppi et al. (2020)	X	X	X
Promote the integration of expert (multidisciplinary) collaboration	Kauppi et al. (2020)	X	X	
Include group work (practical work)	Unger et al. (2022)			X
Promote live discussions (interaction)	Unger et al. (2022)		X	X
Design diverse learning methods and resources for (a)synchronous learning	Usmani (2021)			
Set ways for easy tracking of students' progress and achievement	Vereshchahina et al. (2018)			
Design learning monitoring	Unger et al. (2022)			
Use/prepare accessible video-based materials (digital resources)	Unger et al. (2022)			X
Provide tools that allow for flexible mobility and collaboration	Kauppi et al. (2020)			
Develop transversal competencies, leveraging on digital technology	Pavlidou et al. (2021)			
Enable content/task personalisation (inclusion)	Cundell and Sheepy (2018) Anderson and Krathwohl (2001) Unger et al. (2022)			
Design transparent guidelines to support multidisciplinary online collaboration/ interaction	Kauppi et al. (2020)	X	X	
Use multimodal resources to document and represent the phenomena (digital resources)	Kauppi et al. (2020)		X	
Design (intermediate) teacher/peer feedback	Unger et al. (2022)	X		X
Integrate hands-on work (practical work)	Unger et al. (2022)		X	X
Design learner-learner and learner-content interaction	Anderson and Krathwohl (2001)			
Adopt inclusive teaching practices (e.g., multiformat student responses)	Cundell and Sheepy (2018) Unger et al. (2022)		X	X
Set easy access to curriculum and learning materials	Gao et al. (2021)			

Table 3 Contextual competences

Contextual competences	References	Groups' guidelines	Most relevant	Valid ones
Ensure group diversity: culture, region, discipline, and personality (inclusion)	Taimur et al. (2022)	X	X	
Set flexible learning approaches, such as time and space (inclusion)	Taimur et al. (2022) Unger et al. (2022)		X	
Design and promote peer feedback	Anderson and Krathwohl (2001)	X	X	X
Allow students to continue in-class assignments outside of class on their own time	Unger et al. (2022)			
Develop time-management competencies	Anderson and Krathwohl (2001)			
Require groups to set video-based work meetings outside the class	Unger et al. (2022)			
Send out assignment reminders	Unger et al. (2022)			
Promote activities involving sharing and building on the ideas offered by others	Unger et al. (2022)			
Enable the personalisation of tasks and content delivery	Anderson and Krathwohl (2001)			
Promote peer interaction outside the class (interaction)	Unger et al. (2022)			X
Allow students to choose the mode of participation face-to-face or online	Unger et al. (2022)			
Emphasise teamwork and collaborative knowledge creation	Kauppi et al. (2020)			X
Personalise learning opportunities according to their diverse situations (inclusion)	Kauppi et al. (2020)		X	X
Promote (hybrid) collaboration in projects	Cundell and Sheepy (2018) Kanetaki et al. (2022) Unger et al. (2022)			X
Promote student autonomy and accountability (autonomy)	Kauppi et al. (2020) Vereshchahina et al. (2018)		X	X
Promote teacher-student, student-student, peer-group and group-group communication and engagement (interaction)	Cundell and Sheepy (2018) Vereshchahina et al. (2018); Unger et al. (2022)		X	X
Share supplementary resources	Vereshchahina et al. (2018)			

(continued)

Table 3 (continued)

Contextual competences	References	Groups' guidelines	Most relevant	Valid ones
Promote diverse feedback modes	Anderson and Krathwohl (2001) Kanetaki et al. (2022)		X	X
Promote continuous improvement through peer review activities before submitting final versions	Cundell and Sheepy (2018)			
Organise activities anchored in the collective and individual efforts around a shared object, for example: report, website and presentation	Kauppi et al. (2020)		X	

Table 4 Transformative competences

Transformative competences	References	Groups' guidelines	Most relevant	Valid ones
Develop advanced understanding of suitable pedagogical design principles and knowledge from empirical cases	Kauppi et al. (2020)			
Encourage the identification, sharing and use of relevant open educational resources with peers (digital resources)	Pavlidou et al. (2021)			X
Create engaging, active online activities (interaction)	Cundell and Sheepy (2018)	X		X
Promote well-structured, technology-enhanced, collaboration activities	Cundell and Sheepy (2018)			X
Promote the students' emotional engagement through content customisation (inclusion)	Cundell and Sheepy (2018)	X		X
Integrate in-depth readings into other course activities	Cundell and Sheepy (2018)			

Table 3 shows that out of the 20 contextual competences, 10 were valued by the participants. The table also reveals that the competences related to providing feedback and promoting interaction and involvement of everyone, setting opportunities to develop students' autonomy and accountability, are the most relevant in the context of hybrid teaching and learning scenarios. Peer interaction outside the classroom and the collaboration between the students, either for knowledge creation or within projects, were selected after the design of the scenarios

Concerning the transformative competences (Table 4), the ones listed by the participants at the beginning of the workshops and valued for the creation of the scenarios refer to the effective involvement of students in online activities and the adaptation of resources to stimulate their emotional engagement. The use of Open Educational Resources and the design of technology-enhanced collaborative activities were signaled during the design phase of the workshop.

4 Conclusion

The Hyb-IT-up Project addresses a gap in the literature by proposing a detailed hybrid teaching and learning framework that emphasizes the development of three key categories of competences for designing engaging and effective hybrid learning environments: generic, contextual, and transformative. The research methodology, divided into a systematic literature review and a co-design workshop, followed rigorous and transparent procedures to ensure replicability and high-quality results. The systematic literature review provided a robust basis for identifying relevant guidelines for hybrid teaching and learning approaches. The workshops enriched these findings by involving educators in the co-design process, fostering a user-centred approach that aligns with practical teaching experiences.

The results of the workshops and the literature review culminated in the identification of 45 guidelines categorized into generic, contextual, and transformative competences. Such guidelines convey more importance from the point of view of the workshops' participants as to inclusive practices; interaction and collaboration; the use or development of digital resources; the provision of diverse feedback; and the promotion of practical work. These guidelines are subsumed by other frameworks previously referred to in the introduction, whether specifically stated or interpreted. For instance, the need to design hybrid teaching and learning activities that foresee collaboration, between students, and interaction, among those involved and with diverse digital education resources, are also stressed by Mlotshwa et al. (2020), Hartono et al. (2018) and UNESCO (2023).

Hybrid teaching and learning represent a transformative shift in the educational paradigm, offering numerous benefits over traditional methods. However, the successful adoption of hybrid models requires a comprehensive and practical framework that supports educators in creating effective hybrid learning and teaching environments. The Hyb-It-up project provides such a framework, focusing on the essential competences needed to navigate this new landscape. Moving forward, continuous research and innovation are crucial to refine hybrid approaches, evaluate their effectiveness, and develop new technologies and methodologies to support hybrid education.

By fostering a culture of continuous improvement and collaboration, the educational community can ensure that hybrid teaching and learning remain responsive to the evolving needs of both students and educators. This adaptability will be key to building a resilient, sustainable, and inclusive education system that prepares learners for success in an increasingly complex and interconnected world. Through ongoing efforts to explore, refine, and implement hybrid teaching strategies, we can harness the full potential of this model to enhance the quality and accessibility of education for all.

Acknowledgements This research is supported by the European Union under contract number 2022-1-FI10-KA220-HED-000086605.

References

Anderson, L. W., & Krathwohl, D. R. (2001). *A taxonomy for learning, teaching, and assessing*. Abridged Edition.

Barbera, E., Garcia, I., & Fuertes-Alpiste, M. (2017). A co-design process microanalysis: Stages and facilitators of an inquiry-based and technology-enhanced learning scenario. *The International Review of Research in Open and Distributed Learning, 18*(6). https://doi.org/10.19173/irrodl.v18i6.280.

Bardin, L. (2016). *Análise de Conteúdo*. Edições 70.

Bøjer, B. H., & Brøns, M. G. (2022). How co-design can contribute to the ongoing development of hybrid learning spaces by empowering the users. In E. Gil, Y. Mor, Y. Dimitriadis, & C. Köppe (Eds.), *Hybrid learning spaces. Understanding teaching-learning practice*. Springer. https://doi.org/10.1007/978-3-030-88520-5_4

Cundell, A., & Sheepy, E. (2018). Student perceptions of the most effective and engaging online learning activities in a blended graduate seminar. *Online Learning Journal, 22*(3), 87–102. https://doi.org/10.24059/olj.v22i3.1467

Gao, J., Crossley, S. P., Nollert, M. U., Lance, L. L., & Papavassiliou, D. V. (2021). Online teaching of a lab course amid a pandemic, a challenge and an opportunity. *Chemical Engineering Education, 55*(2), 76–84. https://doi.org/10.18260/2-1-370.660-124795

Guerra, C., & Costa, N. (2021). Can pedagogical innovations be sustainable? One evaluation outlook for research developed in Portuguese higher education. *Education Science, 11*(11), 725. https://doi.org/10.3390/educsci11110725

Hartono, S., Kosala, R., Supangkat, S. H., & Ranti, B. (2018). *Smart hybrid learning framework based on three-layer architecture to bolster up education 4.0.* In Proceeding—2018 International Conference on ICT for Smart Society: Innovation Toward Smart Society and Society 5.0, ICISS 2018, 2017, pp. 1–5. https://doi.org/10.1109/ICTSS.2018.8550028

Kanetaki, Z., Stergiou, C., Bekas, G., Jacques, S., Troussas, C., Sgouropoulou, C., & Ouahabi, A. (2022). Grade prediction modeling in hybrid learning environments for sustainable engineering education. *Sustainability, 14*(9), 5205. https://doi.org/10.3390/su14095205

Kauppi, S., Muukkonen, H., Suorsa, T., & Takala, M. (2020). I still miss human contact, but this is more flexible—Paradoxes in virtual learning interaction and multidisciplinary collaboration. *British Journal of Educational Technology, 51*(4), 1101–1116. https://doi.org/10.1111/bjet.12929

Kentel, A. (2022). Emergency remote teaching of technical drawing during the COVID-19 pandemic. *International Journal of Mobile and Blended Learning, 14*(1), 412–429. https://doi.org/10.4018/IJMBL.314580

Lázár, C., Galambos, A., Váczi, D., & Péter-Both, E. (2021). Learning while doing: Hybrid workshops in Romania and 10+1 conclusions relevant for school education. In *A flexible framework for hybrid lower-secondary education* (pp. 23–30). Tallinn University. Retrieved from https://drive.google.com/file/d/1FO4TpgVJKVGJTbSSaglPTGeYjjuFwJg/view%0

Mlotshwa, N., Tunjera, N., & Chigona, A. (2020). Integration of moodle into the classroom for better conceptual understanding of functions in mathematics. *South African Journal of Education, 40*(3), 1–14. https://doi.org/10.15700/saje.v40n3a1570

Page, M. J., McKenzie, J. E., Bossuyt, P. M., Boutron, I., Hoffmann, T. C., Mulrow, C. D., … Moher, D. (2021, March 29). The PRISMA 2020 statement: An updated guideline for reporting systematic reviews. *BMJ 372*:n71. https://doi.org/10.1136/bmj.n71.

Pavlidou, I., Dragicevic, N., & Tsui, E. (2021). A multi-dimensional hybrid learning environment for business education: A knowledge dynamics perspective. *Sustainability, 13*(7), 3889. https://doi.org/10.3390/su13073889

Sampaio, R., & Mancini, M. (2007). Estudos de Revisão Sistemática: um guia para síntese criteriosa da evidência científica. *Revista Brasileira de Fisioterapia, 11*(1), 83–89. https://doi.org/10.1590/S1413-35552007000100013

Sanders, E. B. N., & Stappers, P. J. (2008). Co-creation and the new landscapes of design. *CoDesign, 4*(1), 5–18. https://doi.org/10.1080/15710880701875068

Sandström, N., Nenonen, S., & Nevgi, A. (2022, September). *Hybrid learning environments in universities: How to manage the co-creation process from design to use*. In C. Tagliaro, A. Migliore, & R. Silvestri (Eds.), Proceedings of the 3rd Workplace Research Conference (pp. 134–143). Politecnico di Milano. Retrieved from http://hdl.handle.net/10138/350474

Scaringella, L., Górska, A., Calderon, D., & Benitez, J. (2022). Should we teach in hybrid mode or fully online? A theory and empirical investigation on the service–profit chain in MBAs. *Information & Management, 59*(1), 103573. https://doi.org/10.1016/j.im.2021.103573

Taimur, S., Onuki, M., & Mursaleen, H. (2022). Exploring the transformative potential of design thinking pedagogy in hybrid setting: A case study of field exercise course, Japan. *Asia Pacific Education Review, 23*(4), 571–593. https://doi.org/10.1007/s12564-022-09776-3

UNESCO. (2023). *Hybrid education, learning, and assessment: A reader; an overview of frameworks, issues and developments in light of COVID-19 and the way forward*. UNESCO. Retrieved from https://unesdoc.unesco.org/ark:/48223/pf0000387639wiposInSet=5&queryId=1e0f9 9fe-8a81-4d03-8846-a7abab1b05c9

Unger, S., Simpson, C., Lecher, A., & Goudreau, S. B. (2022). Student perceptions of hybrid courses in higher education. *Online Learning Journal, 26*(4), 424–448. https://doi.org/10.24059/olj.v26i4.2939

Usmani, S. (2021). COVID-19 pandemic and blended learning: A quantitative assessment of revised Community of Inquiry (RCoI) framework. *Journal of Education and Educational Development, 8*(2), 338–358. https://doi.org/10.22555/joeed.v8i2.544

Vereshchahina, T., Liashchenko, O., & Babiy, S. (2018). English language teachers' perceptions of hybrid learning at university level. *Advanced Education, 10*, 88–97. https://doi.org/10.20535/2410-8286.130734

Wagner, M., Kammerer, L., Ley, T., Helm, C., McGarr, O., Pedaste, M., Leijen, Ä., Rillo, K., & Veskimägi, D. (2022). International good practices on digital skills development of teacher educators. *Report for Deliverable 3*. Federal Ministry Republic of Austria Education, Science and Research.

Zawacki-Richter, O., Kerres, M., Bedenlier, S., Bond, M., & Buntis, K. (2020). *Systematic reviews in educational research: Methodology, perspectives and application*. Springer VS. https://doi.org/10.1016/j.jbusres.2019.07.039

Zeivots, S., & Shalavin, C. (2021). Hybrid teaching workshops: Upskilling educators to deliver hybrid classes. *Journal of Learning Development in Higher Education*, 22. https://doi.org/10.47408/jldhe.vi22.673.

Enhancing Hybrid Teaching with Collaborative Online International Learning

Ana Balula

1 Introduction

Globally, education has been changing faster than at any other time in history, essentially due to digital technological developments. In this context, several EU cooperation initiatives in the field of education and training highlight the need to improve inclusion and mobility, as well as to support green and digital transitions in and through higher education, vocational education and training, and secondary education (Kaleja & Egetenmeyer, 2017).

Internationalization in education has taken many forms, including the mobility of students, teachers, researchers, programs, courses, curricula and projects. Traditionally, this materialized in the geographical relocation of those involved abroad (internationalization abroad); however, it was not open to all those interested in a myriad of personal, professional, logistical and/or financial reasons. For these cases in particular, internationalization at a distance (IaD) has become a relevant possibility, as it refers to all forms of education in which students and teachers (and the educational institutions themselves) are separated geographically and interact through (now digital) technology (Mittelmeier et al., 2019, 2020).

More recently, the understanding of the concept of internationalization in education is broader, focusing on promoting the development of intercultural competencies through dialogical interaction between nationalities to promote global learning. It is from this perspective that internationalization at home (IaH) is becoming more relevant, since it refers to the possibility of students developing intercultural competencies in interaction with elements of other nationalities, for example, foreign

A. Balula (✉)
Águeda School of Technology and Management, CIDTFF, University of Aveiro, Aveiro, Portugal
e-mail: balula@ua.pt

A. Nakata et al. (eds.), *Hyb-IT-up!*,
https://doi.org/10.1007/978-3-031-99743-3_7

students enrolled in their classes or students with different ancestries or links to other nationalities (Beelen & Jones, 2015; Barbosa et al., 2020).

In this context, hybrid learning gains further significance, given it is a model that results of combining face-to-face and online classes simultaneously, with a focus on student-centered teaching, in which the teacher plans, designs and delivers classes for both formats, using ICT infrastructures in order to integrate all those involved (Gao et al., 2021). By integrating both online and in-person elements, hybrid learning enhances the opportunities for students to engage with international peers, fostering intercultural dialogue and understanding while accommodating diverse learning preferences. This approach helps to promote global learning within the local context, making international experiences more accessible and adaptable to students' individual needs. Furthermore, the internationalization of the curriculum (IoC) has also been gaining visibility by incorporating the dimensions of global citizenship, internationalization and interculturality into the curriculum in a formal educational environment—in other words, at the level of content, learning outcomes, resources, teaching and learning methodologies and assessment (Leask, 2015, 2016; Baptista et al., 2022; Balula, 2023). By presupposing the active involvement of students in the learning process and, through this, the systematic and purposeful development of global, international and intercultural learning outcomes, the IoC can be considered strategic for promoting the principles of equity and inclusion in formal education (Baptista et al., 2022; Balula, 2023). This way, the symbiosis between hybrid learning and IoC can serve as an important means to achieving United Nations Sustainable Development Goal 4 (SDG4) on Quality Education. Specifically, it supports the construction of knowledge and the development of skills that promote a culture of peace, non-violence, global citizenship, and an appreciation of cultural diversity, as well as the contribution of culture to sustainable development (SDG 4.7).

This chapter systematizes the implications of the different dimensions and key phases of the life cycle of a COIL project, particularly in terms of planning, enaction, and evaluation. It also offers an overview of how hybrid COIL projects can address the current challenges faced by educational institutions, particularly in promoting high-quality education and fostering greater equity in opportunities. By combining online and face-to-face interaction, the COIL approach may offer flexible and inclusive learning experiences that can bridge gaps in access to education, making global learning more accessible to diverse student populations.

2 Collaborative Online International Learning (COIL)

Although several studies on international collaboration in education can be found in the literature, evidence of collaborative networking experiences for the development of pedagogical practices is not so recurrent (Baptista et al., 2022; Rubin, 2017). One of the possible options for this networking is the development of Collaborative Online International Learning (COIL) projects.

COIL projects are based on the creation of international work teams (involving teachers and students) to develop international collaborative learning experiences, mediated by digital technology, opening up the opportunity for wider participation in internationalization programs that normally required geographical mobility (Baptista et al., 2022; Balula, 2023). The first COIL projects began in the social sciences and humanities and as a way of enabling native speakers to share their culture and language within language courses, but there is now evidence of its development in practically all scientific areas (Rubin, 2017). It is an approach that involves dialogue between teachers and students from different countries, so it necessarily promotes the development of their intercultural awareness in collaborative multicultural learning environments.

2.1 *Dimensions of COIL*

The concept of COIL (Collaborative Online International Learning) integrates three key elements of the learning process: collaboration, the online environment, and internationalization. These dimensions profoundly influence various aspects of planning and implementing teaching and learning processes, making them impossible to overlook (Fig. 1).

The concept of collaboration is defined in the European Commission document "LifeComp into Action" as involvement in group activities and teamwork, recognizing and respecting the other (Sala & Herrero-Rámila, 2022). Collaborative learning is thus rooted in the dynamics of interaction, dialogue, and shared accountability among all participants for both their individual and collective learning, with an emphasis on understanding others' perspectives. Pedagogical approaches based on collaborative learning should, therefore, include activities that foster the development of the collaboration competence by enabling students to:

- Understand and manage interactions with others in different socio-cultural contexts and domain-specific situations;

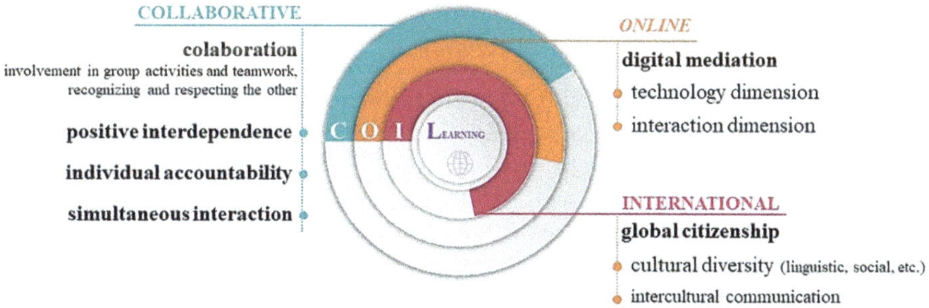

Fig. 1 The pillars of COIL

- Engage in dialogue with confidence, assertiveness, clarity and reciprocity, proactively considering others' perspectives while respecting their emotions, experiences, and values;
- Contribute to the common good, recognizing that others may have different cultural backgrounds, beliefs, values, opinions, or personal circumstances;
- Appreciate the importance of trust, respect for human dignity and equality, and effectively manage conflicts and negotiate disagreements to build and maintain fair and respectful relationships.

According to the recommendations in the European Commission document "LifeComp into Action" (Sala & Herrero-Rámila, 2022), the design of collaborative learning activities should foster a sense of belonging to a group or team. These activities should aim to promote: (1) positive interdependence, i.e., the success of each element is intrinsically linked to the success of the group itself; (2) individual accountability, i.e., each member is individually responsible for their own and the group's learning; and (3) the active participation of students to promote interest and involvement, as well as meaningful learning.

When it comes to hybrid collaborative learning, the environment can add challenges, not only from a technological point of view, but also from a pedagogical point of view. The concept of synchromodal learning, as discussed by Bell et al. (2014), elaborates on different hybrid models, such as the linked classroom and personal portal. Effective implementation of these models requires careful planning, risk tolerance, and ongoing adaptation to evolving technologies, emphasizing the importance of appointing tech navigators and adopting a mindset of continuous improvement.

Various configurations of hybrid learning environments allow for diverse interaction models, such as in-person students engaging with remote peers or teachers, or fully remote teachers guiding in-person student groups. The topologies defined in a COIL project can vary from case to case and can even cross different topologies. For example, in addition to two classes in different countries interacting online, students from the same class can also participate either in person or remotely. Thus, it requires not only selecting and using digital tools but also developing an entirely new approach from the ground up, rethinking both the design of the hybrid learning strategy and the learning environments. Despite these challenges, hybrid teaching offers significant benefits in terms of flexibility, accessibility, and the opportunity to explore technology-enhanced learning methods, encouraging both teachers and students to innovate and continuously improve.

Finally, international learning is highly valuable for those who engage in it, as it offers opportunities to explore and understand other cultures. Making it more globally accessible can be achieved by facilitating online participation. According to the LifeComp Framework (Sala et al., 2020), competencies as empathy, communication and collaboration are essential for developing global citizens. Thus, intercultural communication should be recognized as a significant benefit of international learning, and its impact should be evident in the learning outcomes attained by students.

2.2 *The COIL Life Cycle*

The integration of digital, collaborative, and international dimensions in hybrid teaching and learning processes—central to COIL projects—requires careful planning before implementation. These dimensions should align with the learning outcomes and be reflected in the design of pedagogical strategies and the selection of digital technologies (Alvarez & Steiner, 2019). COIL projects are founded on the following assumptions (Ward, 2016):

- Collaboration between two or more nationalities in defining, developing, and evaluating the project;
- Student activities/assessment must involve working in international teams;
- The project should integrate the development and assessment of intercultural, communication, and digital competencies;
- The learning process and product(s) must be formally included in the students' assessment.

There are no strict limitations on the duration of a COIL project. These projects typically span 5–7 weeks (Rubin, 2017) to allow participants sufficient time to get acquainted with one another, understand the project's scope, and complete their collaborative work. Careful coordination between calendars and time zones of the partnering institutions is essential to ensure smooth project execution.

The development of a COIL project begins with selecting a theme and defining the learning outcomes, followed by identifying one or more partners for collaboration. Partners can be drawn from either the same scientific field or different fields to provide complementary perspectives. Although COIL projects involving multiple scientific areas may be more complex, they offer the benefit of fostering multidisciplinary teamwork, which is increasingly valued in preparing students for the job market (Beelen, 2019). The success of a COIL project requires careful attention to three key phases: planning, enaction, and evaluation, as presented in Fig. 2.

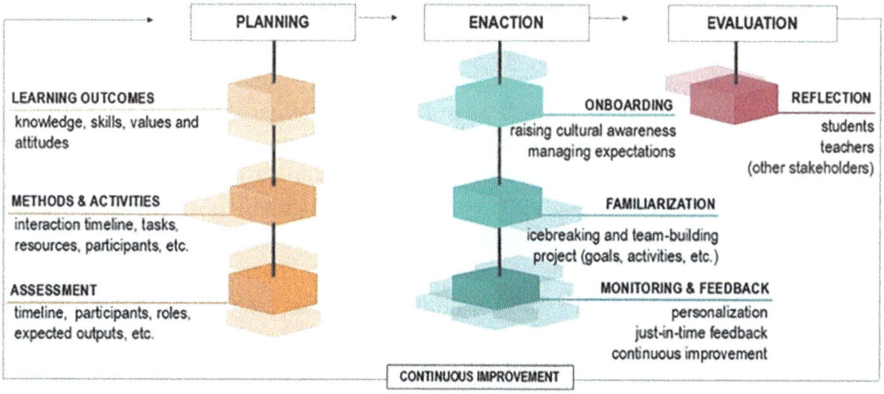

Fig. 2 The life cycle of COIL projects

Planning

Planning a COIL project begins with a clear definition of the learning outcomes and the objectives for developing transversal competencies, specifically intercultural, communication, and digital competencies (Leask, 2016; Baptista et al., 2022). In this stage, the teachers involved should collaboratively explore potential connections between the learning objectives and outcomes of the courses involved. Next, they define the learning activities/assessment methods and criteria, ensuring these integrate international (and intercultural) and digital components. In hybrid learning environments, it is essential to design activities that are adaptable for both in-person and remote students, ensuring equitable access to learning resources and opportunities. This flexibility allows students to engage meaningfully, regardless of their nationality and location. While the project's weight in the overall student assessment may vary across the courses involved, a significant imbalance in these percentages can lead to uneven student engagement and potentially undermine the project's success.

In a learning environment that emphasizes active and student-centered approaches, it is important that assessment goes beyond being predominantly summative ('assessment of learning') and does not center mainly on the final stages of the learning process. Instead, incorporating 'assessment for learning', which involves feedback from peers, teachers, or other sources, offers significant benefits (Balula & Moreira, 2014). This type of approach to assessment helps students identify their strengths and weaknesses, enabling them to make adjustments and improve their learning. By providing ongoing feedback, assessment for learning supports students in better planning their future learning and enhancing their overall educational experience. Learning activities are viewed as assessment moments themselves ('assessment as learning'), integrating feedback processes throughout the learning experience (Balula & Moreira, 2014). This approach helps students develop self-regulation and metacognitive competencies by encouraging them to reflect on and manage their own learning. Thus, a balanced integration of different assessment approaches can enhance the effectiveness and efficiency of the learning process (National Forum for the Enhancement of Teaching and Learning in Higher Education, 2017). In hybrid settings, providing assessment opportunities that cater to both remote and in-person students ensures inclusivity and maintains consistency in feedback and assessment, regardless of how students participate.

Diversifying the roles of participants is also important, including dynamics such as student/content, student/teacher, student/student, student/group, and group/group interaction (Balula & Moreira, 2014). Assessment should not only rely on the teacher; rather, students can take an active role, both individually and in groups or teams, through self-assessment and peer-assessment. These approaches not only make students accountable for their own learning or the collective learning of their team, but also helps them develop critical thinking and assessment competencies. While teachers can provide feedback as needed, incorporating regular, structured feedback moments into the planning process ensures teams can more effectively monitor and manage their progress. In hybrid learning scenarios, fostering student engagement through diverse interactions (both online and in-person) helps bridge the gap between remote and face-to-face participants, enhancing team dynamics.

When selecting digital tools, while class communication and learning output sharing can be negotiated with students, they should also have the opportunity to choose their team's tools, allowing them to work with those they feel most comfortable using. Additionally, giving students the freedom to explore and select tools for creating learning outputs encourages creativity and the development of their own digital competencies. In a hybrid context, the selection of digital tools is crucial; they should support both synchronous and asynchronous collaboration to ensure effective engagement and connection for both in-person and remote students throughout the project.

Overall, COIL activities should be carefully tailored, considering the project's duration, the cognitive workload involved. Additionally, it is important to ensure balanced representation of nationalities within teams. Ideally, including at least two students from each nationality fosters a more supportive and collaborative environment. Teachers should also consider the additional challenges remote students might face, such as time zone differences or access to technology, and adjust the activities accordingly. This balance not only promotes inclusivity but also enhances the team's overall performance and effectiveness.

Finally, after discussing and defining the project's key aspects, teachers should create a comprehensive set of guidelines for students. These guidelines should encompass pedagogical objectives, learning outcomes, project duration, resources, activities (including deadlines and digital tools), and assessment methods. These guidelines should also specify the general interaction and feedback protocols, i.e., how remote and in-person students will engage, communicate, and collaborate, ensuring clarity in how the hybrid model will be implemented. This detailed document will serve as a clear roadmap, ensuring that all participants have a thorough understanding of the project's scope, expectations, and requirements.

Enaction

The enaction of COIL projects, regardless of their specific configurations, generally includes three stages: onboarding, familiarization, and monitoring and feedback (see Fig. 2). The first aim of the onboarding stage is to develop students' cultural sensitivity and awareness of the partner country. Teachers analyze students' readiness for meaningful intercultural communication with their international counterparts and take any necessary measures to ensure all participants are fully prepared. They can, for instance, offer activities that encourage students to explore cultural, political, and social similarities and differences, while also prompting them to reflect on and express new perspectives about their own identities. Authors as Minei et al. (2021) propose intercultural reflection activities based on authentic materials to deconstruct stereotypes and reduce any discomfort or increase students' confidence in communication processes. This type of activity promotes the development of knowledge, attitudes and values that can be mobilized and integrated in the course of the projects themselves and which will contribute to their enrichment. Additionally, managing expectations about working in international teams helps students navigate cultural differences and fosters a collaborative environment.

Following this, the familiarization phase (see Fig. 2) aims to ensure that all students become well-acquainted with the project outline and with one another—an essential foundation for effective collaboration. This phase should begin with a comprehensive presentation of the participants and project itself, ideally based on the various elements outlined in the guidelines developed during the planning phase. It is important to incorporate time for dialogue with students during this presentation, enabling them to make meaningful contributions to the project. Students can actively engage in discussing learning/assessment activities, as this enhances their involvement and fosters a sense of (co)responsibility in the teaching and learning process (Matthews et al., 2018). These opportunities for negotiation should be intentional and aligned with the maturity of the students involved and can pertain to various aspects of the learning process. Examples include (re)defining assessment criteria, selecting digital resources, choosing communication tools, and adjusting deadlines, among others.

Teachers should then incorporate ice-breaking and team-building activities tailored to the hybrid learning topology of the specific COIL project to foster connections and establish rapport among participants. Following this, students organize themselves into international teams based on their interests. To facilitate this process, teachers should provide clear instructions regarding the minimum and maximum number of members per team, as well as guidelines for distributing team members by nationality. Once the teams have been established, they should be encouraged to define the key aspects of their internal interactions, such as the frequency of communication among members, the chosen communication tool(s), and the organization of tasks. Additionally, teams may be asked to create their own identity—such as a name, logo, or motto—to foster a sense of belonging, which is particularly important in an online learning context. This aligns with Salmon's (2013, 2020) five-stage model of e-learning, which emphasizes the importance of online socialization in stage 2.

The monitoring and feedback phase (see Fig. 2) starts when teams start developing solutions to the problem presented in the COIL project. During this period, it is essential for teachers to oversee the teams' interaction dynamics to address any conflicts that may arise, track the progress of the work to ensure compliance with the established timeline, and provide personalized, timely feedback to students. Throughout the process, effectively managing students' expectations concerning communication, interaction, and learning outcomes helps to foster the students' interest and encourages active participation in the project.

Evaluation

First and foremost, the evaluation of a COIL project must consider the perspectives of all participants, including teachers, students, and any relevant external entities (Baptista et al., 2022; Balula, 2023). This triangulation of viewpoints is essential for effectively identifying both the project's strengths and weaknesses, facilitating continuous improvement (see Fig. 2). By gathering insights from diverse stakeholders, teachers can gain a comprehensive understanding of the project's impact and the areas that may require adjustment.

The evaluation of COIL projects can encompass various dimensions, such as student engagement and the effectiveness of communication and feedback strategies. However, it should primarily focus on the overall process—specifically, participants' perceptions of the planning, organization, and execution of the project. This emphasis on process allows for a nuanced understanding of how different components interact and contribute to the overall success of the initiative. Furthermore, encouraging students to pinpoint areas for improvement and suggest constructive alternatives not only tackles existing challenges but also lays the groundwork for future projects. It enables students to reflect on their learning journey in relation to the learning goals, particularly in developing intercultural, communication, and digital competencies. By revisiting their experiences, students can better understand how their participation in COIL projects has enriched their education and prepared them for global citizenship. Such reflection fosters a deeper sense of ownership over their learning, empowering them to recognize the value of diverse perspectives and collaborative efforts.

This evaluative process provides teachers with an opportunity to reevaluate the project from multiple perspectives, allowing for reflection on learning strategies and methodologies (Baptista et al., 2022; Balula, 2023). By considering feedback from students and other stakeholders, teachers can identify effective practices and areas for growth, ultimately refining their approaches to enhance student learning and engagement. This cycle of evaluation and reflection promotes a culture of continuous improvement, ensuring that future COIL projects are even more effective in meeting the needs of all participants.

3 Conclusion

COIL projects represent a dynamic approach to hybrid education that aligns with global educational imperatives and fosters meaningful intercultural interactions. The benefits of COIL projects are multifaceted: they enable educational institutions to advance their internationalization strategies and encourage innovative pedagogical methods that engage both students and teachers in immersive, cross-cultural learning experiences. Furthermore, COIL projects allow students to extend their personal and professional networks, which can enhance future career opportunities in increasingly globalized workplaces. The development of intercultural competence and digital literacy within these projects also supports students' development as global citizens.

COIL projects stimulate the formation of international communities of practice that enable teachers to share experiences, reflect on pedagogical strategies, and collaborate for continuous improvement. Thus, they can play an important role in triggering: (1) the development of international and transdisciplinary communities of practice centered on COIL, to promote the sharing of experiences, as well as in-depth reflection and discussion on pedagogical approaches with a view to their continuous improvement, and (2) the active participation of those involved in other educational initiatives of an international nature. Examples include the European Digital Education Hub, which was created to promote collaboration, the sharing of good practices and the development of solutions with partners from all sectors of education and training in an inclusive environment.

Ultimately, COIL projects embody an approach that promotes excellence in digital education, fostering a culture of continuous pedagogical innovation. The expansion of COIL aligns with a commitment to inclusive, high-quality education underlined in the European Digital Education Action Plan (2021–2027) and fosters the development of competencies for active, informed global citizenship. As such, COIL's potential lies in its capacity to reshape educational practices, making intercultural learning accessible and adaptable, thereby addressing challenges of the digital era and furthering the integration of hybrid learning into global education.

Acknowledgements This work is financially supported by National Funds through FCT—Fundação para a Ciência e a Tecnologia, I.P., under the project UIDB/00194/2020 (https://doi.org/10.54499/UIDB/00194/2020) and UIDP/00194/2020 (https://doi.org/10.54499/UIDP/00194/2020).

References

Alvarez, L., & Steiner, M. (2019). Collaborative online international learning. ASEM education in a digital world: bridging the continents-connecting the people (pp. 18–29).

Balula, A. (2023). Drifts of collaborative online international learning (COIL) towards pedagogical innovation: A foretelling bibliometric analysis, In A. Reis, J. Barroso, J. B. Lopes, T. Mikropoulos & C. Fan (Eds.), *Technology and innovation in learning, teaching and education: Second international conference, TECH-EDU 2020* proceedings (pp. 380–388). Springer. https://doi.org/10.1007/978-3-030-73988-1_30.

Balula, A., & Moreira, A. (2014). *Evaluation of online higher education—Learning, interaction and technology*, Springer Briefs in Education. Springer International Publishing. https://doi.org/10.1007/978-3-319-05425-4_1.

Baptista, D., Balula, A., & Neto, S. (2022). *Business pitching in the communication strategy of a product: A COIL project between Portugal and Brazil*. In L. G. Chova, A. L. Martínez, & I. C. Torres (Eds.), Proceedings of the 16th International Conference of Education, Research and Innovation—INTED2022 (pp. 6578–6584). IATED Academy. https://doi.org/10.21125/inted.2022.1669.

Barbosa, B., Santos, C., & Prado-Meza, C. (2020). There is no one way to internationalization at home: Virtual mobility and student engagement through formal and informal approaches to curricula. *Revista Lusófona de Educação, 47*, 85–98. https://doi.org/10.24140/issn.1645-7250.rle47.06

Beelen, J. (2019). Employability skills as guiding principles for internationalizing home curricula. In *Internationalization and employability in higher education* (pp. 200–212). Routledge. https://doi.org/10.4324/9781351254885-16

Beelen, J., & Jones, E. (2015). Redefining internationalization at home. In A. Curai, L. Matei, R. Pricopie, J. Salmi, & P. Scott (Eds.), *The European higher education area: Between critical reflections and future policies* (pp. 67–80). Springer.

Bell, J., Sawaya, S., & Cain, W. (2014). Synchromodal classes: Designing for shared learning experiences between face-to-face and online students. *International Journal of Designs for Learning, 5*(1).

Gao, S., Takanobu, R., Peng, W., Liu, Q., & Huang, M. (2021). HyKnow: End-to-end task-oriented dialog modeling with hybrid knowledge management. In *Findings of the Association for Computational Linguistics: ACL-IJCNLP 2021* (pp. 1591–1602). Association for Computational Linguistics. https://doi.org/10.18653/v1/2021.findings-acl.139

Kaleja, K., & Egetenmeyer, R. (2017). Internationalization in European vocational education and training. In L. Tran & K. Dempsey (Eds.), *Internationalization in vocational education and training. Technical and vocational education and training: Issues, concerns and prospects* (p. 25). Springer. https://doi.org/10.1007/978-3-319-47859-3_4

Leask, B. (2015). *Internationalizing the curriculum*. Routledge.

Leask, B. (2016). Internationalizing curriculum and learning for all students. In E. Jones, R. Coelen, J. Beelen, & H. Wit (Eds.), *Global and local internationalization. Transgressions: Cultural studies and education*. Sense Publishers. https://doi.org/10.1007/978-94-6300-301-8_8

Matthews, K. E., Dwyer, A., Hine, L., & Turner, J. (2018). Conceptions of students as partners. *Higher Education, 76*, 957–971. https://doi.org/10.1007/s10734-018-0257-y

Minei, E., Razuvaeva, T., & Dyshko, D. (2021). Modern day digital pen pals: A semester-long collaborative online international learning (COIL) project. *Communication Teacher, 35*(4), 1–9. https://doi.org/10.1080/17404622.2021.1887906

Mittelmeier, J., Rienties, B., Gunter, A. W., & Raghuram, P. (2020). Conceptualizing internationalization at a distance: A "third category" of university internationalization. *Journal of Studies in International Education, 25*, 266–282.

Mittelmeier, J., Rienties, B., Rogaten, J., Gunter, A., & Raghuram, P. (2019). Internationalisation at a distance and at home: Academic and social adjustment in a south African distance learning context. *International Journal of Intercultural Relations, 72*, 1–12. https://doi.org/10.1016/j.ijintrel.2019.06.001

National Forum for the Enhancement of Teaching and Learning in Higher Education. (2017, March). *Enhancing programme approaches to assessment and feedback in Irish higher education: Case studies, commentaries and tools*. https://doi.org/10.6084/m9.figshare.5113939.

Rubin, J. (2017). Embedding collaborative online international learning (COIL) at higher education institutions—An evolutionary overview with exemplars. *Internationalization of Higher Education—Policy and Practice, 2*, 27–44.

Sala, A., & Herrero-Rámila, C. (2022). *LifeComp into action: Teaching life skills in the classroom and beyond*. EUR 31141 EN, JRC13000. Publications Office of the European Union. https://doi.org/10.2760/22023.

Sala, A., Punie, Y., Garkov, V., & Cabrera-Giraldez, M. (2020). *LifeComp: The European framework for personal, social and learning to learn key competence*. EUR 30246 EN, JRC120911. Publications Office of the European Union, https://doi.org/10.2760/302967.

Salmon, G. (2013). *E-tivities: The key to active online learning* (2nd ed.). https://doi.org/10.4324/9780203074640

Salmon, G. (2020, February 12). *Five-stage model of e-learning* [video]. YouTube. Retrieved from https://www.youtube.com/watch?v=bqKt8RbEiNU&t=1s

Ward, H. (2016). Internationalization in action (special ed.)—Connecting classrooms: Using online technology to deliver global learning. American Council on Education.

Co-Designing a Micro-Course on Hybrid Learning Competencies for Higher Education Students

Paulo J. M. Santos, Blanca Ruiz-del-Pino, and Armin Weinberger

1 Introduction

Hybrid learning is establishing itself as a prominent model in contemporary education, particularly within higher education contexts (Jiang et al., 2023; Pimmer et al., 2016). Synchronous hybrid learning—defined as a blend of traditional face-to-face instruction and online learning (Raes et al., 2020)—would ideally leverage the strengths of both environments to create a flexible and engaging educational experience.

This chapter aims to propose and operationalize a set of core competencies that enable students to thrive in hybrid learning contexts. We outline a competency framework specific to hybrid education and illustrate its practical application through a micro-course developed for higher education students. In doing so, we respond to the ongoing need for clear guidance on how to support learners' autonomy, collaborative skills, and emotional support in hybrid environments.

From the educator's perspective, hybrid learning necessitates careful orchestration of various elements, including physical spaces, digital platforms, and temporal structures. This integration ensures that both modalities align in terms of objectives, content, and assessments, creating a cohesive educational experience where each element reinforces the other.

Hybrid learning can result in several organizational and pedagogical benefits. For instance, it can reduce workload by eliminating the need to teach the same course multiple times across different campuses (Bell et al., 2014), provide flexibility for both teachers and students to manage their time more effectively (Raes et al.,

P. J. M. Santos (✉) · B. Ruiz-del-Pino · A. Weinberger
Edutech Department, Saarland University, Saarbrücken, Germany
e-mail: p.santos@edutech.uni-saarland.de; bruipin167@g.educaand.es; a.weinberger@edutech.uni-saarland.de

A. Nakata et al. (eds.), *Hyb-IT-up!*,
https://doi.org/10.1007/978-3-031-99743-3_8

2020), and enhance the potential for richer learning experiences through the inclusion of external expertise and diverse perspectives (Bower et al., 2015).

From a student's perspective, hybrid learning offers flexibility in terms of time and location, allowing them to better arrange for their individual circumstances. This adaptability may correspond with a trend towards student-centered models (Childs & Peachey, 2013; Singh et al., 2021; Xiao et al., 2020). Alongside organizational advantages, hybrid learning can also support pedagogical enhancements. If loss of autonomy affects learners' motivation and self-regulation skills in traditional learning environments (Rovai et al., 2007), hybrid learning may allow learners to choose their way of interacting with the content more effectively and to have greater control over their learning process (Abdelmalak & Parra, 2016; Singh et al., 2021). This ability to choose translates into greater equity in the learning process, as it gives access to different avenues for learning (Xiao et al., 2020).

Unlike traditional approaches in which educators solely design instructional content, this study employs a co-design method that directly involves students in shaping learning materials around the competencies relevant to their needs, a perspective not often explored in hybrid learning literature. By engaging students as co-creators, the goal is to bridge potential gaps between institutional objectives and the realities faced by learners.

1.1 Problems of Hybrid Learning

Despite the potential benefits of hybrid models, certain challenges persist, such as attrition in completing courses and low impact on academic results. Online students have often difficulty demonstrating that they are present in class (Weitze et al., 2013) and sometimes feel frustrated and disengaged, resulting in a climate of isolation and lack of community (McInnerney & Roberts, 2004).

One of the great challenges of hybrid learning is being socially present as a remote learner as well as creating and maintaining a sense of belonging to the class group (Raes et al., 2020). Social presence—the perception of others as "real" individuals in a technology-mediated environment (Kreijns et al., 2022)—is key in remote learning when trying to recreate interpersonal dynamics and collaborative engagement found in face-to-face settings. Social presence directly influences how social interactions unfold in online group learning, which in turn impacts learning outcomes (see chapter "A Social Perspective on Hybrid Learning").

Hybrid learning seems to lack group cohesion due to additional communication difficulties, which can hinder group development (Ramsey & Lorenz, 2016). A lack of social presence and connectedness may also reduce student satisfaction and engagement, especially in asynchronous online learning (Arslan, 2021; Kreijns et al., 2022), which negatively impacts effective group dynamics.

The COVID-19 pandemic forced a rapid shift to online and hybrid learning models. Even though students and educators could manage to some extent teaching and learning online, social and emotional interactions often required more specialized skills (Arslan, 2021). This situation suggests the need for a deeper understanding and development of a framework of student competencies to enhance the hybrid learning experience.

1.2 The Need for Student Competencies for Hybrid Learning

Along with greater degrees of freedom and flexibility, online learning may also afford higher levels of self-regulation, which results in being adequately prepared for the lesson, being socially present in the (online) classroom, or communicating adequately through different means. The efficacy of hybrid learning also relies on students' competencies for productively using any higher degree of autonomy (Farrell et al., 2019).

Hybrid learning competencies refer to technological skills such as the ability to use digital tools to access information and collaborate with other online learners, as well as communication and collaboration skills in this environment (Kasiyah et al., 2017). Furthermore, organizational and self-management skills (Xiao et al., 2020) are relevant, such as the ability to set learning goals, manage time effectively and work autonomously (Carter et al., 2020; Raes et al., 2020; Wong et al., 2019). Hybrid learning competencies also encompass social-emotional skills, such as the ability to adapt to change, maintain motivation, and perseverance in learning (Kasiyah et al., 2017; Wong et al., 2019), and work effectively in teams, both in person and online (Johnson et al., 2020).

Existing competency frameworks outline key areas of digital competencies across various contexts. While these frameworks provide a comprehensive understanding of digital competencies and their subareas, none are dedicated specifically to the competencies required for hybrid learning. Although there are clear intersections between the general digital competencies identified in these frameworks and those necessary for effective hybrid learning, there remains a need to adjust these competencies specifically to hybrid contexts.

In the following section, we will present our approach towards developing a hybrid learning competency framework for higher education students, describing the procedure taken and the set of competencies dimensions identified. We will analyse existing digital competencies to extract those central to hybrid learning. Subsequently, we will present the approach for co-creating a micro-course with students, structured around the identified competencies for hybrid learning.

2 Towards a Hybrid Learning Competency Framework

To define the specific competencies required for hybrid learning, we analysed and built upon four existing competency frameworks: the Digital Competence Framework for Citizens (DIGCOMP) by the European Commission (Ferrari, 2013), the Community of Inquiry Framework (Garrison & Akyol, 2012), the Social Cognitive Model of Self-Regulated Learning (Zimmerman, 1989) and the European Framework for Personal, Social and Learning to Learn Key Competence (LIFECOMP) by the European Commission (Sala et al., 2020).

These frameworks, while not specialized in hybrid learning, provided a depth of analysis necessary to extract relevant competencies. These extracted competencies served as the foundation for the hybrid learning competency framework we designed.

With the identified challenges in mind, the competency framework was structured to address the gaps observed in student engagement and performance in hybrid environments. For instance, the difficulty in maintaining a significant social presence in digital settings highlighted the need to develop communicative competencies, such as effective interaction and collaboration through digital technologies. The observed attrition and lack of self-discipline among students underscored the importance of self-regulatory sub-competencies, including time management and effort regulation. Similarly, feelings of isolation and disconnection experienced by students emphasized the importance of emotional competencies, such as the ability to manage emotions and sustain motivation throughout the learning process. Each of these competencies was specifically designed to respond to these challenges.

As a result, hybrid learning competencies were grouped into four facets: technical, communicative, self-regulatory, and emotional competencies.

2.1 Technical Competencies

Firstly, technical competencies are associated with the operational use of digital technologies, encompassing the utilization of hardware and software. This domain involves the safe, critical, and responsible use of digital technologies, as well as engagement with them for learning, work, and participation in society. According to DIGCOMP (Ferrari, 2013), these competencies include activities like searching, filtering and evaluating information, developing digital content, and, in general terms, addressing technical problem-solving issues. In the context of hybrid education, these include the effective use of digital communication platforms, such as configuring and managing digital communication tools (video conferencing, messaging apps, etc.) and understanding their technical affordances. Additionally, technical competencies are required for the use of collaborative tools, such as managing shared workspaces, integrating cloud-based services, and navigating the technical features that facilitate teamwork in digital environments.

DIGCOMP provides the foundational basis for the development of these technical competencies. It offers a structured approach to identifying areas for improvement and fostering continuous growth in students' ability to handle digital tools and technologies effectively. By following the specific descriptors related to technical aspects—such as digital literacy, information management, and problem-solving in digital contexts—students can assess their technical proficiency and seek strategies to enhance their ability to navigate and optimize their hybrid learning environments (Vuorikari et al., 2022).

2.2 Emotional Competencies

Secondly, emotional sub-competencies refer to the ability to identify, express and manage personal emotions that affect the learning process in hybrid situations. According to LIFECOMP (Sala et al., 2020), imparting personal and social competencies in educational contexts can turn education itself into a means to achieve self-fulfilment and personal satisfaction. Programs dedicated to the development of social and emotional skills, such as empathy, problem solving, empathic communication and collaboration, have been shown to have highly positive effects on both students and teachers (Durlak et al., 2011). Social and Emotional Education (SEE) contributes to promoting students' mental health, academic performance and employability over time by increasing prosocial and reducing disruptive behaviours (Sorrenti et al., 2025).

2.3 Communication Competencies

Thirdly, communication competencies are considered essential, as students must be able to communicate effectively in both online and face-to-face contexts and collaborate in group projects and activities. These competencies involve developing strong communication skills, including the ability to work efficiently in teams, provide constructive feedback, and resolve conflicts.

Although both DIGCOMP and LIFECOMP include competencies related to communication, they do not fully address the specific challenges posed by telematic environments, such as those encountered in hybrid learning. Communication and collaboration in these settings often require additional competencies to navigate both physical and digital spaces effectively. To address this gap, we considered key elements from models such as the Community of Inquiry (CoI) (González & Herrera, 2015), which emphasize the importance of competencies that foster meaningful engagement and collaboration in blended contexts. In particular, the CoI model highlights the need for students to develop social, cognitive and teaching presences that support critical thinking, reflection, and the facilitation of group learning processes in both online and in-person interactions.

2.4 Self-Regulatory Competencies

Lastly, self-regulatory competencies play a key role in the learning process, as they help students manage their own learning strategies, time, and effort, which ultimately influences their academic success, whether in face-to-face or online environments (Carter et al., 2020). These competencies involve setting learning goals, planning tasks, monitoring progress, and adapting strategies when necessary.

The Social Cognitive Model of Self-Regulated Learning by Zimmerman (1989) proposes a series of cyclical phases with the aim of helping learners become aware of their learning strategies and metacognitive processes (Wong et al., 2019). In the anticipation phase, learners set their goals, activate their motivation, plan the time they will spend on homework and anticipate possible obstacles (Carter et al., 2020). In the performance phase, they should look for the cognitive and behavioural strategies that work best for them during their tasks and work on attention control and time optimization, seeking feedback when necessary. Finally, in the self-reflection phase, they evaluate the learning process and the results obtained, and they foresee how to introduce improvements and set new goals for future learning efforts (Wong et al., 2019). For an in-depth discussion on how these regulatory processes intertwine with cognitive, motivational, and emotional dimensions, and how they can be applied to hybrid learning settings, see chapter "Regulation of Learning: Cognition, Motivation and Emotion".

Our proposed competency framework for higher education students in hybrid learning environments is presented below (see Table 1), detailing the competence areas, specific competencies for each competence area, and their descriptions.

Table 1 Competency framework for hybrid learning

Areas of competence	Specific competencies	Description
Digital area	1.1 Searching, Filtering, Evaluating and Managing Data, Information and Digital Content	• To explain the information needs with keywords and find data and content in digital environments through simple searches (websites, blogs and databases) • To evaluate the credibility and reliability of sources of data, information and digital content and store the data in an organized way
	1.2 Developing Digital Content	• To use digital tools and technologies in a creative way to create knowledge and to innovate processes and products
	1.3 Safety and Technical Problem Solving	• To be aware of rules of copyright and licenses • To detect risks and threat while using digital learning platforms (saving files, sharing with unknown people, virus checks) • To identify technical problems when operating devices and using digital environments, and to select solutions to solve them
Communication area	2.1 Interacting and Collaborating Through Digital Technologies	• To select appropriate digital communication means and a variety of communication strategies, language registers, and tools that are adapted to context and content for interacting and/or sharing information purposes • To listen to others and cope with conflicts and negotiating disagreements • To fairly share tasks, resources and responsibility within a group considering its specific aim, eliciting the expression of different views and adopting a systemic approach

(continued)

Table 1 (continued)

Areas of competence	Specific competencies	Description
	2.2 Knowing the Netiquette	• To discuss behavioural norms and know-how while using digital technologies and interacting in digital environments • To adapt communication strategies to the specific audience and be aware of cultural and generational diversity aspects to consider in digital environments
	2.3 Managing Social Presence and Digital Identity	• To develop strategies that foster the learner's social presence in online collaborative work following the Community of Inquiry Model • To understand that digital services use a "Privacy policy" to inform how personal data is used
Self-regulated learning area	3.1 Managing Learning Process	• To develop awareness of one's own learning interests, processes and preferred strategies, including learning needs and required support • To plan and implement learning goals, strategies, resources and processes following the social cognitive model of self-regulated learning
	3.2 Developing a Growth Mindset	• Reflecting on other people's feedback as well as on successful and unsuccessful experiences to continue developing one's potential • Reflecting on and assessing purposes, processes and outcomes of learning and knowledge construction, establishing relationships across domains
	3.3 Promoting Critical Thinking	• To compare, analyse, assess, and synthetize data, information, ideas, and media messages to draw logical conclusions • To develop creative ideas, synthesize and combine concepts and information from different sources in view of solving problems
Emotional self-regulation area	4.1 Awareness, Expression and Management of Emotions Related to Learning	• To identify and express personal emotions, thoughts, values, and behaviour that affect the learning process, such as motivation • To manage transitions and uncertainty and to be flexible in digital contexts
	4.2 Pursuit of Mental Health	• To use strategies to avoid stress and anxiety in digital contexts and to avoid health risks and threats to physical and psychological well-being while using digital technologies • To select well-defined and routine ways to protect oneself from mental and physical health dangers in digital environments
	4.3 Care of Social Well-Being	• To indicate well-defined and routine digital technologies for social well-being and social inclusion • To understand another person's emotions and experiences, and the ability to proactively take their perspective

3 Designing a Micro-Course for Supporting Students' Hybrid Learning Competencies

The design of the micro-course, structured around the previously outlined competency framework for hybrid learning, aims to empower higher education students by enhancing their digital, communicative, self-regulatory, and emotional competencies necessary for thriving in hybrid learning environments. It is designed as a self-paced online course, allowing students to engage with the material individually and at their own convenience, addressing the need for flexibility and self-regulation in their learning processes.

The development of the micro-course for hybrid learning competencies was based on a multi-phase co-creation process that involved students actively contributing to the design and content of the course. This process was structured to ensure that the course would be aligned with the needs and perspectives of its target audience. Below, the phases and steps taken during the co-creation process are described.

3.1 Phase 1: Learning Design Lab

The first phase of the co-creation process took place between November and December 2023. A total of 34 participants, all teacher students from the Department of Education at Saarland University, Germany, were involved. This group of teacher students was particularly valuable for the co-design process as they are transitioning to becoming educators themselves. This allowed them to create learning activities with an understanding of pedagogical principles and an awareness of the practical needs of learners.

The students were first introduced to the concept of hybrid learning competencies. They were provided with materials related to different areas of competence, which were drawn from the competency framework previously developed for hybrid learning. Each student was allowed to choose a specific competence or aspect of a competence to explore more deeply.

After studying the relevant materials, the students were asked to create a learning activity that would help develop the competence they had chosen. They were instructed to define the objectives of the activity, estimate the time required to complete it, and determine the task formats, which could include individual projects, written exercises, watching and reflecting on video content, etc. Additionally, they were required to provide a step-by-step outline of how the activity would unfold, specifying its goals and expected outcomes.

After creating the learning activity, students were introduced to the use of CoDeGraph (Kolling et al., 2022), a graphical co-design tool designed to facilitate the co-creation process by enabling different stakeholders to visually represent and connect the elements of a learning unit. The tool allows for the mapping of relationships between agents (e.g., students and teachers) and learning components (e.g., learning objects, assessments, feedback mechanisms) in a structured and visual manner. For this project, the tool was specifically adapted to support the development of a micro-course (MC CoDe-Graph).

Using MC CoDe-Graph, the students were tasked with incorporating their learning activity into the larger context of a module. They used the tool to represent the dynamic flow of their activity and how it connected with other components of the course. This ensured that the designed activities aligned with the intended learning outcomes of the selected competencies.

At the end of this phase, the phase concluded with 34 graphical representations, each illustrating different learning units and activities specifically focused on the targeted competencies. In Fig. 1, you can see an example of one of these graphical representations.

3.2 *Phase 2: International Hybrid Workshop*

The second phase was a hybrid workshop organized under the Hyb-IT-up Project, supported by the European Union's Erasmus+ Programme, in March 2024. The workshop involved participants from several higher education institutions, countries, and educational backgrounds, bringing diversity of perspectives into the design process.

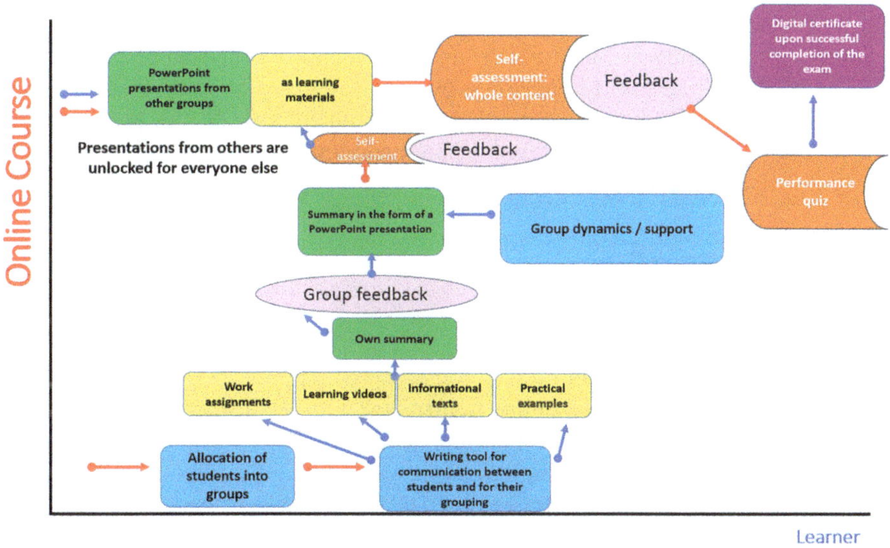

Fig. 1 Example of a CoDe-Graph representing a learning unit to enhance communication skills. Arrows indicate the source of actions: red from the learner and blue from the instructional system. The colour of the boxes represents different categories, such as learning objects, feedback, evaluation

Participants represented institutions such as Saarland University (Germany), University of Oulu (Finland), University of Tartu (Estonia), Open University (Netherlands), and Aveiro University (Portugal). A total of 40 participants (34 online, 6 face-to-face) from diverse backgrounds, cultures, and disciplines took part in the hybrid workshop. The participants' ages ranged from 23 to 45 years, with 73% identifying as female. Participants represented a variety of countries: 28% from Portugal, 14% from Germany, and additional representation from Belgium, Finland, Spain, Estonia, the Netherlands, Colombia, Ghana, and Vietnam. Their education levels were also varied, with 15 participants holding bachelor's degrees, 27 holding master's degrees, and 2 holding PhDs. The participants' fields of study were equally diverse, including Educational Technology, Biology, Environmental Science, and Assessment and Feedback.

The workshop was designed to foster collaboration between participants in both physical and online formats. Drawing from the principles of co-design and participatory design, the workshop utilized a structured format based on the Future Workshop (Müllert & Jungk, 1987). This collaborative problem-solving approach enabled participants to explore challenges and generate solutions related to hybrid learning.

The participants were grouped into four teams, each focusing on one of the core competence areas from the hybrid learning competency framework—Digital Fluency, Communication in Online Environments, Self-Regulation, and Emotional Regulation. These teams were tasked with brainstorming and developing activities and learning units that would enhance students' competencies in the chosen area. As in the first phase, participants were introduced to MC CoDe-Graph, which facilitated the visual mapping of learning components and interactions. This tool allowed participants to represent the structure and flow of their proposed learning units. Each group used the tool to develop a graphical representation of their designed learning activity. The workshop concluded with the creation of four group assignments, each focusing on a specific competence area and visually represented through the MC CoDe-Graph tool.

3.3 The Micro-Course

The course that emerged from this co-design process took the form of a concise guidebook and an interactive online course (see Fig. 2). The guidebook offers a clear and structured approach to developing hybrid learning competencies, while the interactive online course complements it with engaging elements, such as quizzes, reflective exercises, and scenario-based tasks that students can complete at their own pace. The course materials are designed as Open Educational Resources (OERs) and are available in an open-access repository (https://zenodo.org/records/14749106), ensuring broad access for educators and learners. This dual-format approach allows students to engage with the content flexibly, facilitating

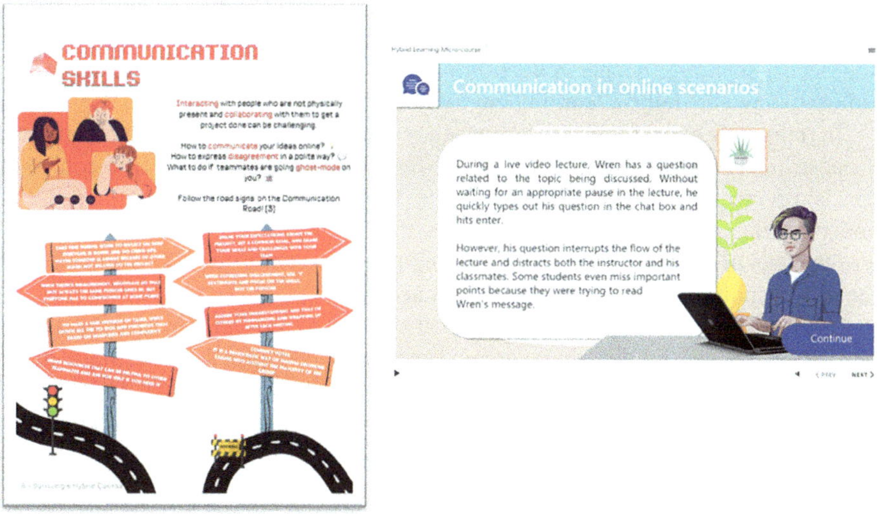

Fig. 2 Micro-course materials: Combined illustration of the guidebook (left), focusing on key communication skills for hybrid learning, and the interactive online course (right), simulating real-life communication challenges in digital learning environments

self-paced, modularized study while encouraging them to reflect on their progress and identify areas for improvement.

4 Discussion and Conclusion

This chapter introduced a framework for hybrid learning competencies building on the premise that despite the rising adoption and clear organizational and flexibility benefits of hybrid learning, a critical gap remains in understanding how students can transform these benefits into positive and effective learning experiences.

The suggested competency framework focused on four core areas: technical, communication, self-regulation, and emotional competencies. This framework was aligned with competencies identified as central through an analysis of existing frameworks, such as DIGCOMP (Ferrari, 2013) and the Community of Inquiry model (Garrison & Akyol, 2012) and was enriched with elements of self-management and emotional regulation, which are crucial for success in online and hybrid learning environments (Zimmerman, 1989; Wong et al., 2019). It provides educators with a guide on which hybrid learning competencies should be developed in students and offers a structure for students to reflect on their own learning needs.

A micro-course was co-created with students, utilizing the framework as its foundation. This course serves as a practical example of how competencies can be developed in a personalized and context-adapted manner. Co-creating the course with students was done to ensure its relevance and applicability. Engaging students in the design process allowed for direct alignment with their real-world experiences and needs, fostering deeper reflection on their competencies and enhancing their ability to navigate hybrid learning environments effectively.

To refine this hybrid learning competency framework, it is essential to explore its purpose and potential as they evolve over time. The relevance of specific competencies is directly influenced by how the aims of hybrid education are defined. As our understanding of hybrid learning expands and adapts, so too would the competencies that needed to be prioritized. Ongoing adaptation ensures that the framework remains responsive to current educational needs.

Emerging trends suggest a fundamental shift in the conception of hybrid learning—from a necessity during pandemic times to an intentional instructional design that builds on the characteristics of hybrid learning. Such designs may hold promise to facilitate transversal skills and shift hybrid learning from a supplementary approach to a central pedagogical strategy, essential for implementing innovative educational practices that integrate the strengths of both physical and digital learning environments.

This shift emphasizes the need to prioritize competencies based on their relevance to the overarching goals of hybrid learning. In scenarios focused on interactive dynamics and collaboration, competencies related to communication and emotional intelligence may become more central than technical skills. This underscores the need for thoughtful selection of competencies to enhance hybrid learning practices based on their relevance to the overarching goal of hybrid learning.

The proposed competency framework and micro-course hold potential to inform program design in higher education institutions seeking to develop robust hybrid learning initiatives. More than this, they can provide a foundation for future studies exploring the specific hybrid learning competencies that have the greatest impact on student engagement and learning outcomes in hybrid settings.

References

Abdelmalak, M. M. M., & Parra, J. L. (2016). Expanding learning opportunities for graduate students with HyFlex course design. *International Journal of Online Pedagogy and Course Design, 6*(4), 19–37. https://doi.org/10.4018/IJOPCD.2016100102

Arslan, G. (2021). Loneliness, college belongingness, subjective vitality, and psychological adjustment during coronavirus pandemic: Development of the college belongingness questionnaire. *Journal of Positive School Psychology, 5*(1), 17–31. https://doi.org/10.31234/osf.io/j7tf2

Bell, J., Sawaya, S., & Cain, W. (2014). Synchromodal classes: Designing for shared learning experiences between face-to-face and online students. *International Journal of Designs for Learning, 5*(1), 68–82.

Bower, M., Dalgarno, B., Kennedy, G. E., Lee, M. J. W., & Kenney, J. (2015). Design and implementation factors in blended synchronous learning environments: Outcomes from a cross-case analysis. *Computers & Education, 86*, 1–17. https://doi.org/10.1016/j.compedu.2015.03.006

Carter, R. A., Rice, M., Yang, S., & Jackson, H. A. (2020). Self-regulated learning in online learning environments: Strategies for remote learning. *Information and Learning Sciences, 121*(5/6), 321–329. https://doi.org/10.1108/ils-04-2020-0114

Childs, M., & Peachey, A. (Eds.). (2013). *Understanding learning in virtual worlds*. Springer.

Durlak, J. A., Weissberg, R. P., Dymnicki, A. B., Taylor, R. D., & Schellinger, K. B. (2011). The impact of enhancing students' social and emotional learning: A meta-analysis of school-based universal interventions. *Child Development, 82*(1), 405–432. https://doi.org/10.1111/j.1467-8624.2010.01564.x

Farrell, O., Brunton, J., Costello, E., Donlon, E., Trevaskis, S., Eccles, S., & Ní Shé, C. (2019). *An investigation of effective online teaching: A needs analysis of online educators and online students*. Openteach Project.

Ferrari, A. (2013). DIGCOMP: A framework for developing and understanding digital competence in Europe. In Y. Punie, & B. Brecko (Eds.). Publications Office of the European Union. https://doi.org/10.2788/52966

Garrison, D. R., & Akyol, Z. (2012). The community of inquiry theoretical framework. In M. G. Moore (Ed.), *Handbook of distance education* (pp. 104–120). Routledge. https://doi.org/10.4324/9780203803738

González, D., & Herrera, L. E. (2015). Tracking the path of communities of inquiry in TEFL: A literature review. *HOW, 22*(1), 80–94.

Jiang, Y., Lin, H. Y., Cheung, L. F., Chan, H. C., & Li, P. (2023). *Hybrid/online teaching: A survey and key issues*. In 2023 IEEE 47th Annual Computers, Software, and Applications Conference (COMPSAC) (pp. 152–157). https://doi.org/10.1109/COMPSAC57700.2023.00028

Johnson, N., Veletsianos, G., & Seaman, J. (2020). U.S. Faculty and Administrators' experiences and approaches in the early weeks of the COVID-19 pandemic. *Online Learning, 24*(2), 6–21.

Kasiyah, D. Sadita, L., Santoso, H. B., Soeradijono, S. H., & Suhartanto, H. (2017). *Assessing students' e-learning competencies in online learning environment*. In 2017 International Conference on Advanced Computer Science and Information Systems (pp. 489–494).

Kolling, A. L., Weinberger, A., & Niegemann, H. (2022). Co-designing MOOCs with CoDegraph. *Journal of Formative Design in Learning, 6*(1), 25–39. https://doi.org/10.1007/s41686-022-00064-2

Kreijns, K., Xu, K., & Weidlich, J. (2022). Social presence: Conceptualization and measurement. *Educational Psychology Review, 34*(1), 139–170.

McInnerney, J. M., & Roberts, T. S. (2004). Online learning: Social interaction and the creation of a sense of community. *Educational Technology & Society, 7*(3), 73–81.

Müllert, N., & Jungk, R. (1987). *Future workshops: How to create desirable futures*. Institute for Social Inventions.

Pimmer, C., Mateescu, M., & Gröhbiel, U. (2016). Mobile and ubiquitous learning in higher education settings. A systematic review of empirical studies. *Computers in Human Behavior, 63*, 490–501. https://doi.org/10.1016/j.chb.2016.05.057

Raes, A., Detienne, L., Windey, I., & Depaepe, F. (2020). A systematic literature review on synchronous hybrid learning: Gaps identified. *Learning Environments Research, 23*, 269–290.

Ramsey, J. R., & Lorenz, M. P. (2016). Exploring the impact of cross-cultural management education on cultural intelligence, student satisfaction, and commitment. *Academy of Management Learning & Education, 15*(1), 79–99.

Rovai, A., Ponton, M., Wighting, M., & Baker, J. (2007). A comparative analysis of student motivation in traditional classroom and e-learning courses. *International Journal on E-learning, 6*(3), 413–432.

Sala, A., Punie, Y., & Garkov, V. (2020). *LifeComp: The European framework for personal, social and learning to learn key competence*. Joint Research Centre. https://doi.org/10.2760/302967

Singh, J., Steele, K., & Singh, L. (2021). Combining the best of online and face-to-face learning: Hybrid and blended learning approach for COVID-19, post vaccine, & post-pandemic world. *Journal of Educational Technology Systems, 50*(2), 140–171.

Sorrenti, G., Zölitz, U., Ribeaud, D., & Eisner, M. (2025). The causal impact of socio-emotional skills training on educational success. *Review of Economic Studies, 92*(1), 506–552.

Vuorikari, R., Jerzak, N., Karpinski, Z., Pokropek, A., & Tudek, J. (2022). *Measuring digital skills across the EU: Digital skills indicator 2.0.* Publications Office of the European Union. https://doi.org/10.2760/897803

Weitze, C. L., Ørngreen, R., & Levinsen, K. (2013, October). *The global classroom video conferencing model and first evaluations.* In Proceedings of the 12th European Conference on E-Learning: SKEMA Business School, Sophia Antipolis France, 30–31 October 2013 (pp. 503–510). Academic Conferences and Publishing International.

Wong, J., Baars, M., Davis, D., Van Der Zee, T., Houben, G. J., & Paas, F. (2019). Supporting self-regulated learning in online learning environments and MOOCs: A systematic review. *International Journal of Human–Computer Interaction, 35*(4–5), 356–373. https://doi.org/10.1080/10447318.2018.1543084

Xiao, J., Sun-Lin, H. Z., Lin, T. H., Li, M., Pan, Z., & Cheng, H. C. (2020). What makes learners a good fit for hybrid learning? Learning competences as predictors of experience and satisfaction in hybrid learning space. *British Journal of Educational Technology, 51*(4), 1203–1219. https://doi.org/10.1111/bjet.12949

Zimmerman, B. J. (1989). A social cognitive view of self-regulated academic learning. *Journal of Educational Psychology, 81*(3), 329–339. https://doi.org/10.1037/0022-0663.81.3.329

Experience-Based Cases of Hybrid Teaching and Learning

Hybrid Problem-Based Learning with Work-Life Clients: A Context of the Educational Technology Project Course

Juuso Kojo, Azusa Nakata, and Kristiina Mänty

1 The Case Context

Hybrid learning skills are important in the current working life contexts (European Commission, Joint Research Centre, et al., 2022). This mode of education enables people to meet from different locations, enriching students' learning experiences by inviting external clients to problem-based collaborative learning (Bell et al., 2014). The Educational Technology Project Course organised by the University of Oulu, Faculty of Education and Psychology (FEP) provided students with opportunities to practice using a hybrid meeting for communicating with external work-life clients.

The Educational Technology Project Course was organised as a part of minor studies of Digital Technologies in Teaching and Learning. The course participants came from the Learning, Education and Technology (LET) international Master's degree programme, the Learning Sciences degree programme (OPTI), and other degree programmes in FEP, including the teacher education programme. The course was mandatory for the LET Master's degree program and Learning Sciences degree program, and optional for other FEP students. The participants included 65% from the LET Master's degree programme, 25% from the Learning Sciences degree programme, and 10% from other FEP programs, including teacher education.

This 10-credit course included 16 hours of lectures, 16 hours of practice sessions, 70 hours of individual sessions (e.g., competence map creation, individual reflection etc.), and 170 hours of collaborative work. During collaborative work, the student teams used hybrid and online means to communicate with work-life clients as well as each other. Course lectures and practice sessions were implemented face-to-face.

J. Kojo (✉) · A. Nakata · K. Mänty
Faculty of Education and Psychology, University of Oulu, Oulu, Finland
e-mail: juuso.kojo@oulu.fi

A. Nakata et al. (eds.), *Hyb-IT-up!*,
https://doi.org/10.1007/978-3-031-99743-3_9

The course aimed to provide the students with the possibility to experience solving authentic working life problems. The students attempted to create solutions in teams of 3–5 people by applying the pedagogical theories they had learnt. Working life problems were provided by the clients such as companies, schools, or other organizations. Thus, the students got a chance to work together with those clients and produced practically purposeful solutions.

2 Learning Goals and Competences

The first main learning objective of the course was to let students apply their theoretical knowledge to solve authentic educational challenges. Students' theoretical knowledge had been established through earlier minor studies courses (e.g., Self-Regulation and Collaborative Learning, Learning Environments and Technologies etc.). For example, students utilised concepts such as technology-enhanced learning, collaborative problem-solving, and other relevant learning theories in designing solutions.

The second main learning objective was to develop students' key working life competences through reflective and project-based learning. At the start of the course, students assessed their existing competences, such as communication, teamwork, or project management skills, by creating competence maps. These maps helped them set personal learning goals aligned with the course content and future professional needs. During the course, students focused on developing competences such as:

- Project management: Planning, implementing, and assessing educational projects.
- Problem-solving: Designing and evaluating practical solutions for authentic educational situations, considering constraints such as resource limitations and diverse learners.
- Reflection and self-regulation: Continuously assessing their development in relation to their competence maps and adjusting their approach accordingly.

The core of the course was students' collaboration in small groups to address authentic challenges presented by real clients, such as companies, schools, and other organizations. The students need to learn how to plan and evaluate their solutions from a practical point of view; what pedagogical and technological solutions are available and possible in authentic educational situations (e.g., fixed choices of applications, limited resources, students with diverse backgrounds etc.).

By the end of the course, students were expected to demonstrate progress in project management, problem-solving, and reflective practices, while also showcasing their ability to tackle real-life challenges collaboratively and effectively.

3 Learning Design

In this course, students addressed real working life problems provided by various clients from the educational technology field. These clients presented authentic challenges forming the foundation of the students' project work. At the start of the course, students were introduced to a set of project overviews prepared by the clients. Based on these overviews, students selected the projects they were interested in, and teams were formed according to their preferences. This approach not only fostered students' motivation and positive group dynamics (Järvenoja & Järvelä, 2013) but also reflected real-world collaborative problem-solving scenarios.

The course structure was supported by a system of Open Badges. Open Badges is a trusted global standard for digital badges, embedding evidence of learning, achievements, and recipient details within a digital image (Open Badge Factory, n.d.). Using competence badges helped to build a visible structure for the course and to make students aware of the phases and subphases of project work by following the self-regulated learning (SRL) framework (planning, implementing, evaluation/reflection; Zimmerman, 2013). The course was designed in such a way that it guides students' decision-making to support their learning, for example, by emphasising the role of planning and setting goals or evaluating the progress in certain subphases (Järvenoja et al., 2020). Badges served as visual representations of the learning goals and competences, giving learners more information on their acquired competences as well as structuring the entire course. Designed Badges, namely phases of the course included four distinct parts: Competence, Project Planning, Project Implementation and Project Evaluation (see Fig. 1).

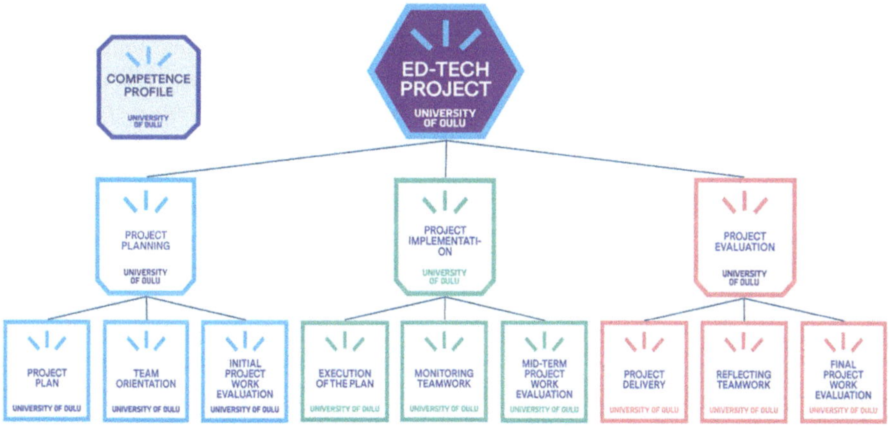

Fig. 1 The badge structure of the course

3.1 Competence

To support students' competence development, the course work started by recognizing and reflecting on students' personal and professional development and working life competences. Reflection was done by an individual essay and a competence map. After this, all the project overviews provided by the clients were introduced to the students. The students selected a few projects they are interested in, and project teams were formulated based on their decision. Forming teams based on individuals' interests is effective to build a motivated group atmosphere (Järvenoja & Järvelä, 2013).

3.2 Project Planning

The first part of the project work, the Project Planning, consisted of the following subsections: the Project Plan, Team Orientation and Initial Project Evaluation. The theoretical bases of project planning, efficient teamwork and understanding of the role of evaluation in project work were introduced in the lectures.

In the practice sessions, student teams started the actual project work under the guidance of the course responsible teacher. The course work was supported by collaboration scripts facilitating students' planning, implementing, monitoring and reflecting on the project work. Scripts were shared in the course's Microsoft Teams platform. All groups are, for example, supported and encouraged in building their own teamwork culture. For student teams working in hybrid settings, providing intentional guidance and guidelines for joint working and settings to get to know each another is essential for establishing productive collaboration and a sense of community (Jeong & Hmelo-Silver, 2016) and for anticipating and regulating the group's cognitive, motivational and emotional challenges (Järvenoja & Järvelä, 2013).

Depending on the needs, the student teams set up multiple on-site, online or hybrid meetings among themselves and with the clients. Students were also instructed to use the course Microsoft Teams platform for their asynchronous communication (e.g., project documentation, messaging and sharing materials). Such digital platforms or learning management systems (LMSs) can capture traces of students' learning, allowing the course teacher to monitor their progress and scaffold students when needed (Perry & Winne, 2006; Sáiz-Manzanares et al., 2021). Using a single platform simplifies the workflow for students to lessen their cognitive load during the task (see Chandler & Sweller, 1991; Kirschner et al., 2018) and supports communication and sharing of materials within the team (Jeong & Hmelo-Silver, 2016). Despite the positive aspect of using digital tools, students were encouraged to arrange the first meeting with their client face-to-face to build better group cohesion for online and hybrid collaboration (Miyake & Kirschner, 2014).

3.3 Project Implementation

The second part of the course was the Project Implementation. This part was also divided into three subsections: Execution of the Plan, Monitoring Teamwork and Mid Term Project Evaluation. In this phase, the lectures provided theoretical grounding for the educational projects, project implementation, and teamwork monitoring. Student teams continued their independent collaborative work, interacting with clients on their chosen platforms and working together to develop solutions to the identified challenges. Student teams also delivered oral presentations about the progress of their projects. During this phase, students had access to consultations with experts in collaborative learning, educational technology, and project-based learning. Expert meetings were organized in both onsite and hybrid modes, allowing clients to participate remotely.

3.4 Project Evaluation

This phase consisted of the following subsections: Project Delivery, Reflecting Teamwork and Final Project Evaluation. In this phase, student teams presented the implementations and deliverables of their projects. Collaborative work was evaluated both at team and individual levels. Finally, the students reflected on how they had developed their competencies by revisiting the competence map they had created at the beginning of the course.

4 Workflow and Interaction

Previous implementations of the Educational Technology Project course included clients either from the university or schools near the university premises. The latest implementation expanded the area: clients were from all around the city area or located in different parts of Finland or even abroad. Also, most of the clients' representatives were teachers whose schedules were often very tight. Thus, it was important to arrange meetings with them as conveniently as possible. For these reasons, working hybrid was a practical solution for enabling fluent and frequent communication with the team and client. This section describes how the hybrid environments were set up and used in this course and facilitated collaborative work with the clients.

In the Project Implementation phase, student teams set up their way of working, meeting on-site, on-line and hybrid. Because of the client's location, some teams mainly used hybrid options (i.e., students get together in one place and clients join a meeting remotely from their workplace). The course instructed students to use Microsoft Teams environment for the course work, but the student teams were allowed to decide their working environments to have more convenient internal and external communication. The students ended up using a wide variety of digital tools such as Zoom, WhatsApp, Notion, Google Meet and Drive, and Microsoft Planner.

As an example, one student team whose client was a private educational game company located in Oulu and Helsinki in Finland implemented a hybrid mode in their meetings. The team reserved a co-working space in the university premise and set up a hybrid setting to communicate with the client using Microsoft Teams (Fig. 2). All the students prepared their laptops and connected to Teams with cameras on, but only one person in the team opened the microphone and speaker to avoid echoing and howling. Some students in the team were knowledgeable about how to avoid such audio issues and competent to set up and handle the hybrid situation, helping other students to connect to Teams and optimise their camera and audio settings.

Another student team also had meetings in a hybrid mode because one member of their clients was joining from Germany. They reserved a small cube in the university premise for their hybrid meetings (Figs. 3 and 4). These cubes are soundproofed and equipped with high-quality audio and video to support online and hybrid group work/learning. There was a main display with a web camera in the cube, but it couldn't capture all the team members. Hence, the student team decided to open two laptops to show the faces of two members each for better social presence.

This student team first met the client and the course teacher in person at the university for the initial kick-off meeting. The students and client introduced themselves and exchanged ideas about the problem and tasks. Meanwhile, the client was trying to show some content from their laptop but found it difficult to show it to everyone without a big screen. From that experience, the student team and client decided to try out a hybrid option for the following meetings and managed to invite another client member from Germany. By sharing the screen from one's laptop, everyone could see the content and had an equal opportunity to discuss the topic.

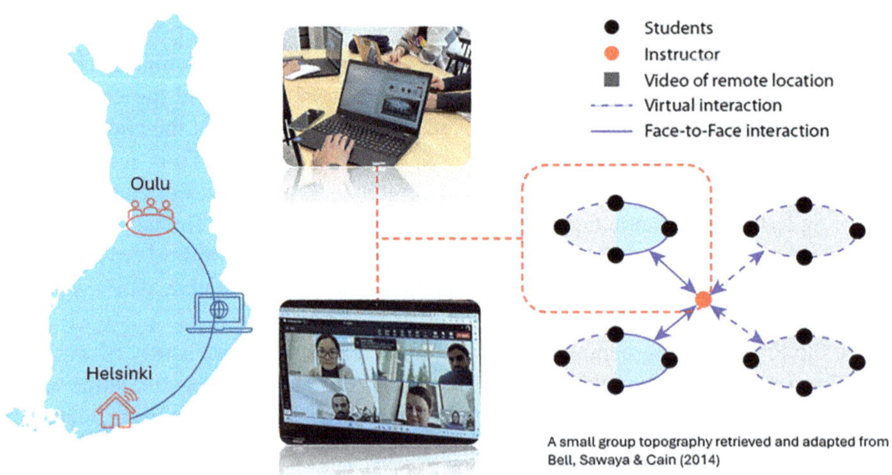

Fig. 2 A hybrid learning model applied in the Educational Technology Project course

Fig. 3 A study cube for group learning at the University of Oulu at Linnanmaa Campus. A picture is retrieved from https://www.oulu.fi/en/news/you-can-now-book-cubes-group-work-and-media-production

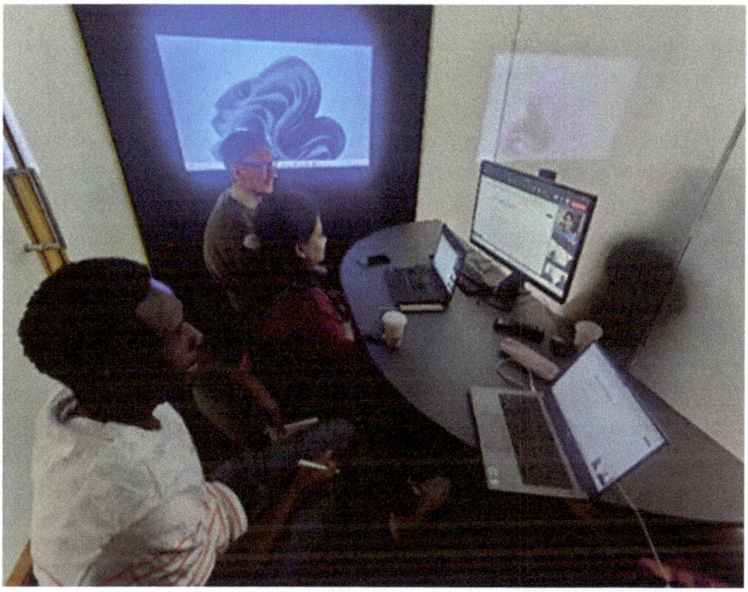

Fig. 4 A student group working in a small soundproof cube designed for online/hybrid group work. production)

In both cases, the students themselves prepared a small space and took care of setting up the hybrid session. This small-scale hybrid meeting did not require any extra equipment such as a video conferencing camera (e.g., Kandao, Meeting Owl, PanaCast), meeting speaker (e.g., Jabra) or a room with a big screen. Although basic knowledge and skills in audio settings of the computer and video conferencing tools are required on the student's end, this approach can help overcome some constraints related to available equipment and resources (Raes et al., 2020).

5 Final Considerations

Hybrid solutions made meetings more effective and efficient in two ways; first, the students and clients did not need to travel to meet each other, and second, meetings could be arranged anytime when both parties agreed, such as daytime between lectures. The feedback from the clients about these flexible meeting arrangements was also very positive—as hybrid meetings have become an "industry standard" in Finnish school life. Because our university provides students with easily accessible spaces and equipment for hybrid working, the arrangement of such hybrid collaborations was relatively easy.

Hybrid teaching also helped students' retention of the course (Lakhal et al., 2017). In some of the practice sessions, some students were not able to participate on-site due to the difficulty of commuting. Hence, the teacher established a hybrid option at the beginning of the course and carried out some lectures allowing remote participation. During the collaborative work part, a remote student could be "present" through their teammate's laptop screen and microphone. As previous studies on hybrid learning have largely suggested, the application of the flexibility of time and place was well recognised in the course (Bell et al., 2014; Raes et al., 2020).

The project cases were based on the client commissions and consisted of open-ended problems. Collaborative problem-solving creates possibilities to work on real-life open-ended and ill-defined problems (Häkkinen et al., 2017). However, working on complex problems, especially when the group interactions are mediated by a hybrid setting, can create various challenges that endanger the collaborative process. In this course, the teacher attempted to minimise possible challenges by applying scripts following SRL and Computer-Supported Collaborative Learning (CSCL) principles, navigating group formation, interactions and task implementation.

We acknowledge that basic skills to use hybrid environments are crucial on both students and clients. Since most client–student meetings were not arranged under the teacher's supervision, a lack of these skills may become problematic. In a future implementation of this course, we can propose a hybrid mode as a standard communication option. We believe this approach can expand opportunities for students by enabling them to work with work-life clients beyond the local area and equipping them with new working skills using hybrid methods.

References

Bell, J., Sawaya, S., & Cain, W. (2014). Synchromodal classes: Designing for shared learning experiences between face-to-face and online students. *International Journal of Designs for Learning, 5*(1). Retrieved from https://scholarworks.iu.edu/journals/index.php/ijdl/article/view/12657/19225.

Chandler, P., & Sweller, J. (1991). Cognitive load theory and the format of instruction. *Cognition and Instruction, 8*, 293–332.

European Commission, Joint Research Centre, Vuorikari, R., Kluzer, S., & Punie, Y. (2022). *DigComp 2.2, The digital competence framework for citizens: With new examples of knowledge, skills and attitudes*. Publications Office of the European Union. Retrieved from https://data.europa.eu/doi/10.2760/115376.

Häkkinen, P., Järvelä, S., Mäkitalo-Siegl, K., Ahonen, A., Näykki, P., & Valtonen, T. (2017). Preparing teacher-students for twenty-first-century learning practices (PREP 21): A framework for enhancing collaborative problem-solving and strategic learning skills. *Teachers and Teaching, 23*(1), 25–41.

Järvenoja, H., & Järvelä, S. (2013). Regulating emotions together for motivated collaboration. In M. Baker, J. Andriessen, & S. Järvelä (Eds.), *Affective learning together. Social and emotional dimensions of collaborative learning* (pp. 162–181). Routledge.

Järvenoja, H., Malmberg, J., Törmänen, T., Mänty, K., Haataja, E., Ahola, S., & Järvelä, S. (2020). A collaborative learning design for promoting and analyzing adaptive motivation and emotion regulation in the science classroom. *Frontiers in Education, 5*, 111.

Jeong, H., & Hmelo-Silver, C. E. (2016). Seven affordances of computer-supported collaborative learning: How to support collaborative learning? How can technologies help? *Educational Psychologist, 51*(2), 247–265.

Kirschner, P. A., Sweller, J., Kirschner, F., & Zambraro, J. (2018). From cognitive load theory to collaborative cognitive load theory. *International Journal of Computer-Supported Collaborative Learning, 13*, 213–233. https://doi.org/10.1007/s11412-018-9277-y

Lakhal, S., Bateman, D., & Bédard, J. (2017). Blended synchronous delivery modes in graduate programs: A literature review and its implementation in the master teacher program. *Collected Essays on Learning and Teaching, 10*, 47–60. https://doi.org/10.22329/celt.v10i0.4747

Miyake, N., & Kirschner, P. A. (2014). The social and interactive dimensions of collaborative learning. In R. K. Sawyer (Ed.), *The Cambridge handbook of the learning sciences* (pp. 418–438). Cambridge University Press. https://doi.org/10.1017/CBO9781139519526.026

Open Badge Factory (n.d.). *What is an Open Badge?* Retrieved from https://openbadgefactory.com/en/.

Perry, N. E., & Winne, P. H. (2006). Learning from learning kits: gStudy traces of students' self-regulated engagements with computerized content. *Educational Psychology Review, 18*(3), 211–228.

Raes, A., Detienne, L., Windey, I., & Depaepe, F. (2020). A systematic literature review on synchronous hybrid learning: Gaps identified. *Learning Environments Research, 23*(3), 269–290. https://doi.org/10.1007/s10984-019-09303-z

Sáiz-Manzanares, M. C., Rodríguez-Díez, J. J., Díez-Pastor, J. F., Rodríguez-Arribas, S., Marticorena-Sánchez, R., & Ji, Y. P. (2021). Monitoring of student learning in learning management systems: An application of educational data mining techniques. *Applied Sciences, 11*(6), 2677.

Zimmerman, B. J. (2013). From cognitive modeling to self-regulation: A social cognitive career path. *Educational Psychologist, 48*(3), 135–147. https://doi.org/10.1080/00461520.2013.794676

Collaborative Hybrid Learning in Developing Health Sciences Competence

Sari Pramila-Savukoski, Tiina Törmänen, Heli-Maria Kuivila, and Kristina Mikkonen

1 The Case Context

The aim was to develop a hybrid education model that can be used nationally and internationally to develop high-quality and flexible higher education, combining face-to-face and remote teaching. The development and evaluation process took place from autumn 2021 until autumn 2023. Hybrid learning and teaching were implemented in courses at the University of Oulu, Faculty of Medicine in Health Sciences degree programme. The course participants were students from Master's degree education (120 ECTS, 2-year programme) in health sciences (including nursing and health management) as their main subject. Most of the degree students lived close to the university (within a zone of 20 km), but some lived in southern Finland like Helsinki which is 600 km from Oulu or remote areas like Kittilä which is 370 km from Oulu (Fig. 1). It was also typical that the students were partly in employment or had families with small children, which favoured the development of hybrid teaching in the degree programme. Experts from different organisations all over Finland and abroad were used as guest lecturers. Thus, hybrid teaching brought economic benefits and flexibility to teaching for the whole study community.

S. Pramila-Savukoski (✉)
Northern Well-being and Services, Lapland University of Applied Sciences, Rovaniemi, Finland

Faculty of Medicine, University of Oulu, Oulu, Finland

Lapland University of Applied Sciences, Oulu, Finland
e-mail: sari.pramila-savukoski@lapinamk.fi

T. Törmänen
Faculty of Education and Psychology, University of Oulu, Oulu, Finland

H.-M. Kuivila · K. Mikkonen
Faculty of Medicine, University of Oulu, Oulu, Finland

A. Nakata et al. (eds.), *Hyb-IT-up!*,
https://doi.org/10.1007/978-3-031-99743-3_10

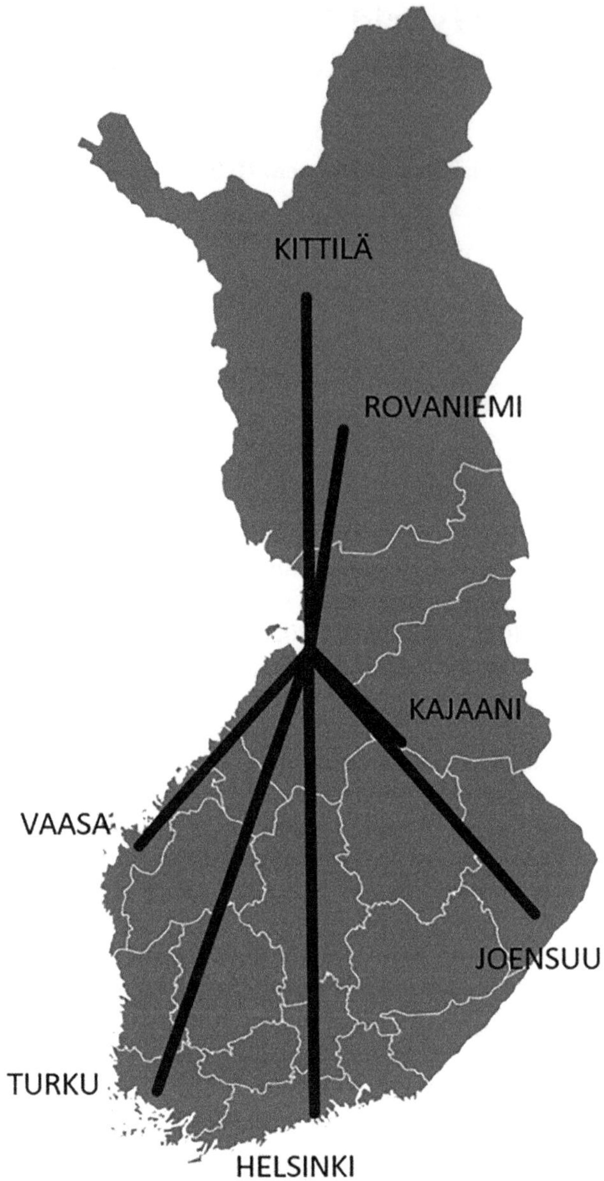

Fig. 1 Students are connecting the University of Oulu all over Finland

Hybrid teaching was implemented in the courses that were part of mandatory studies and had a length of 5–10 ECTS (European Credit Transfer and Accumulation System). To get diverse experiences, hybrid teaching was integrated into small classes of 10–20 students and large classes of 30–50 students. The courses consisted of face-to-face/online participation in the classroom (Fig. 2) and independent and collaborative learning.

Fig. 2 Hybrid teaching with educators and students face-to-face and remote

The courses offered students the opportunity to strengthen their competences together in collaboration, create a supportive learning atmosphere, lead a group, set goals, and plan and monitor activities to achieve competence levels in health sciences. The course contents were built by emphasising evidence-based health care (Jordan et al., 2019), including identifying global health needs, generating evidence by planning research and producing research data, synthesising evidence by summarising and disseminating research data, and applying knowledge by solving collaboratively given tasks.

2 Learning Goals and Competences

Eight key competence areas in health sciences expertise were identified during the hybrid learning course (see Fig. 3; Pramila-Savukoski et al., 2024a). For example, health sciences experts must be proficient in leading people and processes, understanding the economics and management of social and healthcare services (#1), and addressing client needs (people-centred care) in a multidisciplinary manner (#2). This requires knowledge of health promotion (#3), evidence-based practices (#4), and digital solid literacy regarding services, devices, and systems (#5). In addition, experts must manage their work effectively across different timeframes (#6) and collaborate virtually with others engaging in innovative and cognitive problem-solving in multidisciplinary teams (#7), being competent in societal interaction (#8). Each course had specific objectives, emphasising different areas of health sciences to enable students to develop their essential expertise. The objectives of the courses were communicated to students at the beginning of the course. The teaching methods were appropriately tailored to develop these competences.

The hybrid teaching approach was piloted in various courses, including a research methodology course package. The first course of the package aimed to equip students

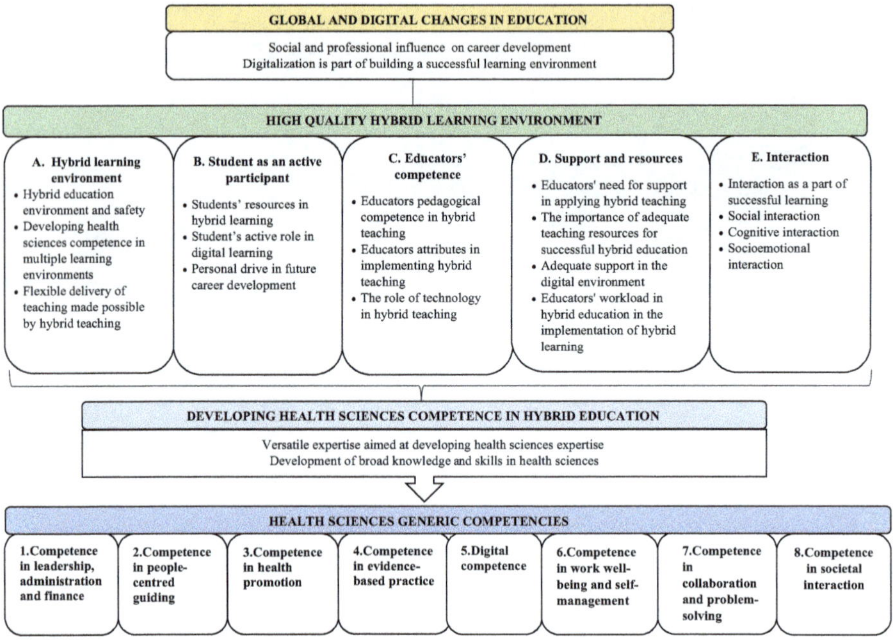

Fig. 3 The theoretical model for high-quality hybrid teaching

with the skills to compare and interpret research methods in nursing and health management sciences, evaluate and apply data collection and analysis techniques, and develop a research plan while considering ethical and data protection issues.

In the second part of the course package, students focused on critically justifying their research topics, identifying key concepts, and applying methodological solutions in their research. They also learned to assess the reliability of quantitative and qualitative research, develop a comprehensive research plan, and present it creatively. The course emphasised the importance of responsible science, ethical research practices, and effective data management. Both parts involved students in close collaboration for problem-solving and decision-making.

3 Learning Design

The developed hybrid education model (Pramila-Savukoski, 2024; see Fig. 3) was used as a learning design with key concepts centred on ensuring that health sciences students develop essential competences through a hybrid learning approach. The model for high-quality hybrid education included the hybrid learning environment, the student's active role, the educators' competence, support and resources, and interaction (Fig. 3). Hybrid teaching supports global and digital transformations while aiming to enhance educational outcomes.

The model guided us to ensure high-quality education by considering a hybrid learning environment with safe and flexible delivery of teaching (see A). According to the experiences and data about learning collected from students (Nyman et al., 2024; Pramila-Savukoski et al., 2023a; Pramila-Savukoski et al., 2023b) and educators (Jämsä et al., 2024; Mensonen et al., 2024), it was found that pedagogical safety and common agreements are important for learning so that health sciences competence can be developed in the best possible way. Hybrid learning makes learning more flexible (Mensonen et al., 2024) but requires high-quality technical environment (Nyman et al., 2024; Mensonen et al., 2024). It may bring new possibilities to connect higher education and working life, which has been identified to be challenging (Pramila-Savukoski et al., 2023a). Students have felt that hybrid learning supports different skills like interaction, technical and working life skills (Nyman et al., 2024). It may cause stress, but on the other hand creates opportunities for social contact and thus enhances well-being (Nyman et al., 2024; Pramila-Savukoski et al., 2023a).

Students were positioned as active and responsible participants who understood their personal drive in their learning and future career development (see B). It is essential that students take that responsibility since educators experience less control in hybrid teaching situations (Mensonen et al., 2024; Pramila-Savukoski et al., 2023b). Based on the evidence, hybrid education seems to support active learners and requires e.g. learners' ability for self-regulation (Nyman et al., 2024; Pramila-Savukoski et al., 2023a). In self-regulated learning, the learner is seen as an active agent who takes responsibility for planning, setting goals, and monitoring and reflecting on the different aspects involved in the learning process (Zimmerman, 2013). These aspects involve cognitive components, such as learning strategies used to solve the tasks, as well as learners' motivational and emotional conditions for learning (Winne & Hadwin, 2008). Interestingly, hybrid learning increased students' motivation to learn (Nyman et al., 2024). Generally, students' own motivation and personal factors influence competence development in digital learning environments (Pramila-Savukoski et al., 2023a). Competence is challenged by continuous change, to which students also have to adapt, but hybrid learning offers great opportunities (Nyman et al., 2024).

To support a safe environment and student's active role, hybrid teaching requires educators to have a wide range of competencies: planning and resourcing, technological, interaction, digital pedagogical and ethical competence (Jokinen et al., 2024; Mensonen et al., 2024; see C). The elements for high-quality hybrid learning were identified (Jokinen et al., 2024; Mensonen et al., 2024; Pramila-Savukoski et al., 2023b) and shared among educators. Good quality hybrid education is based on sound planning and resourcing without forgetting the importance of educators' own attitude and resilience (Mensonen et al., 2024). Educators need to assess the suitability of hybrid learning for the course and the group of students. The success of hybrid teaching depends on how well the educator has planned the teaching event and how teaching and methods are appropriately produced (Mensonen et al., 2024; Nyman et al., 2024). Regarding pedagogical competence, attention should be paid to establishing clear procedures for interaction, such as requesting to speak and consider socio-emotional interaction like expressing feelings and motivational aspects as part of supporting learning. Providing a wide range of interactive applications is essential. Digital pedagogy follows traditional pedagogical methods closely (Mensonen et al., 2024). It is important to support students in taking responsibility for learning, and educators are providing structures and opportunities for learning (Nyman et al., 2024). Educators should facilitate and support interaction to enhance students' motivation (Mensonen et al., 2024; Nyman et al., 2024; Pramila-Savukoski et al., 2023a; Pramila-Savukoski et al., 2023b). In hybrid teaching, assessing and providing feedback should be planned equally and regularly taking care of students who participate in different modes (Nyman et al., 2024). The ethical competence of educators is highlighted as the teaching environment becomes more multidimensional (Mensonen et al., 2024; Nyman et al., 2024). Paying attention to the equal assessment and privacy of students makes learning comfortable for all and enhances the safety. In addition, technology and technological competence play a key role in hybrid education (Mensonen et al., 2024; Nyman et al., 2024) and were perceived to be developed in a national study among educators in higher education (Jämsä et al., 2024). The use of a camera facilitates interaction and promotes the experience of a shared learning situation for students (Pramila-Savukoski et al., 2023a; Nyman et al., 2024), but a safe atmosphere is key to interaction (Nyman et al., 2024). In our study, educators assessed themselves to have excellent competence in interaction, meaning that they feel competent to engage students in interaction and collaboration (Jämsä et al., 2024).

Educators and students need support and resources in hybrid learning (Mensonen et al., 2024; Nyman et al., 2024; Pramila-Savukoski et al., 2023a; see D). Students need support for new ways to interact with peers in digital environments and engage in learning (Nyman et al., 2024). They also need support to be conscious about restructuring new knowledge in interaction with cognitive and socio-emotional aspects (Pramila-Savukoski et al., 2023b). Some students also need help with new teaching methods and the use of technology. Educators need support to deliver quality teaching to support the learning process and develop competence (Mensonen et al., 2024). According to the evidence, educators' training supported their hybrid teaching and increased the motivation to use such types of designs (Kokko et al., 2025). The training also underlined the importance of attitude as part of competence and the adaptation of educators to hybrid teaching (Mensonen et al., 2024).

Learning and developing education is only possible through interaction with educators, peers and the environment (see E). Hybrid learning have revealed challenges in for example group cohesion like feelings of separation, and socio-emotional interaction could be particularly helpful in supporting group formation and cohesion. In a quasi-experimental mixed method study, we found that social, cognitive and socio-emotional interaction emerged in hybrid learning situations, showing students' increase of socio-emotional interaction (Pramila-Savukoski et al., 2023b). Students may need socio-emotional interaction more in online and hybrid than in face-to-face interaction.

All five of these core elements should be considered when developing hybrid teaching. It is essential to understand the learning objectives and the learning process to achieve the desired competencies. The model can be applied to different disciplines by replacing the competences objectives with a set of competences tailored to their own needs.

4 Workflow and Interaction

In concrete terms, the hybrid teaching approach was based on methods that theoretically support student-centred learning and educators' wellbeing according to the research (Mensonen et al., 2024). Initially, the hybrid teaching was designed on previous research, but progressively, the model was refined as the theoretical knowledge developed. Typically, the development work was carried out in courses with two educators. Commonly, one was an educator who was online, and another was physically in the classroom as shown in Fig. 2. Hybrid teaching with one educator was also implemented.

To ensure a safe learning environment, agreements and ground rules on sharing, participation, and taking responsibility as well as the information and communications technology tools needed for teaching were created together with the students before the course/in the info lecture (see Fig. 4).

For educators, their essential competences were identified. When planning teaching, the following issues were considered:

- What kind of knowledge or competencies are to be taught?
- What is the added value of the hybrid teaching?
- How will the educator support and engage the student?
- Regarding resourcing, how much of a role will contact teaching play?
- What facilities/equipment will be used to deliver the hybrid teaching?
- Can part of the teaching be carried out entirely remotely?

To decrease the workload of the educators, team teaching with the theoretical support of hybrid learning/teaching experts was utilised. Good practices were shared, and the roles of both educators varied. Opportunities were built for educators to develop their hybrid teaching competences, and all educators in the degree programme attended 2 ECTS of online or hybrid in-service training. Educators' attitudes were emphasised, and technological equipment was upgraded and harmonised at the level of the whole educational organisation with separate education. Newly qualified educators worked basically with experts. Different kinds of support were provided for students, such as education for Zoom/Teams and guidelines for learning in hybrid mode.

Recognising the importance of interaction, hybrid teaching sought to make the most of valuable time together by creating opportunities to develop learning through collaborative learning methods (Fig. 4). To this end, the purpose and process of the method were discussed and supported by students. Different life situations and time constraints challenged students. Collaborative tasks were created for students to

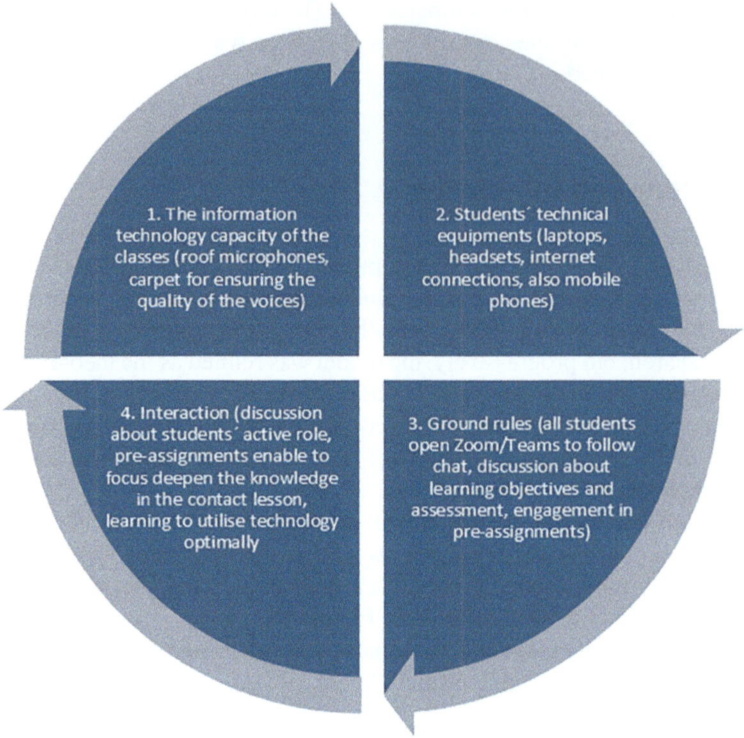

Fig. 4 Technology enablers and ground rules for ensuring safe learning environment

plan, assess and monitor progress and learning. They were also given opportunities for peer assessment and performance in lessons.

Two instruments were developed to evaluate competence development and the effect of hybrid teaching on students and educators. HealthGenericCom was developed and psychometrically tested to self-evaluate students' health sciences generic competence (Pramila-Savukoski et al., 2024a). A theoretical understanding of educators' hybrid teaching competences, both locally and nationally, was needed; therefore, an instrument to assess educators' hybrid teaching competence was developed and psychometrically tested (Jokinen et al., 2024; Jämsä et al., 2024) and utilised in competence development (Fig. 5). As educators needed support, continuous education for educators was also developed (Kokko et al., 2025) and offered free of charge throughout Finland to anyone interested. Throughout the 2 years, large-scale development hybrid events were held throughout higher education to share good practices and create networks. Also, organisation level directions for hybrid learning were developed.

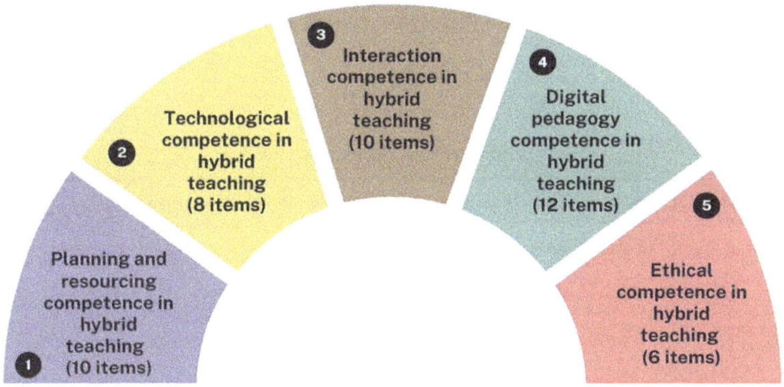

Fig. 5 Factors and items of educators' hybrid competence instrument

5 Final Considerations

As education becomes more digital, flexible teaching solutions become an essential part of higher education. Hybrid learning connects students in different locations, creating a flexible, adaptive learning environment that meets diverse student needs while ensuring psychological safety. In our chapter we presented that global changes and health policies are shaping the competences required of future health science experts, influencing education, training, and resource allocation through public decisions. It is important to emphasise that technological developments, including artificial intelligence (AI), are transforming education and competence by enhancing personalised learning and real-time feedback, and at their best, they support flexible learning and hybrid education. In health sciences, digital competence—especially through the integration of AI—should be further developed to meet the demands of evolving healthcare environments (Pramila-Savukoski et al., 2024b). In our final consideration, we present the theoretical model for high-quality hybrid teaching by integrating AI (see Fig. 6).

Hybrid learning and flexible learning environments, combined with the integration of AI tools, offer dynamic opportunities to enhance student learning by providing personalised, adaptive learning experiences. AI-driven tools can support students by tailoring content to their individual learning needs, monitoring progress, and offering real-time feedback, which allows for more effective and targeted learning. Additionally, these tools enable adaptive evaluation methods, ensuring assessments are aligned with each student's learning pace and style. However, implementing AI in education must prioritise ethical considerations, particularly regarding data privacy, bias, and fairness, to create a safe and supportive learning environment. By balancing innovation with ethical safety, hybrid learning environments can foster academic success and trust in digital education technologies.

In modern digital learning environments, students are expected to take an active role, engaging fully with the content and taking responsibility for their own learning. The integration of AI tools in education can support this by providing

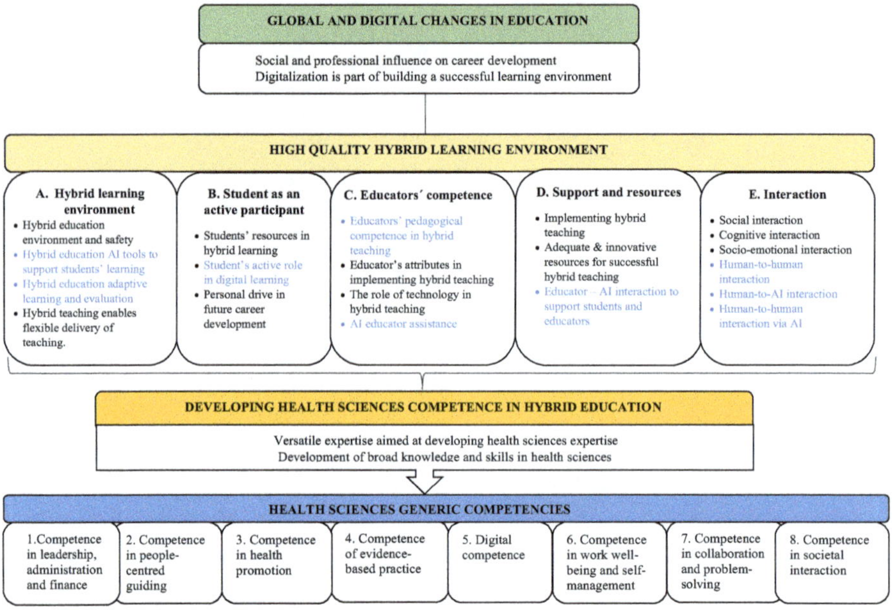

Fig. 6 The theoretical model with integrating AI solutions for high-quality hybrid teaching

personalised learning experiences and real-time feedback, encouraging students to actively and critically participate. However, it is essential that AI complements rather than replaces the learning process, ensuring students remain independent thinkers rather than passive recipients of automated assistance. Educators play a key role in this by developing pedagogical competence in AI literacy and hybrid teaching. AI can assist educators by challenging their thinking and offering new perspectives, but it must not result in complacency among either learners or educators. Instead, AI should enhance the educational process, driving both students and teachers to stay engaged, curious, and proactive in their roles. The interaction between educators and AI can provide valuable support to both students and teachers by offering additional resources and personalised guidance. This collaboration ensures that AI enhances the learning experience without diminishing the active roles of educators and students.

Finally, more research is needed to understand human-to-human interaction facilitated by AI tools, as well as the dynamics of human-to-AI interaction and its impact on wellbeing. Multidisciplinary approaches can support this understanding, deepening the knowledge and skills of many by drawing from diverse fields such as education, health sciences, social sciences, psychology, and technology. This will help ensure AI is integrated in ways that promote both effective learning and the mental and emotional health of students and educators.

References

Jämsä, R., Pramila-Savukoski, S., Kuivila, H., Jokinen, H., Juntunen, J., Koskimäki, M., Törmänen, T., & Mikkonen, K. (2024). The hybrid education competence of educators in the social, healthcare, and health science fields: A cross-sectional study. *Teaching and Learning in Nursing, 19*(3), e550–e556. https://doi.org/10.1016/j.teln.2024.03.012

Jokinen, H., Pramila-Savukoski, S., Kuivila, H., Jämsä, R., Juntunen, J., Törmänen, T., & Mikkonen, K. (2024). Development and psychometric testing of hybrid education competence instrument for social and health care, and health sciences educators. *Nurse Education Today, 132*, 105999. https://doi.org/10.1016/j.nedt.2023.105999

Jordan, Z., Lockwood, C., Munn, Z. & Aromataris, E. (2019). The updated Joanna Briggs Institute Model of Evidence-Based Healthcare. *International Journal of Evidence Based Healthcare, 17*(1), 58–71. https://doi.org/10.1097/XEB.0000000000000155

Kokko, M., Pramila-Savukoski, S., Ojala, J., Kuivila, H., Juntunen, J., Törmänen, T., & Mikkonen, K. (2025). The effect of educational intervention on hybrid teaching competence of health sciences and medical educators' – A mixed methods study. *Scandinavian Journal of Educational Research, 69*, 973–988. https://doi.org/10.1080/00313831.2024.2369860

Mensonen, M., Pramila-Savukoski, S., Mikkonen, K., Törmänen, T., Juntunen, J., & Kuivila, H. (2024). The experiences of social and health care and health sciences educators of implementing hybrid teaching in higher education: A qualitative study. *Nurse Education Today, 133*, 106079. https://doi.org/10.1016/j.nedt.2023.106079

Nyman, E., Pramila-Savukoski, S., Mikkonen, K., Törmänen, T., Juntunen, J., & Kuivila, H.-M. (2024). The experiences of health sciences students with hybrid learning in health sciences education—A qualitative study. *Nurse Education Today, 132*, 106017. https://doi.org/10.1016/j.nedt.2023.106017

Pramila-Savukoski, S. (2024). *Development of hybrid education intervention to ensure health sciences students' generic competences*. Doctoral dissertation, University of Oulu. Oulu University Repository. Retrieved from https://oulurepo.oulu.fi/handle/10024/48258

Pramila-Savukoski, S., Jarva, E., Kuivila, H., Juntunen, J., Koskenranta, M., Kääriäinen, M., & Mikkonen, K. (2024b). Generic competence among health sciences students in higher education - A cross-sectional study. *Nurse Education Today, 133*, 106036. https://doi.org/10.1016/j.nedt.2023.106036

Pramila-Savukoski, S., Kärnä, R., Kuivila, H., Juntunen, J., Koskenranta, M., Oikarainen, A., & Mikkonen, K. (2023a). The influence of digital learning on health sciences students' competence development – A qualitative study. *Nurse Education Today, 120*, 105635. https://doi.org/10.1016/j.nedt.2022.105635

Pramila-Savukoski, S., Kärnä, R., Kuivila, H., Oikarainen, A., Törmänen, T., Juntunen, J., et al. (2023b). Competence development in collaborative hybrid learning among health sciences students: A quasi-experimental mixed-method study. *Journal of Computer Assisted Learning, 39*(6), 1919–1938. https://doi.org/10.1111/jcal.12859

Pramila-Savukoski, S., Kuivila, H., Juntunen, J., Koskenranta, M., Jarva, E., Tuomikoski, A., Hammarén, M., & Mikkonen, K. (2024a). Development and psychometric testing of the Health Sciences Generic Competence (HealthGenericCom) Instrument: A cross-sectional study. *International Journal of Research in Education and Science (IJRES), 10*(1), 21–45. https://doi.org/10.46328/ijres.3306

Winne, PH., Hadwin, AF., (2008). The weave of motivation and self-regulated learning. In D. H. Schunk & B. J. Zimmerman (Eds.), Motivation and self-regulated learning: Theory, research, and applications (pp. 297–314). Lawrence Erlbaum Associates Publishers.

Zimmerman, B. J. (2013). From cognitive modeling to self-regulation: A social cognitive career path. *Educational Psychologist, 48*(3), 135–147. https://doi.org/10.1080/00461520.2013.794676

Hybrid Teaching and Learning in the Context of Vocational Secondary Education

Marlene Wagner, Gerti Pishtari, and Tobias Ley

1 The Case Context

In the 2020/21 academic year, the Waldviertel Business Academy, a collaboration of four rural vocational secondary schools in Lower Austria, introduced the synchronous hybrid classroom. The four schools have partnered to offer four training specializations as part of their curriculum: (1) International Logistics, (2) Health Management and Sports, (3) E-Business Entrepreneurship, and (4) Food & Wood. Students in grades 11–13 choose one of the specializations, which are taught in two 50-min lessons per week. Each school site offers one specialization, and if a student's chosen specialization is not taught at their school, they can still participate via the virtual classroom using the digital platform Microsoft Teams. Overall, the training specializations are taught in a synchronous hybrid classroom, as some students participate on-site, while others participate remotely from different school sites, and the participation mode remains fixed.

The school collaboration has been agreed upon since 2018, and the current application of the synchronous hybrid classroom is the result of a concept developed between school leaders and regional businesses. Once there was a concept, it was followed up by a set of training sessions where teachers mastered the usage of technology and teaching methods for the synchronous hybrid classroom. After 3 years of practice, school leaders aimed to evaluate its implementation in terms of digital

M. Wagner (✉) · G. Pishtari
Center for Digitalization in Lifelong Learning, University for Continuing Education Krems, Krems, Austria
e-mail: marlene.wagner@donau-uni.ac.at

T. Ley
Center for Digitalization in Lifelong Learning, University for Continuing Education Krems, Krems, Austria

Center for Educational Technology, Tallinn University, Tallinn, Estonia

A. Nakata et al. (eds.), *Hyb-IT-up!*,
https://doi.org/10.1007/978-3-031-99743-3_11

technology integration, learning activities, social presence, usability and its impact on student learning and engagement. Quantitative data were collected from students and teachers between December 2022 and February 2023 using an online questionnaire. More detailed results of this study can be found in Wagner et al. (2023) and Wagner et al. (2025).

2 Learning Goals and Competencies

The four topics of the training specializations at the Waldviertel Business Academy have been developed together with the regional business community. This partnership ensures that the curriculum is aligned with the current needs and future trends of the Waldviertel region's labour market. Each specialization aims to equip students with specific competencies and skills that are essential for their professional development in their respective fields. The goal shared by all specializations is to develop students' entrepreneurial competencies.

In the International Logistics module, the curriculum focuses on providing students with a comprehensive understanding of logistics and supply chain management. Key learning goals include an understanding of the fundamentals of logistics, which covers the basic principles and operations such as transportation, warehousing and distribution. Students also study supply chain management, gaining insights into the management of supply chains from procurement to delivery. The module also addresses new business models that are transforming the logistics industry, including e-commerce logistics and green logistics, and equips students with the business planning skills needed to develop and implement effective logistics strategies.

The Health Management and Sports module is designed to address the growing demand for professionals in the healthcare and sports sectors. Learning goals encompass understanding the organisation of healthcare systems, including hospitals, clinics, and community health programs. Students explore the processes involved in healthcare delivery and the importance of networking within the sector. They receive training in personnel planning and management, focusing on recruitment, training, and development specific to healthcare and sports. The module also covers the financial aspects of healthcare services, such as budgeting, billing, and financial reporting, and emphasizes quality assurance and evaluation to maintain high standards in healthcare services.

The E-Business Entrepreneurship module aims to foster an entrepreneurial mindset and provide the tools necessary for starting and managing a business. Students gain an understanding of entrepreneurial thinking, learning the mindset and processes involved in entrepreneurial activities from ideation to execution. The curriculum covers the steps involved in starting a business, including business planning, market analysis, and securing funding. Students also learn about business takeovers and succession, gaining knowledge about acquiring existing businesses and planning for business succession. Additionally, the module focuses on digital business models, covering the creation and management of digital businesses with an emphasis on e-commerce and online strategies.

The Food & Wood module offers a unique blend of food and forestry education, focusing on the specific needs of the food and wood industries. Learning goals include providing students with a comprehensive understanding of these sectors, including production, marketing, and consumer trends. Students study the latest trends and technologies in food and wood production to stay ahead in these dynamic industries. The curriculum includes effective marketing strategies tailored to these industries and imparts skills in business management, such as financial management, resource allocation, and strategic planning, essential for managing businesses within these sectors.

In addition to the content-specific and entrepreneurial competencies, the synchronous hybrid classroom emphasizes the development of digital competencies. Students are trained in using various digital tools and platforms. This training ensures that they can effectively navigate online learning environments, utilize collaboration tools such as Microsoft Teams, Word, PowerPoint, Excel and OneNote, and engage critically with digital content, preparing them for the technological demands of the modern workforce.

3 Learning Design

The following discussion primarily addresses the general learning design of the synchronous hybrid classroom at the Waldviertel Business Academy. It is important to note that specific approaches and activities may vary across the four different training specializations. The general learning design of the synchronous classroom can be described along with the use of different educational technologies and learning activities. This design aims to facilitate effective learning outcomes and engagement among students. The evaluation study (Wagner et al., 2023, 2025) with students and teachers provided interesting insights into the learning designs of the synchronous hybrid classroom in terms of educational technologies used and the implemented learning activities.

The synchronous hybrid classroom employs a variety of digital technologies to support teaching and learning, with Microsoft Teams as the core learning environment. Frequently used technologies include PowerPoint presentations to deliver lectures and present course content, chat services for real-time communication between teachers and students, and electronic texts, often provided as supplementary reading material. Moderately used technologies include online whiteboards for collaborative activities and brainstorming sessions, learning videos (e.g. on YouTube) to complement traditional teaching methods, and feedback systems to gather immediate feedback from students (e.g. Mentimeter, Kahoot). Discussion forums, electronic tests/quizzes and graphic programs are also used, but rarely.

The learning activities in the synchronous hybrid classroom are designed to actively engage students and promote higher-order thinking skills. The evaluation study (Wagner et al., 2023, 2025) highlights the frequency of different learning activities based on the ICAP (Interactive, Constructive, Active, Passive) framework (Chi & Wylie, 2014). Students reported that most often *interactive* learning activities are employed, which include collaborative tasks where students work together, either face-to-face or online, e.g. collaborative development of a digital concept map. Students reported that separate groups are usually formed, i.e. groups on-site in the classroom and groups with students participating online. The ICAP hypothesis states that students' learning performance increases as they engage more with the learning material—from passive to active and constructive to interactive (Chi & Wylie, 2014). The frequent use of interactive learning activities therefore indicates good potential, because these learning activities enable more active engagement with the content. However, they are also amongst the most challenging learning methods to implement, as students need a lot of support. The second most common activity was *passive* learning activities, where students passively receive information from the teacher, for example by listening to a digitally supported presentation. While these learning activities can be effective for delivering foundational knowledge, they may not fully engage students to promote deep understanding. *Active* learning activities, such as completing simple exercises in the form of a digital quiz or cloze test, are sometimes used in the synchronous hybrid classroom, which requires students to actively process and record information during the lesson. *Constructive* learning activities, where students work independently on tasks to build new knowledge, for example by making a video, were the least used. By incorporating more *active* and *constructive* learning activities, teachers could enhance student engagement and promote deeper cognitive processing, leading to better learning outcomes.

4 Workflow and Interaction

This section explores the structure of the workflow in the synchronous hybrid classroom, the nature of interactions among students and teachers, and the impact of these interactions on the overall learning experience.

The synchronous hybrid classroom follows a well-defined workflow that combines synchronous and some asynchronous activities to facilitate a flexible learning environment. Asynchronous elements mostly take the form of traditional homework assignments at school. Classes are scheduled in two 50-min lessons per week, with a mix of on-site and remote participation. This setup requires a robust digital infrastructure, primarily supported by Microsoft Teams, which serves as the central platform for communication, content delivery and collaboration. Additional technological tools available at the schools include 360-degree cameras, VR goggles, 3D printers, Microsoft Surface Pro and Go, interactive tables, flexible furniture, big touchscreen monitors and video conferencing systems.

1. **Synchronous sessions:** During live sessions, students from different school campuses join in the virtual classroom. These sessions include real-time lectures, discussions and interactive activities. Teachers use various digital tools such as PowerPoint presentations, online whiteboards, and chat services to deliver content and engage students. The synchronous nature of these sessions helps maintain a sense of immediacy and connection among participants.

2. **Asynchronous sessions:** To complement live sessions, asynchronous activities are assigned to students. These activities may include watching pre-recorded videos, reading electronic texts, completing assignments and preparing presentations. Asynchronous tasks allow students to work at their own pace and revisit materials as needed, providing flexibility in managing their learning schedules.
3. **Collaborative projects:** Group projects play an important role in the workflow, promoting peer-to-peer interaction and teamwork. The nature of the projects varies depending on the chosen specialization. In the E-Business Entrepreneurship module, for example, students might work on developing a business plan for a startup, requiring them to conduct market research, create financial projections, and develop marketing strategies. In the Logistics International module, a project could involve analysing and optimising a supply chain for a specific product, which includes tasks like route planning, cost analysis, and logistics coordination. At present, these projects mostly involve students working together either face-to-face or online, while mixed groups are rare.

The nature of interactions in the synchronous hybrid classroom has an impact on students' learning experience. The evaluation study (Wagner et al., 2023, 2025) highlighted several key aspects of these interactions (Fig. 1):

1. **Teacher-student interaction:** Effective teacher-student interaction is crucial for fostering engagement and understanding. Teachers employ various strategies to interact with students, including direct instruction during live sessions, personalised feedback on assignments and virtual office hours for additional support. The use of chat services and video calls facilitates real-time communication, helping to bridge the gap between on-site and remote learners.
2. **Student-student interaction:** Peer interactions are essential for collaborative learning and social presence. Social presence refers to the degree to which another person is perceived as a "real person" in computer-mediated communication (Short et al., 1976). Despite the physical separation, digital tools enable meaningful interactions to enhance learning outcomes. However, the study found that social presence is perceived to be lower among remote students compared to those attending on-site, indicating a need for strategies to improve the sense of connection among all students. This low social presence can impact student engagement and satisfaction. To address this, teachers are encouraged to use interactive techniques such as breakout rooms for small group discussions, real-time polling, and virtual ice-breaker activities to enhance the feeling of community and presence in the virtual classroom.
3. **Student-media interaction:** The student-media interaction involves navigating the digital environment, accessing course content, and using various tools to complete assignments and participate in activities. The usability of the digital platform is a critical factor in maintaining student engagement. The majority of students find the digital platform user-friendly. However, teachers pointed out that they would benefit from having a teaching assistant who oversees technology and handles technological issues. Cain (2015) also advocated for the use of "technology navigators" in hybrid classrooms, claiming that these individuals might help teachers and students before and during class. Successful hybrid

Fig. 1 A student group (synchronous on-site and remote) working on a collaborative task (creating a mind map in Padlet) (© Jonas Leutgeb/HAK Zwettl)

instruction depends on clear audio (Zydney et al., 2019) and special attention should therefore be devoted to this component, as this is often the biggest challenge (Raes et al., 2020).

5 Final Considerations

The implementation of the synchronous hybrid classroom at the Waldviertel Business Academy presents a pioneering approach to vocational secondary education. This model has demonstrated significant strengths and areas for improvement, providing valuable insights for teachers, school leaders and researchers.

One of the primary strengths of the synchronous hybrid classroom is its ability to offer a broader range of specializations to students across multiple campuses. This collaborative model enables resource sharing and ensures that students have access to diverse educational opportunities regardless of their location. The integration of digital technologies, particularly Microsoft Teams, has facilitated seamless communication and collaboration among students and teachers. The use of both synchronous and asynchronous activities has been beneficial for students. Synchronous sessions foster real-time interaction and immediate feedback, while asynchronous activities allow students to engage with the material at their own pace. This flexibility is crucial in modern education, catering to the needs of a diverse student population. Furthermore, the hybrid model can enhance students' digital competencies, preparing them for the technological demands of the contemporary workforce. The frequent use of digital tools can not only improve technical skills but also encourage the development of critical thinking and problem-solving abilities through interactive and collaborative learning activities. In the future, more advanced technologies such as augmented/virtual reality tools, 3D printers or 360-degree cameras could be incorporated into the synchronous hybrid classroom to further enhance hands-on learning experiences, stimulate creativity, and better prepare students for cutting-edge developments in the modern workplace.

Despite its many strengths, the synchronous hybrid classroom also faces several challenges. A significant weakness identified is the lower sense of social presence among remote students. The evaluation study (Wagner et al., 2023, 2025) indicated that students attending classes online perceive a weaker connection with their peers and teachers compared to those attending on-site. This reduced social presence can negatively impact engagement and learning outcomes. To address this challenge, pedagogical approaches should be explored in future studies, such as training teachers in methods specifically designed for hybrid settings, like the Community of Inquiry (CoI) framework, which emphasizes social, cognitive, and teaching presence (Garrison et al., 2000). Teachers can also be encouraged to implement more interactive techniques such as collaborative learning, peer-to-peer activities, and group discussions that help bridge the gap between online and on-site students. On the technical side, integrating state-of-the-art approaches could further enhance social presence. For example, virtual environments that simulate more immersive and seamless interactions between on-site and online students could be explored. Avatars or robotic systems, like telepresence robots, could offer a more lifelike interaction for remote students, enabling a smoother collaboration and fostering a stronger sense of community. Additionally, the use of augmented or virtual reality tools could create shared virtual spaces, allowing students to interact in a more engaging and connected manner.

Another challenge is ensuring consistent engagement and motivation among remote students. The findings suggest that remote students may feel less engaged and more prone to distractions. Addressing this issue requires innovative strategies to enhance interaction and maintain student interest, such as incorporating more interactive elements and real-time feedback mechanisms. Technical issues, although not predominant, occasionally disrupt the learning process. Ensuring robust technical support and ongoing training for both teachers and students is essential to mitigate these disruptions and maintain a smooth learning experience.

In conclusion, the synchronous hybrid classroom at the Waldviertel Business Academy has successfully expanded educational opportunities and integrated digital technologies into vocational training. While there are notable strengths in flexibility, competence enhancement, and broad specialization access, addressing the challenges of social presence, engagement, and technical consistency is crucial for optimising the hybrid learning model. Continuous evaluation and adaptation will be key to refining this innovative approach and maximising its benefits for all students.

References

Cain, W. (2015). Technology navigators: An innovative role in pedagogy, design and instructional support. In P. Redmond, J. Lock, & P. Danaher (Eds.), *Educational innovations and contemporary technologies: Enhancing teaching and learning* (pp. 21–35). Palgrave Macmillan.

Chi, M. T., & Wylie, R. (2014). The ICAP framework: Linking cognitive engagement to active learning outcomes. *Educational Psychologist, 49*(4), 219–243.

Garrison, D. R., Anderson, T., & Archer, W. (2000). Critical inquiry in a text-based environment: Computer conferencing in higher education. *The Internet and Higher Education, 2*(2–3), 87–105. https://doi.org/10.1016/S1096-7516(00)00016-6

Raes, A., Detienne, L., Windey, I., & Depaepe, F. (2020). A systematic literature review on synchronous hybrid learning: Gaps identified. *Learning Environments Research, 23*(3), 269–290. https://doi.org/10.1007/s10984-019-09303-z

Short, J., Williams, E., & Christie, B. (1976). *The social psychology of telecommunications*. Wiley.

Wagner, M., Pishtari, G., & Ley, T. (2023). Here or there? Differences of on-site and remote students' perceptions of usability, social presence, engagement, and learning in synchronous hybrid classrooms. In *European conference on technology enhanced learning* (pp. 446–458). Springer Nature Switzerland.

Wagner, M., Pishtari, G., & Ley, T. (2025). The role of learning activities and social presence in synchronous hybrid classrooms: Results from a natural experiment. *Interactive Learning Environments, 33*, 2670–2688. https://doi.org/10.1080/10494820.2024.2414428

Zydney, J. M., McKimm, P., Lindberg, R., & Schmidt, M. (2019). Here or there instruction: Lessons learned in implementing innovative approaches to blended synchronous learning. *TechTrends, 63*, 123–132. https://doi.org/10.1007/s11528-018-0344-z

Connecting in All Ways: A Case on Synchronous Hybrid Education Using a Flipped Classroom Approach

Tine Keulemans, Thomas Elias Cocolios, Sylvia Grommen, Frederik Van de plas, and Annelies Raes

1 General Description of the Case Context

The course "General Physics III: Introduction to Quantum Mechanics and Physics since the 20th Century" is provided by the Faculty of Science, KU Leuven and falls under the responsibility of the Educational Committee for Physics and Astronomy. The course participants are typically enrolled in the bachelor's programs of Physics and Mathematics, the master's program of Industrial Sciences, and the Master of Teaching in Sciences. The course is mandatory for undergraduates in Physics.

The 6-credit course, equivalent to 66 h of work, is divided into two parts: (1) General Physics III: Introduction to Quantum Mechanics and Physics since the 20th Century (4.4 credits), consisting of preparatory individual activities and interactive, hybrid classes and (2) General Physics III: exercises (1.6 credits), which are held entirely on campus.

The overall objective of the course is to provide students with an in-depth understanding of the fundamental principles and applications of quantum mechanics across various fields of physics, from atomic, molecular, solid state, nuclear, and

T. Keulemans (✉) · A. Raes
Centre of Instructional Psychology and Technology, Faculty of Psychology and Educational Sciences, KU Leuven, Leuven, Belgium
e-mail: tine.keulemans@kuleuven.be

T. E. Cocolios
Department of Physics and Astronomy, Institute for Nuclear and Radiation Physics, KU Leuven, Leuven, Belgium

S. Grommen
Tutorial Services, Educational Development and Quality Care, Faculty of Science, KU Leuven, Leuven, Belgium

F. Van de plas
KU Leuven Learning Lab, KU Leuven, Leuven, Belgium

A. Nakata et al. (eds.), *Hyb-IT-up!*,
https://doi.org/10.1007/978-3-031-99743-3_12

particle physics. Students learn about the historical development of quantum mechanics, key theories, and their impact on modern physics research areas, with an emphasis on ongoing research within the institution.

2 Learning Goals and Competences

Students enrolling in the course are expected to have a solid understanding of classical physics, including mechanics, thermodynamics, waves, electromagnetism, and optics. This knowledge should be equivalent to what is covered in General Physics 1 and 2 at KU Leuven, or a similar introductory physics course.

In terms of learning goals, all students who successfully complete the course will: (1) have become familiar with the developments in physics since the beginning of the twentieth century, (2) have gained insight into the physical phenomena that led to the development of quantum physics, (3) be familiar with the basic foundational ideas of quantum mechanics and the first principles of the formal structure of the theory, (4) be capable of solving simple and conceptual problems using specific quantum mechanical methods, (5) understand the indispensable role of these new insights in quantum mechanics in the development of twentieth century research fields, (6) be able to comprehend key models, research methods, and applications within these different research areas and explain the role of quantum mechanics in them, (7) be able to make connections across research fields and have developed a strong intuition about the relevant length and energy scales that play a role in the various domains and processes. In terms of personal development goals, the course aims to foster critical thinking about twentieth-century physics. Students will develop strong analytical abilities by learning fundamental concepts and the formal structures of quantum mechanics, while also acquiring interdisciplinary understanding by making connections across different fields of physics. Furthermore, the course emphasizes scientific argumentation and reasoning, encouraging students to evaluate and construct logical arguments based on quantum mechanical principles. Additionally, it nurtures scientific curiosity, enabling students to articulate, defend, and critically analyse scientific positions.

3 Instructional Design

Various learning contents are covered during the lessons of General Physics III. The main contents include the special relativity theory, the origins of quantum theory, the wave function and the uncertainty principle, the Schrödinger equation, one-dimensional examples, atomic physics, molecules and solids, nuclear physics and radioactivity, elementary particles, and cosmology. The delivery of the content is structured through individual preparatory activities, interactive hybrid classes and individual exercise sessions. Figure 1 visualizes the instructional design using an

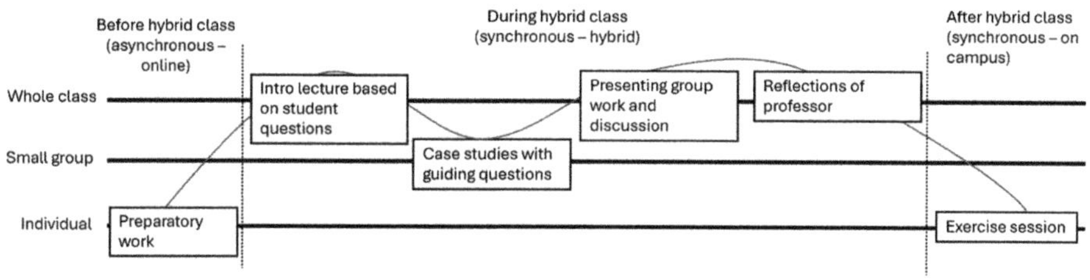

Fig. 1 Instructional design of General Physics III lesson repeated nine times over the semester

orchestration graph, as conceptualized by Dillenbourg (2015). This process is repeated nine times throughout the semester, each iteration covering another topic. In the following, we focus on the learning activities; the hybrid approach is further detailed in Sect. 4.

The course employs a flipped classroom approach, which reverses traditional educational methods (Sun et al., 2017). Students prepare for classroom sessions in advance, allowing in-class time to focus on the application and deeper exploration of the course material. This approach has been associated with positive effects on learning outcomes (Birgili et al., 2021). The professor summarizes his rationale behind it briefly: "*For me, it's about bringing the course material to life and not just guiding students through it.*"

Before the class, students gain access to learning modules asynchronously via the university's learning management system. These modules typically include preparatory materials such as academic texts, short videos, and quizzes designed to assess prerequisite knowledge on the topic. Students are asked to formulate questions and send them in advance to the professor.

The synchronous hybrid class consists of two parts. In the first part, the professor introduces the topic, using exploratory questions proposed by the students themselves during the learning module. In the second phase of the session, the professor deepens students' understanding by introducing case studies with accompanying questions. Students work in groups of six to eight to collaboratively analyze the case studies and answer the questions. After exploring the initial viewpoints on a certain topic, the professor asks the students to gather evidence to support their viewpoint, using some guiding questions, based on the Knowledge Integration approach (Linn, 2001). Students search for arguments in text materials provided by the professor and in scientific databases on the internet. These activities encourage students to enhance their arguments with scientific insights, turning initial ideas into well-founded ones. With limited time to work on the case study, answering all questions often becomes a race against the clock. Professor Cocolios refers therefore to these activities as 'quick reading and thinking activities' and reflect as follows:

> These quick reading and thinking activities boost students' energy levels and encourage them to actively engage with the learning content. Additionally, they foster creativity. Students often collaborate to handle the time pressure, with each person taking on a specific aspect and integrating everything into a shared presentation. It also demonstrates that the task matters to them, showing their genuine engagement with each other and the course.

Towards the end of the hybrid class, the different groups present the result of their work to each other in the form of oral presentations. Afterwards, the professor also shares his own evidence-based ideas on the topic to support knowledge integration. By doing so, he effectively models what a strong argumentation can look like. However, students are under no obligation to adopt the same ideas as the professor. He states that these different viewpoints are essential for the learning process:

> This iterative process of answering statements, going through cases, applying principles and listening to each other's insights is very conducive to the learning curve. By approaching topics from multiple points of view, you will also learn more easily and remember better what matters. The more viewpoints, the more retention.

During the exercise sessions, which are held fully on campus, students solve assignments about the content independently with guidance from teaching assistants. The exercises help students to contextualize the subject matter from the interactive hybrid class by working on concrete cases, by manipulating different physics concepts or mathematical methods and by bringing in numbers and scales from the various physics fields encountered in the course so that students learn how to critically gauge these.

All learning activities were designed in close collaboration with educational support staff from the Faculty of Science and KU Leuven Learning Lab. The educational support staff has served as a sounding board for the professor from the start of the new instructional approach. They regularly discussed the class format, case studies, online learning materials, the interaction between students of the different campuses, and student feedback at the end of the semester. Before the hybrid classes started, they tested the infrastructure and videoconferencing set-up together. After each class, they reflected on the session and made adjustments for subsequent classes. Their collaboration continues to this day.

4 Workflow and Interaction

As a multi-campus university in Flanders, KU Leuven offers a diverse range of study programs across its ten locations. Some programs and their associated courses, including General Physics III, are offered at multiple campuses. This course is available at both the campus Leuven and campus Kortrijk, with about 80 students enrolling annually at campus Leuven and around ten at campus Kortrijk. Figure 2 shows a map of Flanders with all KU Leuven campuses marked, and an arrow indicating the distance between Leuven and Kortrijk.

To prevent the repetition of each class across campuses, the educational team decided to deliver General Physics III in a synchronous hybrid format. Synchronous hybrid education is an educational model where onsite and remote learners participate in learning activities simultaneously (Raes et al., 2020a). Initially, General Physics III employed a traditional lecture format, utilizing livestreams to reach both onsite and remote students. However, Professor Cocolios observed a sense of

Fig. 2 KU Leuven campuses and distance between Kortrijk and Leuven

disconnection with the students, which hindered the learning experience. This observation aligns with the findings of Raes et al. (2020b), Raes (2022), that provided evidence that students following the class through livestream (without interaction or visibility to the teachers) had lower engagement scores compared to remote students following on screen with interaction.

Recognizing the need for change, professor Cocolios drastically reimagined the course and titled his new approach 'Collaborative Multilocation Learning in the Flipped Classroom'. The instructional design, which incorporates both the 'flipped' and 'collaborative aspect', was detailed in Sect. 3. In what follows, we will focus on the 'multilocation aspect' of the course.

Supported by the faculty, two well-equipped collaborative classrooms with hybrid functionalities: one on campus Leuven (see Fig. 3) and one on campus Kortrijk (see Fig. 4) were assigned to the course. Students attend classes in the same classroom, but the professor alternates campuses for each session. In Figs. 3 and 4, the professor is physically present at campus Leuven and visible on a screen at campus Kortrijk. This approach ensures that students alternately enjoy the advantages of attending the hybrid course in person, being in the same room as the teacher. A study by Raes et al. (2020b) confirmed the engagement advantages for onsite students. In this study, engagement levels of four student groups were systematically compared: (1) those who received fully face-to-face instruction, (2) those who received fully online instruction, (3) those who attended a synchronous hybrid class online, and (4) those who attended a synchronous hybrid class in person. The results revealed that students who participated in the hybrid class online were significantly less engaged than students in the other three groups.

To enhance student engagement and ensure comparable learning experiences for all students during General Physics III several design choices are implemented. First, the professor guides students on connecting to screens, sharing content, and using microphones to facilitate active participation. Second, a teaching assistant is present on campus Leuven when the professor is teaching from campus Kortrijk. The teaching assistant ensures that students use the microphone during whole class

Fig. 3 Collaborative classroom at campus Leuven (top left and bottom left)

activities and fosters (whole class and small group) discussions by asking and answering questions as needed. The reverse arrangement is not necessary, due to the small student group in Kortrijk; however, a technical assistant is always nearby. Furthermore, during the debriefing students from campus Leuven and Kortrijk alternate in sharing their findings and thoughts, so that both cohorts are strongly involved in the discussion.

Fig. 4 Collaborative Classroom at campus Kortrijk (top right and bottom right)

The two connected classrooms are equipped with comparable hardware and software components. Each room has two cameras—one at the front and one at the back—to ensure that all students are visible to each other. In the classroom at campus Kortrijk, live footage is shown of the classroom in Leuven. The students and professor at campus Leuven can also see the students at campus Kortrijk on a dedicated screen (see Figs. 3 and 4). For audio, the rooms include speakers, a headset, and a portable microphone, facilitating clear communication between the two locations. The main screen at the front of each room is used during whole class activities to share course materials. An essential part of this setup is the web-conferencing software (Pexip), that connects students across the different campuses. During the group work, the hybrid component becomes less prominent as students primarily engage with peers on their own campus. However, the Pexip software remains active throughout the class, allowing remote students to continue interacting with the professor. Additionally, Poll Everywhere was used, an interactive response system to gather students' initial input.

5 Final Considerations

The interactive format of the General Physics III course is regarded as a good practice for synchronous hybrid education at KU Leuven, owing to its innovative approach. Professor Cocolios goes beyond merely using synchronous hybrid education to technically connect students across different campuses. He also incorporates a flipped classroom approach and employs an interactive response system to enhance interaction, thereby fostering connections in pedagogical-didactical ways. However, some considerations should be made.

Firstly, the current hybrid approach and set-up only facilitates non-mixed-modality group work—where students at campus Kortrijk collaborate separately from those at campus Leuven. While this separation might be simpler from a technical standpoint, authors advocate for mixed-modality group work. Mixed-modality group work allows remote students to better access the in-class experience and prompts the instructor to remain engaged with all students, which results in more equitable learning experiences for all students (Graves et al., 2024; Mohandas, 2022). However, as detailed in Sect. 4, several other design choices were made to foster equitable learning experiences. Additionally, suitable infrastructure for facilitating mixed-modality group work is challenging. Currently, an innovative hybrid classroom at KU Leuven is installed to support this kind of hybrid group work (see "A Next Generation Hybrid Classroom: Facilitating Mixed-Modality Collaborative Learning in a Hybrid Context" chapter).

Secondly, 'Collaborative Multilocation Learning in the Flipped Classroom' is not a "*walk in the park*", according to the professor. This is also recognized in literature. Synchronous hybrid education places an extra 'burden' on the teachers (Zydney et al., 2019; Bower et al., 2015; Ørngreen et al., 2015). Scholars have introduced the notion of teacher orchestration load (TOL) to describe this challenge and try to identify contributing factors, such as unfamiliarity with technology, technological problems, and the need to engage with people in different environments (Carruana Martín et al., 2023; Ortega-Arranz et al., 2024). Moreover, the absence of non-verbal cues from remote students makes it difficult for instructors to gauge their engagement and understanding. Professor Cocolios refers to this challenge as the 'botox effect', highlighting losing connection when facial expressions and other cues are absent.

> There's always something that feels off […] people often say this about individuals with Botox; when you look at someone with Botox, you're unsure how to respond because you can no longer read their expressions. I think this experience is somewhat similar online, where it becomes harder to pick up on spontaneous non-verbal cues.

In addition to the hybrid component, another difficulty is that the students are not accustomed to the highly interactive formats adopted by Professor Cocolios, making it challenging to have them engage. Most courses at the faculty use 'ex cathedra' lecture methods, where less engagement is expected from students.

To lower the burden, Professor Cocolios offers some tips for teaching in hybrid classrooms:

1. **Seek external assistance.** Professor Cocolios collaborated with a faculty member from the Tutorial Services, Educational Development & Quality Care of the Faculty of Science. This partnership was crucial for reflecting on and shaping the course effectively. He emphasizes: *"Having someone from the faculty to think and set things up with me was a very important aspect of the process. I don't think I could have achieved everything I wanted on my own."* In addition, the professor ensured support from someone to assist the students at the remote location during class sessions. He recommends working with someone with both technological and pedagogical-didactical competences: "*Ideally, this person should possess the necessary technological expertise and have enough enthusiasm to break through moments of silence—which can occasionally occur among Flemish students.*"
2. **Use interactive response systems.** Implementing an interactive response system can make it easier to gather and discuss student input from different locations and is a way to encourage students to share their opinions. Professor Cocolios explains: "*With tools like Poll Everywhere, everyone can voice their opinions. It also helps students realize they are not alone in their thoughts or opinions.*" However, it is important to not get caught in technology and not try everything at once.
3. **Be well prepared.** Just as for the students, the flipped classroom approach requires regular additional preparation time that should not be underestimated. Building the course on the students' questions requires rethinking the content for every lecture on short notice. It is thus necessary to reserve time for this preparation.
4. **Don't try to cover too much**. The professor recommends not planning too much content in one hybrid class, in particular a class with a flipped classroom approach: "*I try to schedule much less time than I have, so that students have room to engage.*" Due to the flipped classroom approach, there is room for delivering content in other ways. The approach is also more demanding on the students and on their personal time involvement, which should be compensated for by shorter contact time.
5. **Familiarize yourself with the technology.** Take the time to get comfortable with the technology you will be using and make sure students are also familiar with it. Therefore, include an introductory session at the beginning of the course, to guide them through the tools you'll use to connect the different groups. This helps build confidence and ensures smoother interactions.

While synchronous hybrid education presents challenges for both instructors and students, Professor Cocolios's experience demonstrates that with proper preparation, appropriate technology, and a willingness to adapt, it can offer valuable learning experiences across multiple locations.

References

Birgili, B., Seggie, F. N., & Oğuz, E. (2021). The trends and outcomes of flipped learning research between 2012 and 2018: A descriptive content analysis. *Journal of Computers in Education (the Official Journal of the Global Chinese Society for Computers in Education), 8*(3), 365–394. https://doi.org/10.1007/s40692-021-00183-y

Bower, M., Dalgarno, B., Kennedy, G. E., Lee, M. J. W., & Kenney, J. (2015). Design and implementation factors in blended synchronous learning environments: Outcomes from a cross-case analysis. *Computers & Education, 86*, 1–17. https://doi.org/10.1016/j.compedu.2015.03.006

Carruana Martín, A., Alario-Hoyos, C., & Delgado Kloos, C. (2023). A study of student and teacher challenges in smart synchronous hybrid learning environments. *Sustainability, 15*(15), 11694.

Dillenbourg, P. (2015). *Orchestration graphs*. EPFL Press.

Graves, J. L., Hasan, E., & Varao-Sousa, T. L. (2024). Understanding the hybrid classroom in economics: A case study. *International Review of Economics Education, 45*, 100282. https://doi.org/10.1016/j.iree.2023.100282

Linn, M. C. (2001). Science education: Preparing lifelong learners. In N. J. Smelser & P. B. Baltes (Eds.), *The international encyclopeida of the social and behavioral sciences*. Pergamon. https://doi.org/10.1016/B0-08-043076-7/02441-4

Mohandas, L. (2022). *The impact of interactive synchronous hyflex model on students' perception of social, teaching and cognitive presence in a design thinking course*. Doctoral dissertation, Purdue University Graduate School. https://doi.org/10.25394/PGS.20359989.v1

Ørngreen, R., Levinsen, K., Jelsbak, V., Moller, K. L., & Bendsen, T. (2015). Simultaneous class-based and live video streamed teaching: Experiences and derived principles from the bachelor programme in biomedical laboratory analysis. In A. Jefferies & M. Cubric (Eds.), *Proceedings of the 14th European Conference on E-learning (ECEL 2015)* (pp. 451–459). Academic Conferences and Publishing International Limited, UK.

Ortega-Arranz, A., Amarasinghe, I., Martínez-Monés, A., Asensio-Pérez, J. I., Dimitriadis, Y., Corrales-Astorgano, M., & Hernández-Leo, D. (2024). Collaborative activities in hybrid learning environments: Exploring teacher orchestration load and students' perceptions. *Computers & Education, 219*, 105105. https://doi.org/10.1016/j.compedu.2024.105105

Raes, A. (2022). Exploring student and teacher experiences in hybrid learning environments: Does presence matter? *Postdigital Science and Education, 4*(1), 138–159. https://doi.org/10.1007/s42438-021-00274-0

Raes, A., Detienne, L., Windey, I., & Depaepe, F. (2020a). A systematic literature review on synchronous hybrid learning: Gaps identified. *Learning Environments Research, 23*(3), 269–290. https://doi.org/10.1007/s10984-019-09303-z

Raes, A., Vanneste, P., Pieters, M., Windey, I., Van Den Noortgate, W., & Depaepe, F. (2020b). Learning and instruction in the hybrid virtual classroom: An investigation of students' engagement and the effect of quizzes. *Computers & Education, 143*, 103682. https://doi.org/10.1016/j.compedu.2019.103682

Sun, J. C., Wu, Y., & Lee, W. (2017). The effect of the flipped classroom approach to OpenCourseWare instruction on students' self-regulation. *British Journal of Educational Technology, 48*(3), 713–729. https://doi.org/10.1111/bjet.12444

Zydney, J. M., McKimm, P., Lindberg, R., & Schmidt, M. (2019). Here or there instruction: Lessons learned in implementing innovative approaches to blended synchronous learning. *TechTrends, 63*(2), 123–132. https://doi.org/10.1007/s11528-018-0344-z

A Next Generation Hybrid Classroom: Facilitating Mixed-Modality Collaborative Learning in a Hybrid Context

Tine Keulemans and Annelies Raes

1 Synchronous Hybrid Education at KU Leuven

As a multi-campus university, KU Leuven situated in Belgium has experienced a growing need to synchronously connect students across different locations. To address this need, the university has been implementing Synchronous Hybrid Education (SHE)—an innovative educational model that allows some students to attend learning activities on campus while others participate remotely at the same time—since 2018 (Raes et al., 2019). While the demand was previously limited to specific courses, it has expanded greatly since COVID19 as the pandemic has introduced everyone to the possibilities of hybrid education.

The increased demand led to a large-scale effort to implement two different configurations of hybrid classrooms at KU Leuven as described in the innovation case reports of Universitas 21 (2023).[1] First, we have the frontal teaching configuration, implemented in auditoria at the university. In this configuration, remote students have a clear view of the front of the classroom and can interact with the teacher or speaker through chat, speech, and images. Secondly, there is the interactive teaching configuration, mainly implemented in smaller, flat classrooms. Here, the teaching activity does not only take place in front of the classroom. Remote students are able to see and interact with the entire classroom, rather than focusing solely on the teacher at the front.

Next to large-scale configurations, KU Leuven also invests in high-end hybrid classrooms, which are used for research purposes and can inspire future large-scale

[1] https://universitas21.com/Educational-innovation-case-studies-2023

T. Keulemans (✉) · A. Raes
Centre of Instructional Psychology and Technology, KU Leuven, Leuven, Belgium
e-mail: tine.keulemans@kuleuven.be

A. Nakata et al. (eds.), *Hyb-IT-up!*,
https://doi.org/10.1007/978-3-031-99743-3_13

solutions. Within the context of two research projects—TECOL (2016–2018) and LECTURE+ (2017–2019)—the university collaborated with industry partners to create a high-end synchronous hybrid classroom (see Fig. 1). The projects aimed to make distance learning as seamless and vivid as learning in face-to-face classrooms, without sacrificing the affective features of face-to-face instruction. The classroom became operational in 2017 and won the EUNIS award for the best AV enabled classroom in 2020 (Universitas 21, 2023).

To date, no existing classroom has been adequately equipped to facilitate collaborative learning (i.e., having different groups of students working together) in a hybrid setting at our university. Current learning spaces are designed to support either collaborative learning in face-to-face contexts or (interactive) lectures in hybrid contexts. In September 2024, we addressed this gap by introducing a 'next generation' learning space: **The Hybrid Collaborative Classroom.**

2 The Hybrid Collaborative Classroom

The Hybrid Collaborative classroom is an innovative learning space at KU Leuven designed to facilitate seamless interaction between instructors, onsite students, and remote students during both whole class and small group activities. Furthermore, it provides an ideal setting for conducting research beyond the state-of-the-art within a 'living lab' setting. The space is broadly divided into three zones: the collaborative learning zone, the interactive instruction zone, and the researcher cockpit. Figure 2 presents a floor plan of the classroom.

Fig. 1 Hybrid Classroom campus Kortrijk

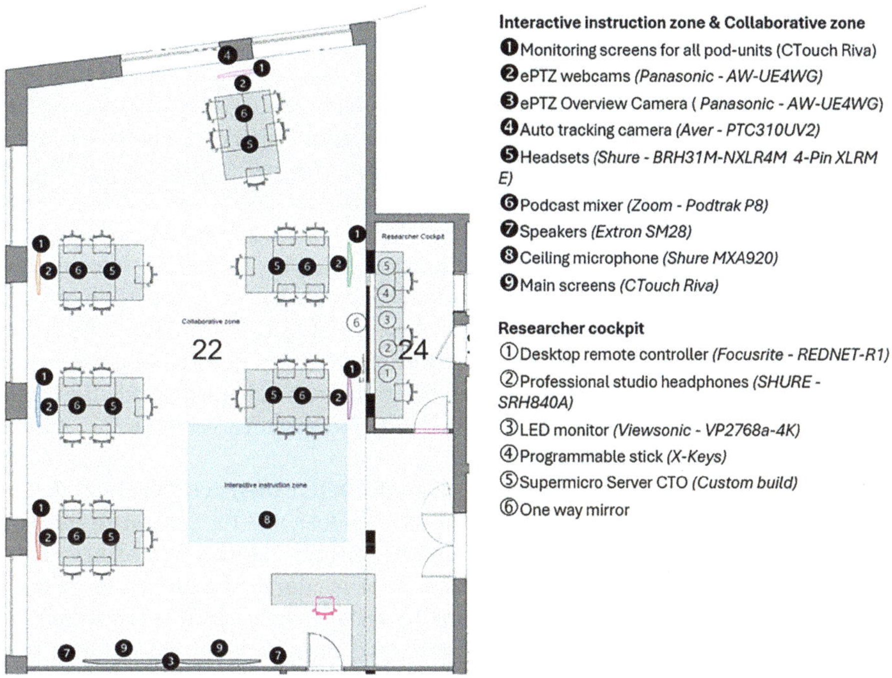

Fig. 2 Floor plan of the Hybrid Collaborative Classroom and its technical components

The largest part of the classroom is the **collaborative learning zone**. This zone consists of six group worktables, each accommodating up to four onsite students and four remote students which can be displayed on the group screen. Additionally, there is one extra chair for the teacher to physically join the group work, resulting in 30 rollable chairs. This set-up enables mixed-modality group work—connecting both remote and onsite students to work synchronously in the hybrid environment.

To distinguish our set-up from others, it is worth mentioning that some teachers at KU Leuven have already explored collaborative learning in a hybrid setting. One approach has remote students working together in online breakout rooms during the hybrid class, while onsite students collaborate face-to-face on campus—a non-mixed-modality approach. The teacher supports remote students by joining their breakout rooms and checks in on the onsite students by moving around the physical classroom. While this approach might be simpler from a technical standpoint, several reasons can be given to advocate for a mixed-modality approach. In a non-mixed-modality approach remote students might have the feeling of being excluded from the classroom. By contrast, a mixed-modality group approach—where onsite and remote students collaborate within the same group—allows remote students to better access the in-class experience. This approach also encourages the instructor to remain engaged with all students, which results in more equitable learning experiences for all students (Graves et al., 2024; Mohandas, 2022). Such mixed-modality approach is already applied in some courses at KU Leuven. To do so, teachers let all students—both onsite and remote—log-in on their own device and join online breakout rooms during a hybrid class. Each breakout room includes a mix of onsite and remote students. The teacher supports the various groups by joining the different breakout rooms to provide guidance. Research has been conducted in this kind of context by Purdue University (Interactive Synchronous Hyflex case at Purdue University; Mentzer et al., 2025). However, in this approach the advantages of being physically present on campus may be diminished when all students are primarily focused on their own screens. So, what sets our approach apart? Our aim is to foster mixed-modality collaborative work in a hybrid context, where remote students can have the in-class experience and on campus students have real interactions. Internationally we are aware of one other classroom that had comparable ambitions, which is the Hybrid Active Learning Classroom (HALC) at Utrecht University. Today the room is no longer operative. Despite positive user experiences, there were two major challenges in the HALC: (1) the various audio channels made the classroom noisy during collaborative work, and (2) the distance between the teacher during the plenary session was too large.

Situated at the front of the classroom, **the interactive instruction zone** is distinguished by a coloured nudging area. This zone is designed for students to receive instructions or to participate in whole class discussions (either while sitting on the rollable chairs or standing). The instruction zone is equipped with two large main screens for content presentation and a smaller rollable screen to display all remote participants. Creating a distinct instruction zone separate from the collaborative work zone clarifies the boundaries between different learning activities. Additionally, this setup also minimizes the distance between students and the teacher, enhancing engagement.

The **researcher cockpit** is a dedicated area from which researchers can observe both remote and onsite students, as well as the teacher(s), in action. The inclusion of the researcher cockpit transforms the classroom in a 'living lab'. Living labs are put forth as a new research, development and innovation (RDI) model for twenty-first century innovation (Chesbrough & Appleyard, 2007). The research setting enables us to study innovative practices and technologies in situ and in vivo, and creates the opportunity to capture how technology use from an ecological perspective. Potential research questions include: 'What teacher orchestration actions contribute to the orchestration load in a hybrid collaborative setting?', 'What is the impact of delivery mode on student engagement?', 'To what extent are teachers' actions influenced by the information presented on teacher dashboards?', etc.

3 Technical Components of the Hybrid Collaborative Classroom

The three zones are equipped with advanced hardware and software technologies (see Fig. 2), which are further described below. For the collaborative zone and the interactive instruction zone, we structure the text around four key subareas: image, audio, production and content sharing (as suggested by SURF, the ICT cooperative of Dutch educational and research institutions).

3.1 The Collaborative Zone

Image. During collaborative work, remote students from the respective group are shown on the monitoring screen at each of the pod-units ❶. A webcam mounted beneath the screen captures the onsite students ❷. When the teacher physically joins the small group discussion by taking a seat at the end of the group work table, he/she is included in the webcam view (see Fig. 3). Additionally, remote students can view both a comprehensive video feed of the entire classroom and a dynamic video feed of the teacher, thanks to cameras installed at the front and back of the room ❸, ❹.

Audio. During collaborative sessions, onsite students use professional single ear headsets, commonly employed in broadcast settings. These headsets with build-in microphones allow onsite users to hear remote peers and ensures that onsite students are audible to remote participants ❺. Each table is equipped with a podcast mixer to which the headphones are connected ❻, minimizing the audio latency. For optimal audio quality, remote students are also encouraged to use headsets. The teacher has the option to simultaneously speak to the group, while also wearing a single ear headset.

Production. To facilitate communication among all participants in the classroom, a platform-independent solution has been designed. Currently, Engageli has been selected due to its robust collaborative features and built-in analytics, which could

Fig. 3 Group work tables in the collaborative zone

provide valuable insights for the future research. However, the classroom setup also works with other web conferencing platforms. During collaborative work, each physical table in the room with a maximum of four onsite students will function as one participant within the platform's breakout room, ensuring seamless integration between onsite and remote students. Engageli would typically work in 'Table Mode', the mode for small group interactions, in this situation.

Sharing Content. Engageli allows both remote and onsite participants to share various types of content from their devices. Students can digitally share documents to collaborate on them together. The content can also be shown on the monitoring group screen next to the remote participants.

3.2 The Interactive Instruction Zone

Image. During instruction, remote students are shown on one of the monitoring screens (the one closest to the nudging area ❶. This screen is easily moveable, allowing the remote students to be positioned behind, in front of, or alongside onsite students (see Fig. 4). Remote students can view both a comprehensive video feed of the entire classroom and a dynamic video feed of the teacher, thanks to cameras installed at the front and back of the room ❸, ❹.

Audio. During interactive instruction, onsite students can hear their remote peers through speakers installed at the front of the classroom ❼. A ceiling microphone ensures that remote students can hear their onsite classmates and the teacher and eliminates the need for passing around a handheld microphone among onsite students or using a push-and-talk button ❽. Due to its functionalities, the interactive

Fig. 4 The interactive instruction zone

instruction zone itself represents a compact version of the interactive teaching configuration found in other classrooms at KU Leuven.

Production. To facilitate communication during moments of whole class instruction or discussions, the room mode in Engageli is used. In this mode, the teacher receives audio from all students, and students can hear one another, regardless of their seating arrangement.

Sharing content. The teacher can share content on the two main screens at the front of the classroom. This includes lesson slides, a digital whiteboard, and collaborative work from one or more groups ❾. Additionally, Engageli also offers the possibility to launch polls and quizzes.

3.3 *The Researcher Cockpit*

The audiovisual infrastructure described in the previous paragraphs serves a dual purpose. Next to making interaction possible between both groups of students and the teacher(s), all cameras, microphones and speakers are also used for observation and data collection. The signals converge in a central hub, the researcher cockpit (see Fig. 5).

All audio signals are routed to the monitor controller in the cockpit (①). The device allows switching between different audio signals and speakers, which enables the researcher(s) to capture to the conversations within different groups. Additionally, high-quality headphones are available for the comfort of the researcher(s) (②). Similar, all camera feeds are directed to a central server on which Open Broadcaster Software (OBS) (③) is installed. The OBS software and the multitrack recording enable a possibility for real-time switching between multiple video sources, enhancing the observation process. To facilitate this, a programmable stick can be utilized (④). The large micro server computer also serves as a temporary data storage unit (⑤) before the data is transferred to a centrally managed storage.

In addition to digital monitoring techniques, the cockpit features a one-way mirror that enables researchers to observe all participants unobtrusively. However, participants' informed consent is always obtained beforehand (⑥).

Fig. 5 Researcher cockpit

4 Stakeholders

In 2022, the initial concept for the hybrid collaborative classroom was proposed by Professor Annelies Raes in the project application for research infrastructure. The development of the Hybrid Collaborative Classroom, however, was only possible through close consultation with various stakeholders at each stage of the process.

After gaining support from educational policy at the university level, a design team comprising IT/AV specialists, researchers, educational experts and an interior designer collaborated to conceptualize the space. Following the initial design phase, a researcher from the team presented the room concept to 21 KU Leuven teachers experienced in synchronous hybrid education to gather their feedback and ideas. Various scenarios were considered during this process.

During the development phase, IT/AV and furniture suppliers were involved in setting up the hardware in the hybrid collaborative classroom. On the software side, the IT/AV specialist collaborated with Engageli's engineers. Given that Engageli is primarily an online education platform, several modifications were required to adapt its software to the mixed-modality hybrid collaborative approach we were aiming for. For example, adjustments were needed to ensure that only remote students were visible on the screens during the collaboration phase. To make sure the classroom remains a sustainable educational and research environment, the research and development team recognizes the importance of ongoing support from the university.

5 Final Considerations

Reflecting on the Hybrid Collaborative Classroom, it is crucial to acknowledge both the strengths and the weaknesses of the space, based on insights from market research and competitor analysis.

5.1 Strengths

The first key strength of the Hybrid Collaborative Classroom at KU Leuven is its advanced audio component (Sects. 3.1 and 3.2), which distinguishes it from other setups like the HALC at Utrecht University. Unlike the HALC, where onsite students need to use a 'push-and-talk button' to engage with remote participants—potentially disrupting communication—the KU Leuven setup ensures smoother interaction. The headphones in the KU Leuven classroom minimize noise from simultaneous conversations, enhancing the overall user experience. Furthermore, the 'single-ear' design allows for more natural conversations than full headsets, as onsite students can hear each other's natural voices and other classroom sounds.

A second notable strength of the room is its flexibility in supporting various software solutions. The technical setup is designed to be independent of the software used, allowing for seamless integration with different platforms. Currently, Engageli software (Sect. 2) has been chosen for application in the research project, but initial pilot tests with MS Teams—the default conferencing tool at KU Leuven—have also proven to work successfully in the current setting.

A third strength is that the design of the classroom has been informed by previous research and teacher interviews. As Norgard (2021) pointed out: "*In a post-pandemic world, learning will now face the challenge of moving beyond technical solutions, shiny platforms, technological set-ups and tech trends to focus on broader and deeper questions of learning.*" While our classroom indeed looks 'shiny' (a colleague even called it "the Ferrari of hybrid classrooms"), its design is rooted in a deeper evidence-based vision that seeks to promote equitable learning experience for both onsite and remote students (Graves et al., 2024). Additionally, from the teacher perspective, the setup may simplify classroom orchestration by reducing the 'split attention effect' during collaborative activities. Compared to a non-mixed-modality hybrid design, it becomes easier to pay equal attention to both online and onsite students because they are visible at one glance (Wang et al., 2018). However, future research is needed to further validate these assumptions.

5.2 *Weaknesses*

A first notable weakness is that the room is designed for a relatively small audience. However, the innovative classroom can be seen as a sandbox which can inform future configurations within the university.

Secondly, while teachers acknowledged the intuitive design of the environment, most of their feedback expressed concerns about the additional burden of teaching in this space and the need for adequate support. We agree that, in addition to the support requested for in research projects, a sustainable long-term solution is necessary. We are exploring the possibility of appointing a lab manager—independent of funded research projects—to oversee room availability and provide essential didactical, research, and/or technical support. Furthermore, our ambition is to conduct research on the 'additional burden' that teachers experience in hybrid settings. Literature often refers to this as teacher orchestration load, "the effort necessary for the teacher—and other actors—to conduct learning activities" (Cuendet et al., 2013).

In summary, with its mixed-modality approach and integrated research facilities, we believe we have created a distinctive and innovative learning space. While it does present certain challenges, we are dedicated to addressing these through a design-based research approach (McKenney & Reeves, 2018), and ongoing collaboration with various stakeholders. Our commitment is to continuously optimize and refine the Hybrid Collaborative Classroom in the years ahead.

References

Chesbrough, H. W., & Appleyard, M. M. (2007). Open innovation and strategy. *California Management Review, 50*(1), 57–76. https://doi.org/10.2307/41166416

Cuendet, S., Bonnard, Q., Do-Lenh, S., & Dillenbourg, P. (2013). Designing augmented reality for the classroom. *Computers and Education, 68*, 557–569. https://doi.org/10.1016/j.compedu.2013.02.015

Graves, J. L., Hasan, E., & Varao-Sousa, T. L. (2024). Understanding the hybrid classroom in economics: A case study. *International Review of Economics Education, 45*, 100282. https://doi.org/10.1016/j.iree.2023.100282

McKenney, S., & Reeves, T. (2018). *Conducting educational design research* (2nd ed.). Routledge. https://doi.org/10.4324/9781315105642

Mentzer, N., Mammadova, E., Koehler, A., Mohandas, L., & Farrington, S. (2025). Analyzing the impact of basic psychological needs on student academic performance: A comparison of post-pandemic interactive synchronous hyflex and pre-pandemic traditional face-to-face instruction. *Educational Technology Research and Development, 73*, 91–114. https://doi.org/10.1007/s11423-024-10417-2

Mohandas, L. (2022). *The impact of interactive synchronous hyflex model on students' perception of social, teaching and cognitive presence in a design thinking course*. Doctoral dissertation, Purdue University Graduate School. https://doi.org/10.25394/PGS.20359989.v1

Norgard, R. T. (2021). Theorising hybrid lifelong learning. *British Journal of Educational Technology, 52*(4), 1709–1723. https://doi.org/10.1111/bjet.13121

Raes, A., Pieters, M., & Bonte, P. (2019). Hyflex learning within the Master of Teaching Program@ KU Leuven: KU LEUVEN, Belgium. In B. J. Beatty (Ed.), *Hybrid-flexible course design: Implementing student-directed hybrid classes*. EdTech Books. Retrieved from https://edtechbooks.org/hyflex

Universitas 21. (2023). *Educational innovation case studies 2023: Learning lab*. Retrieved from https://universitas21.com/Educational-innovation-case-studies-2023

Wang, Q., Huang, C., & Quek, C. L. (2018). Students' perspectives on the design and implementation of a blended synchronous learning environment. *Australasian Journal of Educational Technology, 34*(1), 1–13. https://doi.org/10.14742/ajet.3404

Shaping Sustainable Urban Landscapes Through Picturebooks: An Interdisciplinary COIL Journey

Ana Margarida Ramos, Marnie Campagnaro, Małgorzata Cackowska, and Susana Caixinha

1 The Case Context

The project "The Child and the City: Shaping Sustainable Urban Landscapes through Picturebooks" was a Collaborative Online International Learning (COIL) experience led by Marnie Campagnaro from the University of Padova, Italy. It involved 21 students and three teachers from three European universities: Padova (Italy), Gdansk (Poland), and Aveiro (Portugal). From October 25th to December 19th, 2023, participants engaged in five online sessions comprising lectures, workshops, and interactive group work. The project analysed picturebooks to explore the relationship between urban landscapes, childhood, and architectural perspectives in children's literature, with a particular emphasis on ideologies, cross-cultural perspectives, and sustainability.

The diverse group included bachelor's and master's degree students, selected through an open call (Fig. 1) within their respective universities. While the majority came from teacher training programs, the cohort also included students in

A. M. Ramos (✉)
Department of Languages and Cultures, University of Aveiro, Aveiro, Portugal
e-mail: anamargarida@ua.pt

M. Campagnaro
Department of Philosophy, Sociology, Pedagogy and Applied Psychology, University of Padova, Padova, Italy
e-mail: marnie.campagnaro@unipd.it

M. Cackowska
Faculty of Social Sciences, University of Gdańsk, Gdańsk, Poland
e-mail: malgorzata.cackowska@ug.edu.pl

S. Caixinha
University of Aveiro, Aveiro, Portugal
e-mail: sazevedo@ua.pt

A. Nakata et al. (eds.), *Hyb-IT-up!*,
https://doi.org/10.1007/978-3-031-99743-3_14

Fig. 1 Call for participation (with the project information)

psychology, publishing studies and communication. International representation extended beyond the three host countries, with mobility students from Brazil and Spain enriching the cultural diversity of the class.

Each session featured theoretical contextualization and practical group work, analysing picturebooks from various countries. Students presented their analyses, linking them to theoretical approaches and reflecting on their work. The project included a face-to-face International Seminar at the University of Padova, 'Urban Visions. Exploring the City through Illustrated Books', consolidating online learning and providing hands-on experience with diverse children's literature from different countries and languages.

The purpose of this initiative was to provide a valuable international learning opportunity for the teaching of children's literature. It aimed to promote theoretical frameworks that incorporate cross-cultural perspectives and establish a pioneering European didactic-research collaboration, providing students with global perspectives within their study programs.

2 Learning Goals and Competences

This COIL project was designed to achieve multiple learning goals and develop various competences among the participants, including the teachers involved. At its core, the program exemplified key features of hybrid and blended teaching and learning through its innovative use of virtual mobility, which enabled meaningful international collaboration without physical travel. The program's objectives were to foster international virtual mobility, promote critical thinking, and enhance global citizenship skills. Prerequisites for participation included the ability to communicate in English (both orally and in writing) and an interest in children's literature, particularly picturebooks, as well as environmental, social justice and ideological issues. Building on these foundational skills, the project aimed to equip students with the knowledge and soft skills necessary to excel as efficient children's literature educators in multicultural environments.

A primary goal was to provide an enriching and highly effective international learning experience based on the principles of Active Learning (Misseyanni et al., 2018). This approach was achieved through virtual mobility (internationalization at home) and collaboration with partner universities, involving the design of shared teaching materials and reading activities. The project actively engaged participants in the learning process, encouraging them to take ownership of their education through interactive and collaborative methods. It sought to develop cross-cultural knowledge transfer, build international relations, and promote mutual understanding among participants. Moreover, it aimed to expand, consolidate, and deepen knowledge about picturebooks, both theoretically and practically, through exposure to books from different countries. This strategy facilitated comparative readings and established connections between distinct cultures, broadening participants' reading encyclopedias and interpretive horizons.

The aim of this learning experience was to explore the dynamic relationship between urban landscapes, childhood, ideologies, and architectural perspectives within the city. The course investigated how architecture, as represented in children's literature, both literarily and visually, serves as a crucial lens for reflecting on the importance of urban environments in promoting children's well-being. Central to this exploration was examining picturebooks' critical role in shaping the visual representation of these scenarios. By exploring these fictional realms, participants gained valuable insights into how imaginative narratives and visual storytelling contribute to our understanding of urban spaces versus rural environments. The project considered how the portrayal of cities in picturebooks influences our perception of urban environments—such as apartment buildings, pedestrian streets, squares, cultural centres, urban parks, treehouses, residential neighbourhoods, or commercial districts—and how these stories can be harnessed to inspire and inform child-centric architectural approaches.

This learning experience aimed to improve teaching practices by infusing international, intercultural, and sustainable dimensions into the curriculum. Ultimately, the project aimed at establishing a pioneering European didactic-research collaboration, offering students global perspectives within their program of study and preparing them for the growing diversity of the twenty-first-century educational landscape.

3 Learning Design

The project was designed as an innovative, interdisciplinary learning experience that brought together students from diverse academic backgrounds within the Humanities. Participants hailed from fields such as Primary Teacher Education, Publishing Studies, and Psychology, united by their shared passion for analysing children's literature and exploring broader literary themes through an interdisciplinary lens.

The program consisted of five online lessons (2 h each) scheduled from October to November 2023, culminating in a final group assignment due in December (Fig. 2). The project fostered rich multimodal interaction through diverse communication channels, allowing participants to engage meaningfully across both digital and physical spaces. While email served as a formal communication tool, face-to-face interactions provided opportunities for immediate and personal exchanges. The integration of Padlet enhanced asynchronous collaboration, enabling participants to share comments, reflections, and resources at their own pace. Each online lesson was strategically structured to include dedicated discussion periods and Q&A sessions, creating dynamic spaces for real-time dialogue and knowledge exchange. Additionally, students took initiative in establishing WhatsApp groups, which became informal but vital platforms for peer-to-peer interaction, fostering a sense of community beyond the formal learning environment.

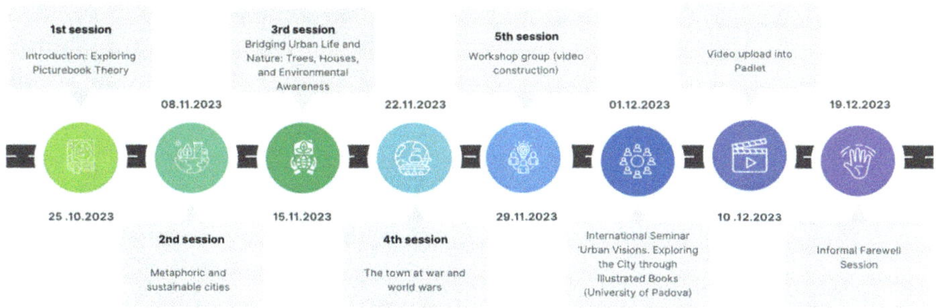

Fig. 2 Project timeline (with additional sessions)

To conclude the project, an international face-to-face seminar titled "Urban Visions: Exploring the City through Illustrated Books" was organized at the University of Padova on December 1st, 2023 (Fig. 3). During this seminar, the three scholars of the COIL project were physically present, offering a unique opportunity to meet and exchange ideas with the students involved in the COIL project and other students interested in the topic. This in-person interaction fostered a dynamic exchange of perspectives and deepened the engagement with the subject matter. The learning design incorporated diverse sources, including literature, case studies, and expert insights.

Additionally, at the request of the students, an informal farewell online meeting was held on 19 December. Each session was carefully designed to balance both theoretical contextualization of key themes and practical group work. Using Zoom breakout rooms, students interacted in groups, practicing the application of newly gained knowledge.

To further promote collaboration, interaction, and intercultural dialogue, the 21 participants were divided into seven working groups, each comprising one student from the three participating universities. This structure fostered a rich mix of interdisciplinary and cultural perspectives, drawing on the participants' diverse academic backgrounds and personal experiences.

Theoretical frameworks were introduced during the first part of each lesson. In the second part, students engaged in interactive exercises, comparisons and case studies drawn from picturebooks. When physical picturebooks were unavailable, PDFs or aloud readings available online were provided. The third and final segment of each session included a global discussion and the presentation of the key conclusions.

The final assignment was a three-minute video analysis of a chosen picturebook (Fig. 4). Students were encouraged to provide a summary of the book, a detailed examination of at least one double page, and a reflection on how the book portrays the child's interaction with the city. This assignment consolidated the learning outcomes and encouraged creative expression and ecocritical analysis. English was the working language throughout the project, which added to the experience's worldwide and intercultural quality. This approach improved communication across the

Fig. 3 Scholars engage in lively discussions with students during the seminar in Padova, December 1st 2023

Fig. 4 Two examples of three-minute video analyses of a selected picturebook, created as the final assignment

heterogeneous group and prepared students for future international collaborations in their academic and professional careers and personal lives.

The COIL project combined children's literature with critical urban studies, focusing on essential notions of space, place, and architecture. Henri Lefebvre's (1967) research on inclusive urban spaces that cater to all, including children, and Colin Ward's *The Child in the City* (Ward, 1978), which investigates children's responsibilities in urban planning, were important historical studies for this project. Christophe Meunier's (2023) research shed light on how children's literature depicts urban landscapes, whilst Campagnaro and Goga's (2022) study highlighted the value of ecocritical engagement with picturebooks. Their work supported the project's goal of fostering child-centred, ecologically sensitive urban architecture. Furthermore, Schmiedeknecht et al. (2020) investigate how modern architecture in children's literature influences future impressions of the built environment enriched student's knowledge. These paradigms brought together urban studies and children's literature, emphasizing the need for environmental awareness in developing future cities.

The first lesson introduced key aspects of picturebook theory, setting the foundation for the course. The plenary session explored the definition of picturebooks, elements such as peritexts, design, and materiality, and the underlying ideologies in challenging themes. In the subsequent workshop, groups analysed the chosen picturebooks, identifying critical aspects from the theoretical presentations, such as materiality, peritexts (cover and back cover, endpapers, title page, etc.), illustrative style (techniques, colours, page composition, lettering), page rhythm, and anthropocentric versus ecocritical perspectives.

The second lesson examined the concept of metaphoric and sustainable cities in picturebooks. The plenary focused on a Portuguese picturebook featuring a symbolic city that became a Cultural Centre. During the workshop, groups engaged in a comparative analysis of urban and rural spaces depicted in the picturebook *The World in a Second*, identifying main ideas and connotations.

The third lesson explored the interconnections between urban environments, architecture, green awareness, and children's literature. Drawing on works like *The Baron in the Trees* and *The Circus in the Mist*, the workshop addressed how urban settings impact our lives and how they are portrayed in children's literature. The workshop focused on Kaori Takahashi's *Knock! Knock! Where's My Bear?* namely the influence of sound in landscape planning and design.

The fourth lesson examined picturebooks depicting war as cultural and political artefacts. The plenary explored the Ukrainian picturebook *How War Changed Rondo* in the context of Russia's invasion of Ukraine. The workshop delved into the wordless Polish picturebook *I am the City, Warsaw*, examining Warsaw's historical evolution and its role in fostering urban and environmental awareness.

The final class session included a workshop where students worked on their final assignment. The course culminated with each group submitting their digital video assessments to Padlet.

4 Workflow and Interaction

This COIL project exemplifies the principles of hybrid learning (Whitelock & Jelfs, 2003), particularly in its use of online tools to facilitate individual and group work (Campagnaro & Ferrari, 2024). This approach created a rich digital ecosystem that supported effective international collaboration and learning across three European universities.

To prevent inequity and exclusion in online intercultural communication and to foster critical digital literacy (Dooly & Darvin, 2022), educators guided learners in understanding effective interaction and communication using various online tools. It used a synchronous and asynchronous strategy, incorporating multiple platforms such as Zoom, Padlet, Kahoot, and Mentimeter, significantly enhancing the project's impact.

This COIL was based on the educational approach of collaborative learning. This approach improves learning using groups of students working together, creating a relationship between their knowledge to create a shared understanding (Häkkinen et al., 2017). Zoom was the primary tool for synchronous sessions, providing a space for theoretical presentations and group discussions via breakout rooms. The weekly sessions followed a consistent format: brief theoretical presentations, practical group work in breakout rooms, and whole-group discussions. This structure balanced instructor-led content, collaborative work, and whole-group reflection, fostering active engagement and critical thinking.

While synchronous communication is important in a collaborative learning approach, it is also essential to incorporate tools that facilitate asynchronous communication. These tools offer greater flexibility, allowing students to interact without needing to be engaged simultaneously (Jeong & Hmelo-Silver, 2016). Additionally, they give learners more time to reflect on their participation and contribute thoughtfully to sharing knowledge.

Padlet (Fig. 5) acted as the central asynchronous collaboration tool, hosting key information, bibliography, and multimedia learning resources, including PowerPoints, videos, digitized picturebooks, and photo documentation of all meetings. It also facilitated contact sharing and the submission of final group work. Using Padlet as a collaborative digital wall enhanced student engagement and fostered a sense of community in the online learning environment.

To further enhance interactivity and provide immediate feedback, tools such as Kahoot and Mentimeter (Mayhew et al., 2020) were employed for online quizzes and presentations, allowing instructors to monitor progress, critical digital literacy, interest, and satisfaction in real-time. To facilitate ongoing communication and collaboration, students created WhatsApp groups for exchanging ideas and developing

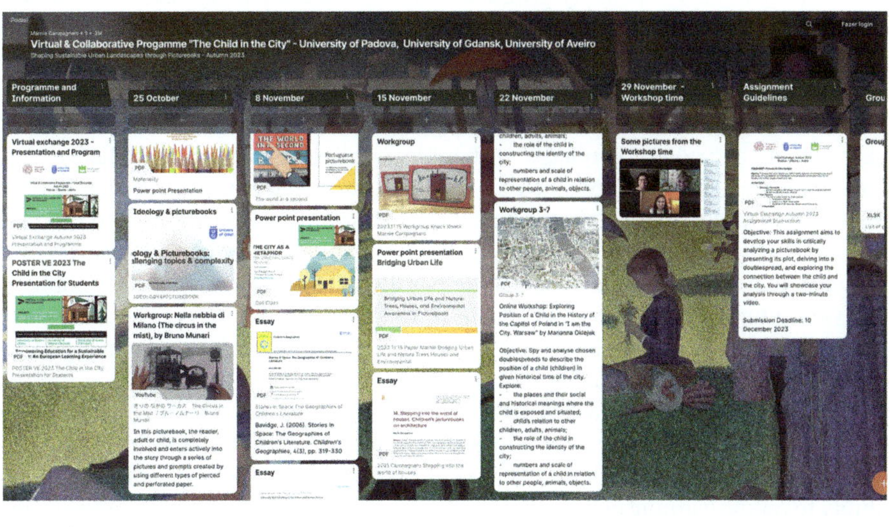

Fig. 5 Partial view of the Padlet

collaborative work outside of formal sessions. This extended the learning experience beyond scheduled meetings, allowing for deeper connections and more comprehensive exploration of the project themes.

Students also utilized various video recording and montage techniques for their final project videos, developing digital literacy skills that are increasingly crucial in today's educational and professional landscapes (Fischer & Neumann, 2012; Marín & Castañeda, 2023). The final assignment required students to create a three-minute video analyzing a picturebook of their choice, relating it to the project's themes. This task consolidated their learning and encouraged creative expression and critical analysis.

Between synchronous sessions, students engaged in self-directed learning, managing their time and pace effectively to balance online and offline components. This approach fostered the development of self-regulated learning skills and digital literacy, crucial for success in both academic and professional contexts. The hybrid teaching and learning model significantly enriched the project by fostering self-regulated learning and digital literacy, which are critical for academic and professional success (Anderson, 2018). Furthermore, the hybrid approach offered opportunities for virtual mobility, enabling students from diverse socioeconomic backgrounds to access educational resources equitably and collaborate in a diverse and inclusive environment. This not only helped mitigate social and economic disparities but also facilitated the development of oral and written communication skills across formal and informal registers, essential for cultivating global citizenship. The adaptability developed by participants as they navigated online learning environments aligns with the increasing demands of contemporary education. The literature on hybrid learning underscores its ability to integrate flexibility, inclusion, and engagement into educational processes, making it a valuable model for fostering comprehensive skill development (Garrison & Vaughan, 2008).

The project design actively promoted cross-cultural exchange and communication. International groups were formed, each comprising students from different universities, fostering diverse perspectives and intercultural dialogue. Language barriers were addressed proactively, with a focus on effective communication over perfect language use. Students were encouraged to use translation tools and help each other overcome language difficulties, reflecting a more inclusive and communication-focused approach to English use in international academic contexts. Students collaboratively translated texts from various languages into English, broadening their exposure to picturebooks from different countries. This process not only enhanced their language skills but also deepened their understanding of diverse cultural perspectives. The sharing of picturebooks by both lecturers and students served as a gateway to cultural exchange, significantly expanding participants' knowledge of international children's literature.

The workflow and interaction design of this COIL project effectively leveraged digital tools and pedagogical strategies to create a rich, collaborative learning environment. By emphasizing digital literacy, cross-cultural communication, and adaptability to online learning environments, the project not only explored the intersection of children's literature, urban landscapes, and sustainability from diverse international perspectives but also equipped students with crucial skills for success in an increasingly globalized and digitalized world. This comprehensive approach to workflow and interaction created a transformative learning experience that transcended geographical boundaries, preparing participants for future academic and professional challenges in international contexts.

5 Final Considerations

This COIL project not only achieved its learning objectives but also demonstrated the potential of online and hybrid learning contexts in higher education. This approach to international collaboration proved particularly relevant in exploring the intersection of children's literature, urban landscapes, and sustainability—themes that inherently benefit from diverse cultural perspectives.

The project's success, evidenced by participant feedback and high-quality outputs, underscores the effectiveness of virtual mobility in creating rich, transformative learning experiences. One student commented that he spent the whole week waiting for the meetings and that they had become a particularly important part of his training. By leveraging digital platforms, students from Aveiro, Padova, and Gdansk engaged in meaningful cross-cultural exchanges, expanding their understanding of how picturebooks can shape perceptions of urban environments and sustainability.

The methodologies used facilitated the development of crucial twenty-first century skills, including digital literacy, online collaboration, and adaptability to virtual learning environments. These competencies are increasingly vital in today's globalized world and job market, preparing students for future academic and professional challenges. By combining technological platforms with the exploration of picturebooks' materiality, the project identified both the potential and challenges of hybrid learning. It enabled participants to develop skills and strategies for differentiated learning and collaborative work, particularly valuable in partnerships spanning different countries, languages, and cultures.

Despite challenges such as recruitment difficulties and scheduling across two time zones, and researching picturebooks without physically touching them, yet still experiencing their materiality, the project's online nature allowed for flexibility and inclusivity that might not have been possible in a traditional, face-to-face setting. This adaptability is a key advantage of online and hybrid learning contexts in higher education, enabling participation from diverse student groups and fostering international collaboration without the need for physical travel. Moreover, the improvement in participants' English language skills and their increased confidence in international academic settings highlight how online learning can break down language barriers. These outcomes are particularly significant in the context of higher education's growing emphasis on internationalization and cross-cultural competence.

In conclusion, this COIL project successfully explored the relationship between children, urban and rural landscapes, and picturebooks and showcased the transformative potential of online and hybrid learning in higher education. It demonstrated how virtual collaboration can effectively bridge cultural divides, expand students' perspectives, and prepare them for an increasingly interconnected world. As we look to the future of higher education, projects like this pave the way for more inclusive approaches, underlining the importance of embracing digital technologies and international partnerships in creating meaningful, boundary-crossing learning experiences.

References

Anderson, T. (2018). *The theory and practice of online learning* (2nd ed.). Athabasca University Press.

Campagnaro, M., & Ferrari, L. (2024). Children's literature, ecocritical dialogues, and social-emotional learning: Developing integrated teaching practices. *Excellence and Innovation in Learning and Teaching, 9*, 86–104. https://doi.org/10.3280/exioa1-2024oa18035

Campagnaro, M., & Goga, N. (2022). Material green entanglements: Research on student teachers' aesthetic and ecocritical engagement with picturebooks of their own choice. *International Research in Children's Literature, 15*(3), 308–322. https://doi.org/10.3366/ircl.2022.0465

Dooly, M., & Darvin, R. (2022). Intercultural communicative competence in the digital age: Critical digital literacy and inquiry-based pedagogy. *Language and Intercultural Communication, 22*(3), 354–366. https://doi.org/10.1080/14708477.2022.2063304

Fischer, H. E., & Neumann, K. (2012). Video analysis as a tool for understanding science instruction. In D. Jorde & J. Dillon (Eds.), *Science education research and practice in Europe: Retrospective and prospective* (pp. 115–140). Sense Publishers.

Garrison, D. R., & Vaughan, N. D. (2008). *Blended learning in higher education: Framework, principles, and guidelines*. Jossey-Bass.

Häkkinen, P., Järvelä, S., Mäkitalo-Siegl, K., Ahonen, A., Näykki, P., & Valtonen, T. (2017). Preparing teacher-students for twenty-first-century learning practices (PREP 21): A framework for enhancing collaborative problem-solving and strategic learning skills. *Teachers and Teaching, 23*(1), 25–41.

Jeong, H., & Hmelo-Silver, C. E. (2016). Seven affordances of computer-supported collaborative learning: How to support collaborative learning? How can technologies help? *Educational Psychologist, 51*(2), 247–265.

Lefebvre, H. (1967). *Le droit à la ville*. Anthropos.

Marín, V. I., & Castañeda, L. (2023). Developing digital literacy for teaching and learning. In M. Y. M. Lam, S. S. J. Lam, & H. T. Lam (Eds.), *Handbook of open, distance and digital education* (pp. 1089–1108). Springer. https://doi.org/10.1007/978-981-19-2080-6_64

Mayhew, E., Davies, M., Millmore, A., Thompson, L., & Pena Bizama, A. (2020). The impact of audience response platform Mentimeter on the student and staff learning experience. *Research in Learning Technology, 28*. https://doi.org/10.25304/rlt.v28.2397

Meunier, C. (2023). The child and the city. Images, narratives, spaces. *Strenæ, 23*. https://doi.org/10.4000/strenae.10340

Misseyanni, A., Papadopoulou, P., Marouli, C., & Lytras, M. (2018). *Active learning strategies in higher education: Teaching for leadership, innovation, and creativity*. Emerald Publishing Limited.

Schmiedeknecht, T., Rudd, J., & Hayward, E. (Eds.). (2020). *Modern architecture in picturebooks: Representations of the built environment in children's literature*. Routledge.
Ward, C. (1978). *The child in the city*. Penguin Books.
Whitelock, D., & Jelfs, A. (2003). Editorial: Journal of educational media special issue on blended learning. *Journal of Educational Media, 28*(2–3), 99–100.

Fostering Tourism and Hospitality Students' Language and Career Skills: A Blended and Hybrid Approach

Sandra Vieira Vasconcelos

1 The Case Context

As Higher Education Institutions (HEI) are increasingly being challenged to update their curricular and come up strategies to meet current and future societal and market demands, there is a growing interest in developing collaborative university-industry initiatives, that can support students' work readiness, as well as their career and employability skills (Paviotti, 2020). These skills, which are linked to students' readiness to work, stem from the combined "assessments made by stakeholders of higher education, namely graduates and employers" (Suleman, 2016, p. 170), and can comprise different activities, from dedicated counselling and fairs to workshops and/or activities within different courses.

Having been described as a "vital educational source for soft skills training" (Lavrysh, 2017, p. 517), ESP courses have, often under the guise of written communication exercises, acted as catalysts for the development of employability skills. Covering activities that require students to analyse ads and write CVs and cover letters, these training modules can help increase their awareness of personal skills, goals and ambitions and their knowledge about recruitment and the labour market in general (Bridgstock, 2009; Paviotti, 2020).

Based on these premises, and acknowledging the current skills gap within this scope (Vasconcelos, 2024), this chapter puts forward a set of activities designed to assist tourism students in applying for jobs, through the development of personal digital portfolios that are aligned with the industry's demands, as well as with current recruitment trends. The activities described, whose key outputs included a CV,

S. V. Vasconcelos (✉)
UNIAG, ESHT, Polytechnic of Porto, Vila do Conde, Portugal

CIDTFF – Research Centre on Didactics and Technology in the Education of Trainers, University of Aveiro, Aveiro, Portugal
e-mail: s.vasconcelos@esht.ipp.pt

A. Nakata et al. (eds.), *Hyb-IT-up!*,
https://doi.org/10.1007/978-3-031-99743-3_15

a personal statement, a cover email and a personal video pitch, were carried out within the scope of ESP courses, having involved 65 undergraduate students in their final semester. Considering the number of working students, as well as previous experiences both face-to-face and online, the activities were developed in a hybrid mode, making it possible for participants to simultaneously engage in both in-person and online learning.

Although the course was mainly conducted in a blended mode, the activities described within this chapter refer to a hybrid module, which involved different workshops and tasks focussing on the development of the digital portfolios. In addition to the use of technology-driven learning platforms (i.e., Moodle—Learning Management System and Zoom—Videoconferencing service), students also had access to both online and onsite mentoring and support, making it possible to create a mostly seamless experience for both in-person and remote students throughout the sessions. This hybrid, technology-facilitated approach made it possible to provide timely and ongoing feedback from multiple sources, as well as a establish new collaboration strategies that fostered students' autonomy and their understanding of "education, training, and qualifications systems and models" (Vasconcelos, 2024, p. 7649), at the same time it made them more aware of as their personal competences and aspirations.

2 Learning Goals and Competences

Having been developed within different ESP courses, the activities described aimed to develop a similar set of language and career skills in final year undergraduate students. There were no prerequisite skills and knowledge, even though students should have completed previous courses, being expected to have a B2 level of English (Council of Europe, 2001).

Despite being tailored to different tourism subsectors (i.e., tourism, hospitality and catering), the syllabi follow a common structure, each featuring a specific module on careers and job applications. In addition to more general field-related content focusing on profiles, job descriptions and responsibilities, topics include recruitment advertisements, CVs and application letters and job interviews. Considering the pertinence of the topic and the students' profiles, it was decided to implement this module in a hybrid mode, giving all students the opportunity to take part in the activities (conversely, the other modules are taught face-to-face, with students sitting written and oral tests). In terms of learning goals, this module aimed to enhance students' opportunities for securing employment and navigating recruitment processes, as they were expected to: (1) describe profiles, tasks, requirements and responsibilities of tourism-related jobs; (2) write and analyse recruitment advertisements, CVs and applications; (3) identify procedures and techniques involved in job interviews; and (4) take part in simulated job interviews.

Language-wise, the key goals involve: (1) using the target language (English) to carry out meaningful tasks, complemented by priming of key vocabulary, specific terminology and/or grammatical constructs; and (2) noticing, focusing on form and the syntactic, pragmatic and semantic value of language structures and lexicalized expressions.

3 Learning Design and Workflow

Considering the learning goals and competences, the different activities followed a task-based approach that aimed to help students develop their communication and interpersonal skills and prepare for job interviews within their respective fields. As a result, there was a cumulative approach, in which activities were introduced gradually (see Table 1), making up a digital portfolio to be used as part of a final simulated activity involving external experts (Human Resources managers). Within the scope of the module, online and in-person instruction occurred simultaneously, with students being able to complete the tasks and interact with the instructor, experts and their peers in real time, both online and face-to-face. In addition to Moodle, the instructor used the video-conferencing system Zoom, connecting from the classroom.

The activities described in Table 1 were designed taking into consideration current market trends, particularly within the scope of the tourism industry, having been framed by language and communication frameworks. Moreover, they are also aligned with experiential learning (EL) principles, which aim to support the develop knowledge and skills through practical activities, followed by an iterative process of reflection.

Defined as "the process whereby knowledge is created through the transformation of experience" (Kolb, 2014), the concept of EL hinges on "the linkage between the theory and practice" (Hyasat, 2022, p. 293), combining "experience, perception, cognition, and behaviour" (Kolb, 2014). According to Kolb's framework, when engaging with EL, learners should be brought into contact with concrete experiences (Stage 1: Concrete Experience), being given the opportunity to reflect on that

Table 1 Learning design: key development stages and activities/outputs

Development stages	Activities/outputs
1. Preliminary work	Vocabulary introduction (reading and writing, concept mapping and brainstorming activities focusing on industry related and individual skills (hard and soft skills) Research and text analysis (reading and listening comprehension and noticing activities involving job advertisements, profiles and CVs) Workshop on personal branding and pitching
2. Digital portfolio	Artefact production (writing and speaking activities involving the creation of a CV, personal statement, application letter and personal video pitch)
3. Simulation	Simulated job interview (speaking activity).
4. Feedback	Interactive session with experts

experience and what they have learned form it (Stage 2: Reflective Observation). Based on their observation and the ensuing reflection, they should be able to come up with new propositions, which they can test in practical situations (Stages 3: Abstract Conceptualization and 4: Active Experimentation).

Drawing from this framework, within the scope of this hybrid module, initially, as preliminary work, students were introduced to specific terminology pertaining to different jobs and career paths within their field of studies, at the same time they were asked to identify their unique set of skills. Following this introduction, they were presented with job ads from their respective fields, having been asked to not only identity the most relevant skills, but to also crosscut them with their personal profiles, reflecting on whether they matched the different positions' requirements and to what extent. Carried out both in regular classes and in a dedicated workshop with an HR expert, these activities made it possible for students to draw individual concept maps based on their own path and career goals.

Further elaborating on these maps and working with templates, students were then asked to write 80–120 words personal statements and select an actual position, for which they could apply. After deciding on a position, they were required to build their CV, write a cover letter and produce a 1-min video pitch showcasing their skills and personality, with all these artefacts being compiled into a digital portfolio to be submitted in Moodle. Following up on their application, they would then be invited for a job interview (simulated activity).

Having taken place in synchronous hybrid sessions (both online and face-to-face), the interviews were led by the course's professor together with an HR manager or recruiter (taking advantage of the school's partnerships with the industry and its alumni network), and included topics and questions previously discussed in class, as well as the information featured in students' portfolios. In addition to being assessed on their speaking and comprehension skills, students were also given feedback on their CVs and overall stance throughout the interview, having had the opportunity to interact with the different HR managers/recruiters taking part in the activity (one for each tourism subsector, i.e., tourism, hospitality and catering).

In addition to the widespread use of online recruitment (based on digital platforms, dynamic application forms and Artificial Intelligence—AI), the activities also addressed the growing importance video CVs and pitches, as these are increasingly becoming key for job seekers wanting to showcase their creativity and soft skills (Soares & Pataco, 2017; Iglesias, 2019; Balula & Vasconcelos, 2020).

4 Workflow and Interaction

As mentioned in the previous section, the learning activities described were task-oriented and cumulative in nature, having been designed to include successive additions that built on students' existing knowledge. As a result, students were able to become familiar with procedures and specific terminology, before moving on to more complex tasks that required them to be self-aware, as well as effective communicators, whose message could come across in different formats and platforms. Also relevant in terms of workflow, was creating a safe environment for students to gradually engage in more interactive and collaborative activities involving external partners. That being so, the initial activities were led by the teacher, working from the classroom, interacting both with face-to-face and online participants). Following this initial stage, the activities were gradually decentred, with students and experts participating online taking on a more active stance.

Considering the learning outcomes and goals, and despite the fact students had to work on their personal portfolios (i.e., individual assignments), the activities called for different types of interaction, namely when it came to discussions and workshops and the work with the mentors/experts. In addition to a workshop, there was a planned mentoring section, with students also being able to set up additional sessions with designated HR experts (see Table 2).

The pre-planned mentoring sessions were held both face-to-face and over Zoom (using breakout rooms) with the lead teacher and a HR expert meeting with the students to answer queries and provide feedback on ongoing tasks. Overall, three sessions were held (one for each class), with only six students requesting additional sessions. There was no set division between the groups participating online and onsite, i.e., students could decide based on their convenience.

While most face-to-face interaction took place during group discussions, online interaction took place mostly one-on-one, as needs varied considerably according to each student. This was made easier by the use of breakout rooms and Moodle's feedback tools. Moodle's feedback was mostly used to provide asynchronous feedback on the assignments submitted in the platform. Despite having been provided with different templates (stemming from Microsoft Word, Canva and Europass),

Table 2 Instruction methods and digital tools/environments used in developing the digital portfolios

Development stage	Methods of instruction	Digital tools/environment
1. Preliminary work (week 1)	Teacher-led instruction (lecture/seminar) Learner-led instruction (concept mapping and brainstorming) Interactive instruction (class/small group discussions)	Moodle (Institutional Learning Management System) & Zoom
2. Digital portfolio (weeks 2–5)	Learner-led instruction (individual) Mentoring	Moodle (Institutional Learning Management System) Hybrid (individual work and mentoring sessions over Zoom)
3. Simulation (week 7)	Experiential and interactive learning (simulation/ role-play)	Hybrid (individual interviews)
4. Feedback (weeks 7–8)	Interactive instruction (teacher/expert-led)	Blended approach (feedback provided onsite/online—synchronously- and using Moodle feedback tools)

students were free to choose the style and format of their CV, cover letters and video pitch, provided they complied with previously agreed on guidelines.

In general, by adopting a hybrid approach, the strategy succeeded in balancing schedules and accommodating the needs of both students and mentors/experts. Even though face-to-face activities can be perceived as instrumental in developing a rapport with students and getting them to engage in hands-on exercises pertaining to their skills, the fact that other students and experts were able to participate online was key to ensure participation and establish authenticity, bridging the gap between academia and the labour market. Overall, this was perceived as an advantage, with participants highlighting the module's inclusivity and diversity, referencing the fact that the use of videoconferencing made the process more convenient for the external experts taking part in the activities.

5 Final Considerations

Relying on the use of digital portfolios and a hybrid approach, the teaching and learning strategy described as part of this case consisted of a wide set of activities involving job applications and recruitment, combining both face-to-face and distance interactions. Having been implemented within the scope of three ESP courses, these activities aimed to enhance students' knowledge and career skills, taking advantage of technology-driven learning platforms and interactive classroom experiences to bridge an existing gap when it comes to these skills, as well as potential university-industry collaboration.

Drawing from the literature, and based on students' final outputs, it was possible to establish the potential benefits of hybrid learning within the scope of career skills development in today's dynamic setting. The collaboration with recruiters and the use of authentic materials, such as job advertisements, created opportunities for hands-on learning, paving the way for simulated activities, mimicking current recruitment situations by applying a hybrid mode of participation. This made it possible to create safe and meaningful learning experiences. Moreover, the fact participants were able to explore different tools and platforms, allowed them to showcase their knowledge, experience, and fitness for the desired job. This diversity and complementarity, combined with the flexibility and scalability allotted by technology and hybrid approaches, is perceived as a key strength.

On the other hand, however, in order to successfully integrate career and employability skills into tourism education, there needs to be a more significant collaboration between academia and industry, with a focus on further aligning curricula with the needs of the workforce/market. This collaboration, albeit necessary, is time-consuming and demanding, which might become a hindrance for similar initiatives. Even though this collaborative effort is facilitated by technology, there is still work to be done. Research on career development and career management suggests a growing need for targeted educational interventions that can further integrate career education into academic curricula. This integration can be better achieved by further exploring the affordances of digital platforms, particularly when it comes to expediting communication, collaboration and feedback. Rather than relying only on academic work, HEI should encourage cross-sectorial activities that leverage the development of career skills. Within this scope, language and communication courses can play a pivotal role and hybrid teaching can facilitate such cross-sectorial collaboration.

As for potential the hybrid teaching, even though it was possible to observe that face-to-face participants spent more time interacting with each other, as the sessions moved forward, there was a better integration, with all participants providing feedback and engaging with the mentors/experts. There was also a matter of adjusting activities to a different model. The fact this was a unique model within a broader, more traditional, course, caused some initial disruption that needed to be overcome. The experts' involvement and the realization that the hybrid mode actually made it possible to involve more people in the activities (hence augmenting feedback possibilities), which was instrumental in this process. Overall, despite its tentative and experiential nature, it is believed that this experience can be expanded to other modules, thus enhancing its potential and leveraging future work within this scope.

References

Balula, A., & Vasconcelos, S. (2020). Personal branding and storytelling: Tales from the tourism ESP classroom. *Journal of Tourism & Development, 34*.

Bridgstock, R. (2009). The graduate attributes we've overlooked: Enhancing graduate employability through career management skills. *Higher Education Research & Development, 28*(1), 31–44. https://doi.org/10.1080/07294360802444347

Council of Europe. (2001). *Common European framework of reference for languages: Learning, teaching, assessment*. Cambridge University Press.

Hyasat, A. S. (2022). The experiential learning theory as base for tourism and hospitality courses and internship programs. *Indian Journal of Economics and Business, 21*(1), 291–303.

Iglesias, M. (2019). To apply or not to apply for a job efficiently: That is the question. In *International conference on research in education proceedings* (pp. 28–41). https://doi.org/10.5038/9781955833042

Kolb, D. (2014). *Experiential learning: Experience as the source of learning and development*. Pearson Education.

Lavrysh, Y. (2017). Soft skills acquisition through ESP classes at technical university. *Journal of teaching English for specific and academic purposes, 4*(3), 517–525. https://doi.org/10.22190/JTESAP1603517L

Paviotti, G. (2020). The challenge of career education. *Education Sciences and Society, 1*, 360–381. https://doi.org/10.3280/ess1-2020oa9576

Soares, G., & Pataco, T. (2017). My video CV, or how to impress the hotel industry. In *CAPSI 2017 proceedings* (pp. 95–110). https://doi.org/10.18803/capsi.v17.95-110

Suleman, F. (2016). Employability skills of higher education graduates: Little consensus on a much-discussed subject. *Procedia-Social and Behavioral Sciences, 228*, 169–174. https://doi.org/10.1016/j.sbspro.2016.07.025

Vasconcelos, S. (2024). Fostering tourism students' career skills: An experience report. In *EDULEARN24 proceedings* (pp. 7649–7652). IATED. https://doi.org/10.21125/edulearn.2024.1799

Telepresence Robots and Chatbots in Hybrid Teaching and Learning: A Case of Interdisciplinary Focused Environment

Sirje Virkus

1 The Case Context

Tallinn University has a long history of implementing synchronous hybrid teaching and learning methods, dating back to 1998 (Virkus & Sponberg, 1999; Virkus, 2011, 2013). During the spring semester of 2023/2024, the university offered a hybrid course titled "Enhancing Elderly Care Through Telepresence Robots" as part of its Learning in Interdisciplinary Focused Environment (LIFE) initiative. This university-wide initiative challenges the traditional subject-based approach to education by prioritizing problem-solving and fostering interdisciplinary collaboration. The LIFE initiative aims to bridge the gaps between academic disciplines by bringing together students, faculty, and external partners to develop practical or research-driven solutions to real-world challenges. Unlike conventional subject-based education, this initiative fosters collaboration by bringing together students from diverse academic backgrounds across the entire university to combine their expertise and work on innovative projects. Participation in the LIFE initiative is mandatory for all Bachelor's and Master's students, with successful completion earning them six ECTS credits, equivalent to 156 h of academic work.

Course ideas within the LIFE initiative originate from a diverse range of sources, including university lecturers, student teams, and external partners such as entrepreneurs, NGOs, and organizations. These ideas are then developed into courses, where students are organized into interdisciplinary teams of six. Each team carefully incorporates members from at least three different academic disciplines, ensuring a rich diversity of perspectives and fostering creative problem-solving. Depending on the complexity of the project, one to four teams may collaborate within a single

S. Virkus (✉)
School of Digital Technology, Tallinn University, Tallinn, Estonia
e-mail: sirje.virkus@tlu.ee

A. Nakata et al. (eds.), *Hyb-IT-up!*,
https://doi.org/10.1007/978-3-031-99743-3_16

course. This collaborative environment allows students to tackle a wide range of challenges, from practical applications to in-depth research questions.

The LIFE course, “Enhancing Elderly Care Through Telepresence Robots,” brought together nine students from diverse disciplines, including Social Work, Law, Interdisciplinary Humanities, Cross-media, Psychology, International Relations, and Russian Philology. Conducted entirely in English during the spring of 2024, this iteration of the course attracted a multinational cohort of both undergraduate and graduate students. The course was co-taught by two faculty members from the School of Digital Technologies and an expert in social work from the School of Governance, Law, and Society.

The course structure comprised 26 h of contact sessions, 60 h of individual work (including literature reviews, interviews, and reflective assignments), and 70 h of collaborative team activities. The course format combined face-to-face interactions, Zoom meetings, and the use of a telepresence robot (TPR; Fig. 1) and a virtual

Fig. 1 Telepresence robot Double 3 by Double Robotics

assistant, providing a flexible learning environment. Telepresence robots are remote-controlled, mobile devices equipped with cameras, speakers, microphones, a screen, sensor-assisted motion control, and other interactive features, specifically designed to facilitate remote communication and collaboration (Virkus et al., 2023).

This course adopted a synchronous hybrid learning approach, chosen for its flexibility, inclusivity, and adaptability. Designed to accommodate the diverse needs of an international group of undergraduate and graduate students, this model was particularly well-suited to those managing family responsibilities, health issues, time constraints, and varying geographical locations. By adopting this approach, the course ensured equitable access for students juggling multiple commitments, facing health challenges, or residing far from campus.

2 Learning Goals and Competences

The LIFE course "Enhancing Elderly Care Through Telepresence Robots" was designed with both general learning goals and objectives specific to the project's topic.

The primary goal of the LIFE course is to support the development of students' general competencies and teamwork skills, which would foster the development of the competence of resolving interdisciplinary problems. The supervisor's role is to actively engage student groups in the learning process, with a key focus on developing their critical thinking, problem-solving, and argumentative skills (González-Pérez & Ramírez-Montoya, 2022). This, in turn, enhances students' metacognitive abilities, supporting their growth into independent, self-directed learners capable of managing their own learning and applying their knowledge in real-world contexts. The course seeks to equip students with practical skills that can be applied across various disciplines, promoting lifelong learning. By working in interdisciplinary teams, students develop the ability to approach complex problems from multiple perspectives—an essential skill for academic achievement, professional success, and lifelong learning.

The objective specific to the project's topic is to develop an understanding of TPRs and their potential to enhance elderly care and well-being. The course focuses on the applications of TPRs in providing support and companionship for the elderly, exploring how these technologies can improve social interaction, reduce isolation, and enhance overall quality of life. Students also assess the technological, social, and ethical implications of integrating TPRs into elderly care environments.

By the end of the course, students are expected to develop key competencies that prepare them for real-world challenges. These include teamwork and time management, enabling them to work collaboratively, divide roles, share responsibilities, and manage their time effectively. They also gain interdisciplinary problem-solving skills, allowing them to integrate diverse perspectives and tackle complex issues by collaborating across different fields. Students refine their research and analytical abilities through systematic literature reviews, needs assessments, and stakeholder interviews, while improving their critical thinking and argumentation to support decision-making (González-Pérez & Ramírez-Montoya, 2022). Technological competency is enhanced by learning to assess the suitability of TPRs in elderly care, alongside developing an understanding of the ethical and social implications of integrating such technologies into healthcare. Additionally, students gain skills in project planning and execution, from developing to presenting solutions for real-world problems. They also improve their presentation skills, communicating project outcomes effectively to stakeholders. Finally, students are expected to provide actionable insights and recommendations for the practical use of TPRs to enhance elderly well-being, grounded in thorough research and analysis.

3 Learning Design

The pedagogical approach of this course integrated face-to-face interaction with technology-enabled interactive methods, creating a dynamic hybrid teaching and learning environment. The learning design was informed by HyFlex (Hybrid Flexible Learning) principles introduced by Beatty (2019), a learning approach that gives students the flexibility to select the mode of learning that best suits their needs—either face-to-face or online. This approach is based on four key principles: learner choice, equivalency between participation modes, reusability, and accessibility.

Additionally, the pedagogical framework of Challenge-Based Learning (CBL) was employed to solve authentic, real-life challenges (Nichols & Cator, 2008).

> Challenge Based Learning is an engaging multidisciplinary approach to teaching and learning that encourages students to leverage the technology they use in their daily lives to solve real-world problems. Challenge Based Learning is collaborative and hands-on, asking students to work with peers, teachers, and experts in their communities and around the world to ask good questions, develop deeper subject area knowledge, accept and solve challenges, take action, and share their experience (Nichols & Cator, 2008, p. 1).

Originally developed by Apple Inc., CBL is now widely used in universities, schools, and institutions worldwide. It integrates aspects of problem-based learning, project-based learning, inquiry-based learning, design thinking, and draws on Vygotsky's sociocultural theory. CBL has the potential to empower students, as well as teachers, field experts, and community members, to actively address real, complex, and relevant-to-their-environment challenges while acquiring deep content knowledge and advanced soft skills (Gallagher & Savage, 2023; Leijon et al., 2022).

The LIFE course itself also presents a unique challenge for students, departing from the usual academic path with specific requirements. Mandatory tasks for all LIFE projects include:

1. Collaborating with team members to create a project plan, outlining goals, actions, timeline, assessment criteria, and a media plan.
2. Completing and presenting a mid-term team report.

3. Attending a feedback session during the semester's mid-point to receive constructive input from a university expert.
4. Compiling a project portfolio, including the project report, action plan, stakeholder communications, and evaluation.
5. Writing a self-reflective report on individual roles and team dynamics.
6. Presenting the final project results to the university's expert panel as a team.

The course combined face-to-face interaction with digital engagement through the use of Zoom videoconferencing, a TPR, and a chatbot to facilitate both learning and communication. These technologies address the diverse needs of students from various academic backgrounds, nationalities, and education levels (Bachelor's and Master's), particularly in a course that differs from traditional university formats. Additionally, providing timely feedback remains a challenge due to the differing pace of student progress.

Two key reasons justified the integration of a TPR into the course. First, since the course focused on improving elderly care through the use of TPRs, incorporating a TPR familiarised students with this technology, aligning directly with course objectives. To further support student understanding of telepresence technology, we also included multimedia resources such as videos and interactive simulations. Second, although not yet widely adopted, TPRs are becoming increasingly popular due to their potential to reduce costs and time, enhance communication, and foster a sense of social presence. TPRs help bridge geographical barriers, enabling individuals with chronic illnesses, disabilities, or mobility limitations to engage in remote events (Virkus et al., 2023). Research highlights the potential of TPRs in synchronous hybrid learning environments. A comprehensive review by Means et al. (2010) found that blended or hybrid learning, which combines face-to-face and online components, has emerged as one of the most promising educational approaches (Gleason & Greenhow, 2017; Kasuk & Virkus, 2024).

However, integrating TPRs into education requires addressing several challenges, including aligning learning goals, choosing suitable pedagogical approaches, ensuring technical readiness, providing training and support, promoting accessibility, safeguarding privacy, and implementing ethical and evaluative frameworks. Careful consideration of these factors ensures meaningful and pedagogically sound integration of TPRs in education (Cain et al., 2016; Charteris et al., 2022; Gleason & Greenhow, 2017; Kasuk & Virkus, 2024).

To enhance student support in navigating the course's complexity, a chatbot was introduced as a virtual assistant in the synchronous hybrid course. It provided personalised guidance, facilitated access to course materials, tracked project milestones, and assisted in managing deadlines. The chatbot also offered specialised content support on the application of TPRs in improving elderly care and well-being. Additionally, it functioned as a central repository, enabling students to explore supplementary readings and case studies pertinent to their research. By being available 24/7, the chatbot ensures equitable access to resources, accommodating diverse schedules and individual learning paces. Beyond assisting students, the chatbot also alleviate the workload of instructors by automating administrative and instructional tasks, allowing them to dedicate more time to higher-level teaching and student engagement. This integration of chatbot technology demonstrates a commitment to leveraging innovative tools not only as subjects of study but as practical assets in the educational process.

The course was designed with a strong emphasis on student-centred learning and research-driven methodologies. Students played an active role in shaping their educational experience, engaging directly with literature reviews, needs assessments, stakeholder interviews, and technological exploration. This approach fostered critical thinking, problem-solving, and hands-on learning, encouraging students to take a proactive stance rather than passively receiving information. Faculty members served as facilitators and mentors, offering guidance and support students' inquiries, rather than directing every step. The research foundation was built on both literature reviews and primary data collection, including needs assessments and stakeholder interviews. This student-led research and development process provided a foundation for future initiatives in the field of elderly care.

The course was assessed using a non-differentiated grading scale, meaning it employed a pass/fail evaluation system. Evaluation was based on the quality of the literature review, effectiveness of the needs assessment, innovation in the technology exploration, thoughtful consideration of social and ethical aspects, and the clarity and depth of the final report.

This hybrid teaching and learning model was especially effective in accommodating diverse learning needs and schedules, providing greater accessibility and flexibility for students across various disciplines (Beatty, 2019).

4 Workflow and Interaction

This section outlines the setup and utilisation of the hybrid environments in the LIFE course, as well as the rationale behind the selection of technological tools.

The student teams commenced the project work under the supervision of the course instructors. An introductory session outlined the project requirements and key milestones. The coursework was further supported by various guidance documents, accessible via the course's Moodle platform. Additionally, Google Drive was used for uploading articles related to the systematic literature review, while Google Docs facilitated collaboration on the joint literature review and the development of interview questions.

Hybrid teaching and learning were incorporated into both contact sessions and collaborative team activities, fostering increased student engagement. This approach minimized travel requirements and provided greater flexibility, enabling students to better balance work and family commitments, while aligning with modern workplace practices (Beatty, 2019). Students participated in virtual meetings via Zoom on their laptops, keeping their cameras on and unmuting their microphones only when speaking to minimize background noise. Each student appeared to be technically proficient and required no additional assistance. They effectively managed the technological setup for the hybrid sessions and independently organised their meeting spaces.

The students and their supervisory team held weekly hybrid meetings to discuss a range of topics, including interdisciplinary teamwork, project planning, and progress updates. These meetings aimed to address key issues and plan future activities to ensure the milestones of the LIFE project were met. Three main interaction formats were used: (1) Teachers were physically present in the classroom, while students participated remotely via Zoom. (2) Students were physically present, while teachers joined using a TPR. (3) A mix of in-person and remote participation, with some students and a teacher in the classroom and others joining via Zoom or through a TPR.

During team-based collaboration, the student team established its own working methods, meeting on-site, online, and in hybrid formats. While the course encouraged the use of the Moodle environment for coursework, student teams were given the flexibility to choose their communication platforms for both internal and external collaboration. As a result, students adopted a variety of digital tools, including Zoom, WhatsApp, Facebook, and Google Drive. They effectively integrated these tools to ensure seamless communication and document sharing among team members. Although research suggests that the learning design should minimize extraneous cognitive load (Young et al., 2014), this course followed the principle of learner choice (Beatty, 2019).

The course chatbot, accessible through the university's learning management system Moodle, assisted with both course logistics and content-related inquiries. Students leveraged its extensive functionality to enhance their learning experience, quickly retrieving essential information on course content, upcoming deadlines, and specific requirements for the final project, course portfolio and presentations. By customising interactions, the chatbot was able to provide tailored recommendations based on individual learning needs. Through personalised resource recommendations, the chatbot supported deeper research and encouraged broader exploration of the subject matter. The course supervisory team evaluated multiple chatbot platforms, including Melibo, Rasa, Google Dialogflow, IBM Watson Assistant, ChatterBot, Mitsuku, Chatbase, and Botpress. Chatbase was ultimately selected for its flexibility, cost-effectiveness, and superior performance. It leverages advanced natural language processing (NLP) and machine learning to convert uploaded data into a structured knowledge base, enabling context-aware responses. By identifying and categorizing user intents, Chatbase ensures robust handling of diverse queries.

The Double 3 by Double Robotics was chosen for this course due to pragmatic reasons, as it was readily available at Tallinn University. TPRs share common features, such as a wheeled base with a large battery compartment, a screen for video communication, Wi-Fi and Bluetooth connectivity, and built-in microphones, speakers, and cameras for facilitating two-way communication. TPRs enable users to remotely control their movement and interact with their surroundings via a computer, tablet, or smartphone. The Double 3 is equipped with two 13-megapixel cameras (a wide-angle and a superzoom lens) that can tilt up and down to adapt to various scenarios, such as reading documents on a desk or zooming in on specific points of interest. However, it has the shortest battery life, lasting up to 4 h on a single charge, with a 2-h recharge time. One of the Double 3's key features is its built-in obstacle avoidance technology, which provides navigational guidelines using floor markings to help guide the robot safely. Users can click anywhere on the floor, and the TPR will navigate to the selected point, avoiding obstacles along the way. Additionally, the Double 3 has an adjustable height, ranging from 120 to 152 cm. Furthermore, the Double 3 can accommodate multiple participants within a single robotic unit. While one person takes the lead role and appears prominently on the robot's display, others can also engage and interact through this technology (Virkus et al., 2024). The TPR was deployed to bridge the gap between remote and in-person participants. The TPR projected the live video feed of the remote's face on its screen and allowed mobility, enabling the teacher or student to navigate around the classroom, engage in discussions, and interact with onsite participants in real time. This setup fostered a sense of physical presence and social inclusion, significantly improving engagement for remote participants. Through this bidirectional communication channel, remote and onsite participants collaborated seamlessly, simulating the dynamics of a fully co-located learning environment.

The implementation of hybrid learning approach in the course exemplifies a pedagogically meaningful approach to integrating digital technology, teacher facilitation, and active student participation. Digital tools such as Moodle, Google Drive, Zoom, the Double 3 TPR and chatbot were thoughtfully selected to enhance learning experiences while accommodating diverse student needs. These technologies were not mere adjuncts to teaching but central components in fostering engagement, collaboration, and accessibility (Beatty, 2019).

The role of teachers extended beyond content delivery to active facilitation of hybrid sessions. By alternating between physical presence and virtual participation, instructors modelled the adaptability and flexibility inherent in modern professional practices (Beatty, 2019). Teachers also supported students through tailored guidance, weekly hybrid meetings, and the deployment of innovative tools such as chatbots for continuous, personalized assistance. These efforts ensured that students could focus on meaningful learning without being hindered by technical or logistical barriers.

Students played a pivotal role as active participants in this hybrid learning environment. By autonomously adopting and integrating various digital platforms, they demonstrated self-directed learning and collaboration skills essential for their academic and professional futures. Their ability to manage hybrid meeting spaces and leverage technology for communication, research, and documentation underscored their readiness to navigate the complexities of contemporary work environments.

Hybrid learning in the LIFE course bridged traditional classroom practices and modern digital workflows, aligning with pedagogical principles that prioritize flexibility, engagement, and learner choice (Beatty, 2019). By reducing travel requirements and enabling diverse participation formats, this model not only catered to students' personal and professional commitments but also mirrored the dynamics of real-world collaborative projects. The seamless integration of digital tools, proactive teacher involvement, and empowered student engagement illustrate the potential of hybrid learning to transform education into an inclusive, dynamic, and meaningful experience (Figs. 2, 3, 4, and 5).

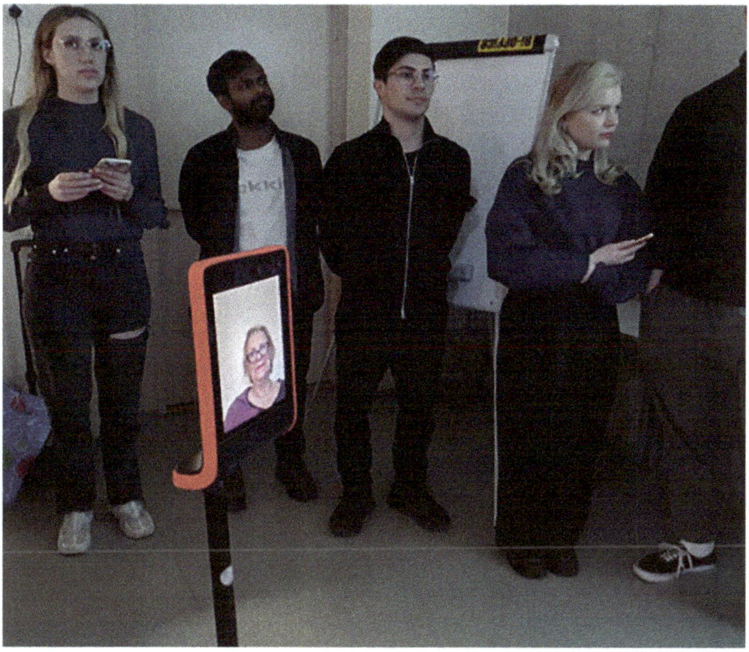

Fig. 2 Students are presenting their project results and the teacher is participating through TPR. Photo taken from the class

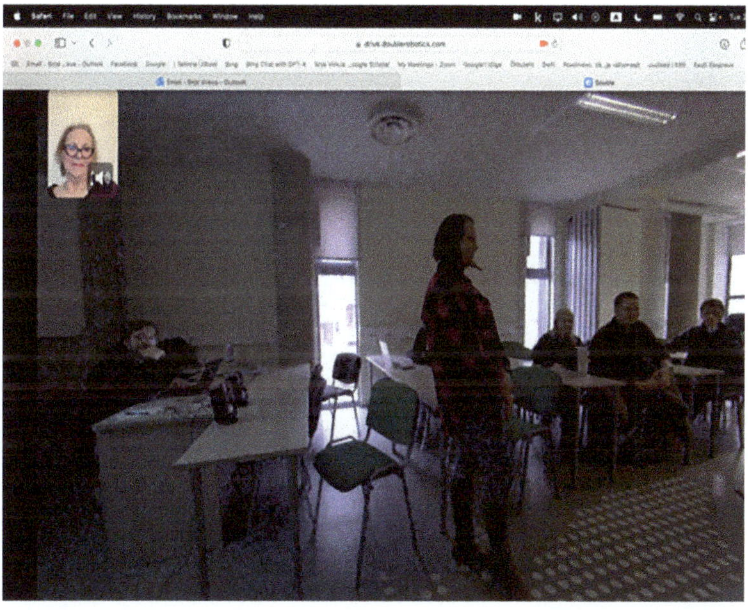

Fig. 3 Students are presenting their project results and the teacher is participating through TPR. Photo taken from the TPR

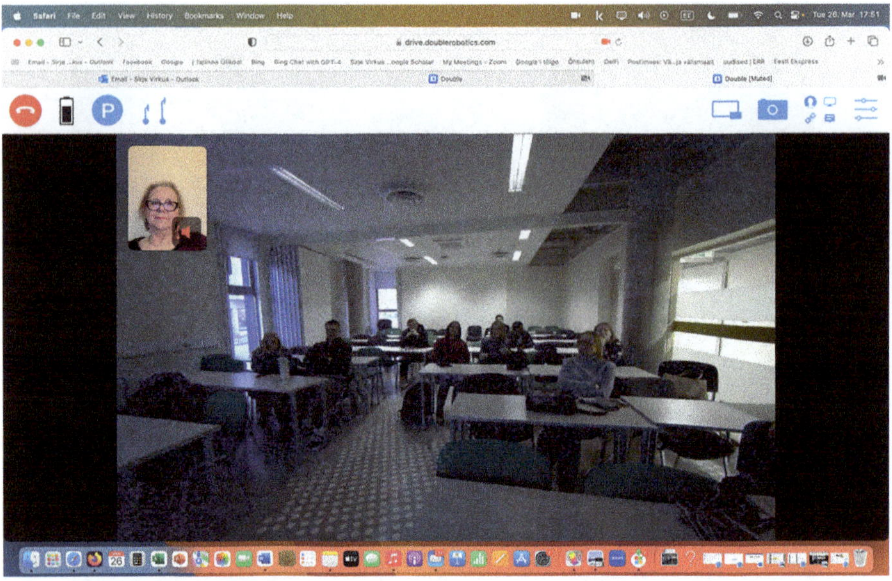

Fig. 4 Students are participating in the class with one supervisor and another supervisor is participating through TPR. Photo taken from the TPR

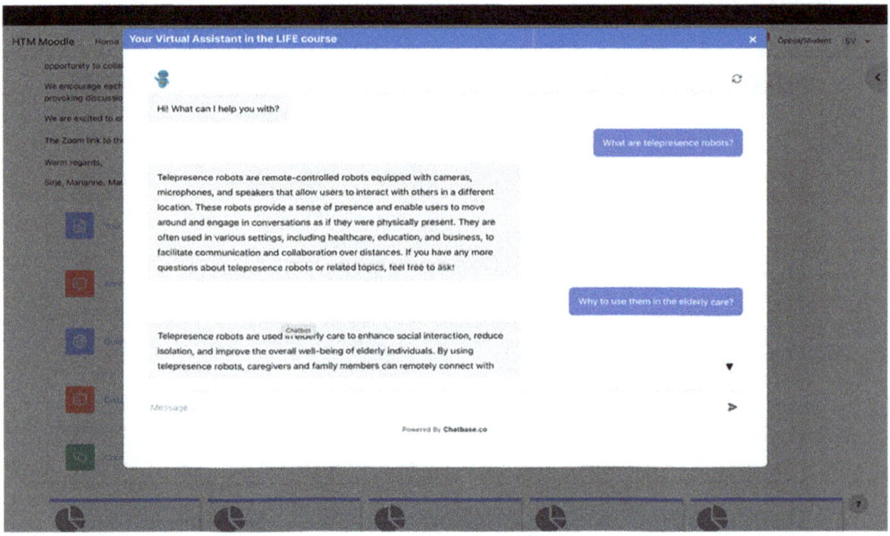

Fig. 5 Example of the Chatbot (Virtual Assistant in the LIFE Course)

5 Final Considerations

The LIFE course, designed around HyFlex principles, fostered a flexible and inclusive learning environment. This hybrid approach, blending in-person, online, and remote interactions, catered to diverse student needs while mirroring contemporary workplace realities. By integrating face-to-face, online, and telepresence technologies, the course enhanced accessibility and fostered interdisciplinary collaboration, preparing students for the demands of modern professional settings.

The incorporation of chatbots and TPRs in the course introduced innovative tools relevant to both education and the rapidly growing field of elderly care. While these technologies offer significant potential, challenges related to technical readiness, ethical considerations, and equitable access must be carefully addressed for their successful and meaningful integration.

Interdisciplinary collaboration was a cornerstone of the course. Students from diverse academic backgrounds worked together to explore the use of TPRs in elderly care, developing crucial problem-solving and teamwork skills highly valued in today's professional world. The course prioritized student autonomy and lifelong learning, emphasizing critical thinking, research, and problem-solving. Students actively engaged in their learning through tasks such as conducting literature reviews, interviewing elderly individuals, and undertaking team-based projects. The use of chatbots provided 24/7 personalized support, enhancing student engagement while also streamlining instructor workload.

By focusing on real-world challenges, the course empowered students to take ownership of their learning journey. The holistic assessment approach, emphasizing research quality and ethical considerations, encouraged deeper engagement and fostered a broader skillset beyond traditional academic metrics.

In conclusion, Tallinn University's LIFE course serves as a model for forward-thinking education. By leveraging hybrid learning methodologies, innovative technologies, and collaborative approaches, the course equips students with the essential competencies necessary to thrive in a rapidly evolving and interconnected world.

References

Beatty, B. J. (2019). *Hybrid-flexible course design: Implementing student-directed hybrid classes*. EdTech Books. Retrieved September 17, 2024, from https://edtechbooks.org/hyflex

Cain, W., Bell, J., & Cheng, C. (2016). Implementing robotic telepresence in a synchronous hybrid course. In *2016 IEEE 16th international conference on advanced learning technologies (ICALT)* (pp. 171–175). IEEE. https://doi.org/10.1109/ICALT.2016.79

Charteris, J., Berman, J., & Page, A. (2022). Virtual inclusion through telepresence robots: An inclusivity model and heuristic. *International Journal of Inclusive Education, 28*(11), 2475–2489. https://doi.org/10.1080/13603116.2022.2112769

Gallagher, S. E., & Savage, T. (2023). Challenge-based learning in higher education: An exploratory literature review. *Teaching in Higher Education, 28*(6), 1135–1157. https://doi.org/10.1080/13562517.2020.1863354

Gleason, B. W., & Greenhow, C. (2017). Hybrid education: The potential of teaching and learning with robot-mediated communication. *Online Learning, 21*(4), 159–176. https://doi.org/10.24059/olj.v21i4.1276

González-Pérez, L. I., & Ramírez-Montoya, M. S. (2022). Components of education 4.0 in 21st century skills frameworks: Systematic review. *Sustainability, 14*(3), 1493.

Kasuk, T., & Virkus, S. (2024). Exploring the power of telepresence: Enhancing education through telepresence robots. *Information and Learning Sciences, 125*(1/2), 109–137. https://doi.org/10.1108/ILS-07-2023-0093

Leijon, M., Gudmundsson, P., Staaf, P., & Christersson, C. (2022). Challenge based learning in higher education: A systematic literature review. *Innovations in Education and Teaching International, 59*(5), 609–618. https://doi.org/10.1080/14703297.2021.1892503

Means, B., Toyama, Y., Murphy, R., Bakia, M., & Jones, K. (2010). *Evaluation of evidence-based practices in online learning: A meta-analysis and review of online learning studies*. U.S., Department of Education. Retrieved September 17, 2024, from https://www2.ed.gov/rschstat/eval/tech/evidence-based-practices/finalreport.pdf

Nichols, M., & Cator, K. (2008). *Challenge based learning white paper*. Apple. Retrieved September 17, 2024, from https://www.challengebasedlearning.org/wp-content/uploads/2019/03/CBL_Paper_2008.pdf

Virkus, S. (2011). Blended learning in 3-country digital library masters degree. *Multimedia Information & Technology, 37*(1), 18–21.

Virkus, S. (2013). Blended learning in a digital library learning programme. In A. Sigal (Ed.), *Advancing library education: Technological innovation and instructional design* (pp. 238–249). IGI Global.

Virkus, S., Alemu, G., Paimre, M., Mandre, S., Leoste, J., Talisainen, A., Marmor, K., & Pöial, J. (2024). The potential of telepresence in libraries: Students' perspectives. *Libri, 74*(2), 105–118. https://doi.org/10.1515/libri-2023-0082

Virkus, S., Leoste, J., Marmor, K., Kasuk, T., & Talisainen, A. (2023). Telepresence robots from the perspective of psychology and educational sciences. *Information and Learning Sciences, 124*(1/2), 48–69. https://doi.org/10.1108/ILS-09-2022-0106

Virkus, S., & Sponberg, H. (1999). Collaborative learning and teaching: Co-operation between Estonia and Norway. In *Proceedings of the ENABLE99. Enabling network-based learning, international conference, Espoo-Vantaa Institute of Technology (EVITech)* (pp. 69–74).

Young, J. Q., Van Merrienboer, J., Durning, S., & Ten Cate, O. (2014). Cognitive load theory: Implications for medical education: AMEE guide no. 86. *Medical Teacher, 36*(5), 371–384.

Experimenting with Hybrid Learning in Distance Education: Experiences, Results, and Lessons Learned

Olga Firssova, Peter ten Hacken, Maartje Henderikx, and Femke Nijland

1 The Case Context

For the last two decades, synchronous hybrid learning has been developing as an innovative educational approach with the potential to connect learning and teaching in a physical classroom with online learning and teaching, thus offering students more flexibility in choosing how to study and creating new opportunities for interacting between students in and outside the classroom (Abdelmalak & Parra, 2016; Bell et al., 2014; Miller et al, 2013; Raes et al., 2020; Zydney et al., 2019). The COVID-19 pandemic led to an increase in the use of hybrid teaching and learning (cf. Carruana Martín et al., 2023; Kreijns et al., 2024; Raes, 2022). Both in early experiments and in recent upscaled implementations of hybrid learning, teaching and learning in the physical classroom were extended beyond its borders with the help of technology. The possibility to join face-to-face campus-based lessons, lectures, or seminars remotely to interact with the teacher and fellow students constituted the core of the innovation (Meylani, 2024).

In the presented pilot, the point of departure in the innovation was different: the online (virtual) classroom as a space, which standardly hosts synchronous interaction between the teacher and (distance) students, was extended to include a teaching and learning activity in a physical classroom and to create affordances for interaction between students online and students in this classroom.

This pilot was conducted in a distance learning course of the Open University of the Netherlands (OU) in 2021 during the period of the COVID-19 pandemic when the restrictions for direct contact and organizing live events were partially

O. Firssova (✉) · M. Henderikx · F. Nijland
Faculty of Educational Science, Open University of the Netherlands, Heerlen, Netherlands
e-mail: olga.firssova@ou.nl

P. ten Hacken
Faculty of Management Sciences, Open University of the Netherlands, Heerlen, Netherlands

A. Nakata et al. (eds.), *Hyb-IT-up!*,
https://doi.org/10.1007/978-3-031-99743-3_17

temporarily lifted. Both OU teachers and OU students felt the need for more human contact and communication after months of work and study in relative isolation. At the same time, another round of pandemic and further or new measures restricting contacts were expected soon. The need for interaction formats that would minimize the risk of infection spread yet would provide affordances for interactive and rich learning experiences was the driving force of this small-scale pilot.

The OU students are adult learners who combine their studies with work and other commitments and prefer the flexibility of supervised self-study at their own pace, place, and time. The OU strives to meet the demands of flexibility while offering active and interactive academic-level programs supported by advanced technologies (Schlusmans et al., 2016). Electronic learning management systems, groupware, and social media are intensively used to facilitate distance learning, teaching, and communication. Most student-teacher and student-student interactions and learning activities, such as lectures and seminars, demonstrations, presentations, and discussions take place online, either asynchronously, in the electronic learning environment of the OU, or synchronously, in the Virtual Classroom available in all OU courses. Some courses may include in-person activities designed to add value for students or required for graduation and certification, such as face-to-face training for certified psychologists or museum visits for students of Arts and Cultural Sciences. Live events may also be organized for academic socialization, participation in academic debates, and networking, as seen in the master's in educational science program science (Henderikx & Vrieling, 2023; Nijland et al., 2023).

Advancements in streaming technology, availability of and experience with distance conferencing tools, social media, and dedicated groupware have made it possible to conduct learning activities as hybrid learning events in which students simultaneously participate in physical and online spaces and can interact across spaces. One of the first documented experiences with hybrid learning at the OU is a pilot during the introductory Management Science course in Quantitative Research Methods (QnRM; Ten Hacken, 2022).

2 Learning Goals and Competences

The core curriculum of the OU Bachelor Management Science in Research Methods and Techniques is organized as a series of one European Credit Point (ECTS) introductory and intermediate-level courses. Having completed these courses, students are expected to be able to critically read and evaluate research literature on the topics of study in Management Science, conduct and report bachelor-level thesis research, and participate in academic debate on relevant issues.

The learning goals of the QnRM course, during which the hybrid learning approach was piloted, are basic knowledge and skills in methods and techniques of statistical data analysis, such as reliability analysis, principal component analysis, correlation, and regression. In this course, students learn to work with the statistical package SPSS.

3 Learning Design

Cohorts enrolling in the QnRM course comprise around 150–200 students. They are standardly divided into classes of 16–20 students. For group assignments groups of 4–5 students are formed in each class at the beginning of the course. Course design is based on individual self-study assignments to be done at one's own pace, interactive assignments with fellow students, and at least one synchronous 4-h online event in the Virtual Classroom conducted in the second half of the course. During the course, students share their drafts, discuss the material, and communicate with each other asynchronously in the discussion forum of the electronic learning environment. The teacher uses a one-to-many message tool for just-in-time information and announcements relevant to all students or specific groups and discussion forums to answer questions posed by students.

The standardly provided online synchronous 4-hour event is organized for each class separately in the second part of the course. The event includes a lecture and a workshop with hands-on group assignments. In the lecture, which is given in the course Virtual Classroom, the teacher goes in-depth into the material, elaborating on the quantitative research methods studied and demonstrating how SPSS statistical package is used to analyze data. In the workshop, students apply the (new) knowledge and train technical research skills in the "learning by doing" mode in small groups in break-out rooms of the Virtual Classroom. After the synchronous session, each group completes and submits three group assignments, receives feedback on each, and is assigned a pass or fail grade for each assignment. To complete the course, students must have a passing grade for all three assignments. If one or more assignments are graded below the passing score, they may be retaken.

In 2021, the synchronous event of the Quantitative Methods course was designed and piloted in two different formats: as a regular online session in the Virtual Classroom (VC condition) and as a hybrid session with in-person and online participants (Hybrid condition). Classes of students were randomly assigned to one of the conditions. Students of four classes ($N = 64$) were assigned to the VC condition and took part in the regular 4-h online event in the Virtual Classroom. Students of five classes were assigned to the Hybrid condition ($N = 90$). These classes were invited to participate in the event in one of the OU Study Centres or join the session from home. Students were free to join the meeting in either mode without any further announcements.

In both Hybrid and VC conditions, the learning activities were structured in the same way: in the lecture, the students listened to the teacher and made notes, in the hands-on session students discussed the assignment and completed it in groups of four or five that had been formed at the start of the course. Teacher feedback was similarly provided to each group: the teacher joined the group, listened to the discussion, asked questions, and provided tips and considerations. Teacher feedback on drafts submitted after the hands-on session did not differ per condition either. From the teacher perspective, the pilot objectives were to gain experience in teaching online and in-person students simultaneously and experience the difference in orchestration and delivery between the fully online setup and a more complex hybrid setup. From the student perspective, the objectives were testing the feasibility of extending the virtual classroom with an in-person set-up without exchanging one for the other and experimenting with student interaction across spaces to gain insights into the possible added value of such interaction for student learning (Ortega-Arranz et al., 2024).

4 Hybrid Condition: Event Setup, Workflow, and Interaction

For the teacher, the preparations for the hybrid event included choosing a fitting hybrid setup at the designated location with the help of the OU Hybrid Virtual Classroom manual and informing and inviting participants. The OU Hybrid Virtual Classroom manual describes the process of organizing and setting up hybrid events in MS Teams such as generating the meeting link and sharing it via invitations. Invitations were sent as course announcements for each class separately.

In the Hybrid condition, students were either present in person, in the physical classroom, or connected to the classroom through MS Teams. A large TV screen connected to a beamer was installed in the middle of the classroom to display the presentation. A Mobile Teams Room set (MTR-set) which consists of another large TV screen, a webcam, and a sensitive microphone attached to it, was positioned at a 45° angle to the TV with the presentation screen and was facing students in the classroom. The teacher's stand was placed at a 45° angle on the other side of the TV with the presentation. The webcam with the sensitive microphone supported capturing the lecture and conversations in the physical classroom. This setup ensured that all participants in the event could see each other and have eye contact. Students in the classroom could see online students who joined the session via MS Teams and were visible on the TV screen of the MTR set. The online students could see and hear the classroom conversations and follow the students present in the classroom via the camera and microphone. Online students could not see the presentation on the central TV screen but on their own screen as it was shared with them through MS Teams. Both in-person and online students could ask a question or request clarification by raising a hand, online students had to switch on their microphones to speak up. Figure 1 is a graphical representation of the described setup.

During the workshop, student groups engaged in hands-on assignments using the SPSS statistical package. The teacher briefly joined each group to check the progress and give just-in-time tips and advice. As groups had been formed in advance, group interaction was organized and facilitated in three different ways, as illustrated at Fig. 2. When all group members were present in the physical classroom at the OU study center (F2F groups), they could use one of the available open spaces for group work where the teacher would physically join them (Fig. 2a). When all group members were online (online groups), the group received access to an MS Teams breakout room where the group could communicate, exchange materials, and work together on the group assignments. The teacher would join the breakout room in MS Teams on his laptop from the OU venue. Figure 2b illustrates this setup. The groups

Fig. 1 A graphical representation of the hybrid lecture setup

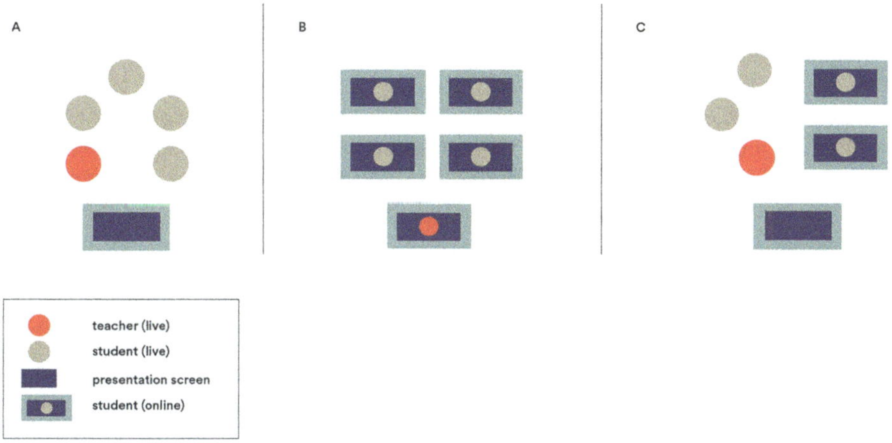

Fig. 2 (**a–c**) A graphical representation of the hands-on session setup: in-person, online, and hybrid

with some group members present in person and some online (hybrid group, Fig. 2c), used separate study rooms at the OU study center for live interaction and a breakout room in MS Teams for communication with online group members and collaboration on SPSS-related tasks on the shared screen in MS Teams. All group members had access to the breakout room on their laptops. The teacher joined such a group physically and interacted with the whole group through the connection to the breakout room in MS Teams on his laptop.

5 Course Outcomes

The assessment scores for the three completed assignments were collected with the information about retakes needed to get a positive grade. Thus, the course assessments for students who attended the 4-hour synchronous study session either in person or through MS Teams (Hybrid condition) could be compared with the results of students who participated in this session online in the regular virtual classroom (VC condition). As shown in Table 1, the average assessment scores of the hybrid condition students taken together are 0.52 points higher than those in the VC condition. These results are significant, $t\,(152) = 2.164$, $p = 0.016$. Students who followed the lecture and participated in the hands-on group activity in person scored significantly better than students in the VC condition ($t\,(103) = 1.825$, $p = 0.035$). Hybrid condition students who followed the session online also scored significantly better than students in the VC condition ($t\,(111) = 1.792$, $p = 0.038$). The difference between in-person and online participants of the hybrid session is not significant.

A student could retake from zero to all three assignments. Table 2 shows how many assignments are retaken on average per condition. Notably, the standard deviation in the VC condition is higher than in the hybrid condition. Students in the VC condition had 0.45 more retakes than those in the Study Centre (in-person hybrid condition, $t\,(103) = 2.871$, $p = 0.003$). Online hybrid condition students had to retake assignments 0.29 times more often than students who attended the session live, this difference is also significant ($t\,(88) = 1.976$, $p = 0.025$). The difference between the VC condition and the online hybrid condition is not significant.

Table 3 shows that students who had attended the synchronous activity in person needed a retake less often than students who had participated in the regular VC

Table 1 Outcomes of hybrid and VC conditions on assessment grade average on a 10-point scale

Condition		*N* participants	Assessment grade average	SD
Hybrid	In-person participants	41	6.49	1.3
	Online participants	49	6.51	1.63
VC		64	5.98	1.44
Total		154	6.28	1.48

Table 2 Comparison of conditions on the average number of retaken assignments

Condition		*N* participants	Average retaken assignments	SD
Hybrid	In-person participants	41	0.22	0.571
	Online participants	49	0.51	0.820
VC		64	0.67	1.040
Total		154	0.50	0.880

Table 3 Number of Assignments Retaken per Condition: Counts and Percentage per Condition

Condition		0 Retake	1 Retake	2 Retakes	3 Retakes	Total
Hybrid	In-person participants:					
	Count	35	3	3	0	64
	Percentage	85.4%	7.3%	7.3%	0	100%
	Online participants:					
	Count	34	5	10	0	49
	Percentage	69.4%	10.2%	20.4%	0	100%
VC	Count	39	16	0	9	64
	Percentage	60.9%	25.0%	0%	14.1%	100%
Total	Count	108	24	13	9	154
	Percentage	70.1%	15.6%	8.4%	5.8%	100%

session: 85.4% of those who attended the session physically did not have to retake any assignments. In comparison, 14.1% of the students in the VC condition had to retake three assignments. The relationship between the condition and the number of retakes is significant (X^2 (6, $N = 154$) = 34.9, $p = 0.000$).

6 Hybrid Setup Evaluated: The Students' Perspective

To collect the students' experiences a course evaluation questionnaire was developed and distributed together with the study materials among students in Hybrid condition. Seventy-three of ninety students filled in the questionnaire, with a total response rate of 81%. Forty-one (56%) respondents had participated in the session in person and 32 (44%) had joined the session online. The evaluation questionnaire included items on the organization and technical aspects, on the communication about the event, experienced comprehensibility of the lecture and the demonstrations, readability of the presentation slides, the quality of interaction between the teacher and the audience, the group work in the hands-on session, experienced relevance of group assignments and teacher feedback. All the aspects were evaluated on a 5-score Likert scale. Ratings ranged from 3.8 on average (SD = 0.86) for the quality of the lecture to 4.5 (SD = 0.75) for the comprehensibility of the lecture.

Answers to the open questions showed that students valued the possibility of asking questions and getting answers directly. They also appreciated the teacher's expertise and involvement during the session. Online students particularly complimented the small-scale set-up that made it feasible for the teacher to pay equal attention to all students. Opinions about the length of the session varied. Some students indicated they would prefer a more extended meeting and more elaboration on the topics. For others, the 4-h session was too long.

Critical remarks concerned information about the expected preparation and workload communicated before the event; this information seemed to be overlooked by the students. Some students felt unprepared and suggested that the invitation to the session should emphasize the importance of joining the session well-prepared. Technical aspects that the students mentioned concerned the connection to the session through MS Teams and the noise in the physical classroom that hindered when following the lecture.

An interesting question about the preference for a session format was included in the general course evaluation questionnaire to which the whole cohort responded. All students were asked what type of synchronous sessions they would prefer to attend in all RM courses if COVID-19 had not imposed constraints for physical meetings. Table 4 shows that all students strongly prefer hybrid or face-to-face synchronous sessions. Notably, students who participated in the hybrid session in person gave regular face-to-face sessions as the preferred participation mode. Students who joined the hybrid session online preferred hybrid sessions over the regular online (virtual class) option.

Table 4 Students' preferences for participation in synchronous events

Question: If it were not for COVID-19, how would you prefer all synchronous events to be organized in all RM courses?	All students	In-person participants in the hybrid session	Online participants in the hybrid session	Total preferences
As face-to-face sessions	29 (42.4%)	22 (56.4%)	7 (22.6%)	58
As hybrid sessions	37 (50.7%)	17 (43.6%)	20 (64.5%)	74
As VC online sessions	4 (5.5%)	–	4 (12.9%)	8
Total	70 (100%)	42 (100%)	31 (100%)	143 (100%)

7 Final Considerations

In the conducted pilot, the fully online learning (VC condition) was compared to hybrid learning (Hybrid condition) realized in three different formats: fully in-person, fully online, and hybrid, i.e. with learners online and in-person learning together. Strictly speaking, only those students who collaborated with fellow students across online and physical spaces crossed the boundaries of the online or physical space during the group task and were actively experiencing hybrid learning.

The teacher, though, had additional tasks in preparing and setting up the session in a hybrid format and had a varied hybrid teaching experience, giving a lecture to two audiences at the same time and supervising student groups in three different formats during the same workshop.

Students in the in-person hybrid condition seemed to have benefited from this session the most. They scored highest on the assessment and needed fewer retakes of one or more assignments. Notably, students in the online hybrid condition also scored somewhat better on the assessment than students from the VC condition. Students in the hybrid condition seemed positive about the experience. They also expressed their preference for face-to-face or "hybrid" setups compared to fully online synchronous meetings in future courses. This might suggest that students experience a hybrid learning environment as a richer setting for a synchronous session even when they participate in such a session online. Overall, this pilot implies that students see added value in participating in a hybrid event even when they remain online.

The results of this pilot indicate that further exploration of hybrid learning as an alternative to fully online classes in a distance education curriculum is relevant. This small-scale experiment also showed that such explorations require the dedicated attention of the teacher to prepare, organize, and orchestrate the event, specifically, the setup, technology, and physical space needed. Juggling between the students and student groups in the physical space, fully online student groups, and students who interact in a hybrid way across spaces requires flexibility and high-level interaction skills from the teacher above the regular domain and pedagogical expertise (Ortega-Arranz et al., 2024).

For the teacher, organizing the regular session in a hybrid format was an experiment, a way to innovate education using technology. Based on the outcomes, this pilot can be considered successful even though it was a small-scale pilot and only concerned one 4-h learning activity in a distance learning programme of 180 ECTS. However, it still contains lessons for the practice of distance education that are interesting and worth considering when the potential and caveats of hybrid learning are put under the magnifying glass.

References

Abdelmalak, M. M. M., & Parra, J. L. (2016). Expanding learning opportunities for graduate students with HyFlex course design. *International Journal of Online Pedagogy and Course Design, 6*(4), 19–37. https://doi.org/10.4018/IJOPCD.2016100102

Bell, J., Sawaya, S., & Cain, W. (2014). Synchromodal classes: Designing for shared learning experiences between face-to-face and online students. *International Journal of Designs for Learning, 5*(1), 68–82. https://doi.org/10.14434/ijdl.v5i1.12657

Carruana Martín, A., Alaryo-Hoyos, C., & Delgado Kloos, C. (2023). A study of student and teacher challenges in smart synchronous hybrid learning environments. *Sustainability, 15*(15), 11694. https://doi.org/10.3390/su151511694

Henderikx, M., & Vrieling, E. (2023). Facilitating peer feedback in online higher education using modelling. In T. Bastiaens (Ed.), *Proceedings of EdMedia + innovate learning* (pp. 210–217). Association for the Advancement of Computing in Education (AACE). Retrieved from https://www.learntechlib.org/primary/p/222506/

Kreijns, K., Yau, J., Weidlich, J., & Weinberger, A. (2024). Towards a comprehensive framework of social presence for online, hybrid, and blended learning. *Frontiers in Education, 8*, 286594. https://doi.org/10.3389/feduc.2023.1286594

Meylani, R. (2024). An in-depth literature review of remote, online, and hybrid learning with case studies of successful and failed attempts. *International Journal of Studies in Education and Science, 5*(1), 29–42. https://doi.org/10.46328/ijses.87

Miller, J. B., Risser, M. D., & Griffiths, R. P. (2013). Student choice, instructor flexibility: Moving beyond the blended instructional model. *Issues and Trends in Learning Technologies, 1*(1). https://doi.org/10.2458/azu_itet_v1i1_16464

Nijland, F. J., Firssova, O., Robbers, S., & Vermeulen, M. (2023). The networked student. *Teaching and Teacher Education, 131*, 104169. https://doi.org/10.1016/j.tate.2023.104169

Ortega-Arranz, A., Amarasinghe, I., Martínez-Monés, A., Asensio-Pérez, J. I., Dimitriadis, Y., Corrales-Astorgano, M., & Hernández-Leo, D. (2024). Collaborative activities in hybrid learning environments: Exploring teacher orchestration load and students' perceptions. *Computers & Education, 219*, 105105. https://doi.org/10.1016/j.compedu.2024.105105

Raes, A. (2022). Exploring student and teacher experiences in hybrid learning environments: Does presence matter? *Postdigital Science and Education, 4*, 138–159. https://doi.org/10.1007/s42438-021-00274-0

Raes, A., Detienne, L., Windey, I., et al. (2020). A systematic literature review on synchronous hybrid learning: Gaps identified. *Learning Environment Research, 23*, 269–290. https://doi.org/10.1007/s10984-019-09303-z

Schlusmans, K., Munckhof, R., & Nelissen, G. (2016). Active online education: A new educational approach at the Open Universiteit of the Netherlands. In G. Ubachs & L. Konings (Eds.), *Proceedings of the online, open and flexible higher education conference* (pp. 163–176). EADTU.

Ten Hacken, P. (2022). *Evaluatie Hybride bijeenkomst bij Blok 3, Kwantitatieve methoden, van de cursus Methoden en technieken van onderzoek, MB0116* [Evaluation of the hybrid meeting in block 3, quantitative methods in the course research methods and techniques, MB0116]. OUNL, Unpublished report.

Zydney, J. M., McKimmy, P., Lindberg, R., & Schmidt, M. (2019). Here or there instruction: Lessons learned in implementing innovative approaches to blended synchronous learning. *TechTrends, 63*(2), 123–132. https://doi.org/10.1007/s11528-018-0344-z

Hybrid Classroom Scenarios and Academic Teaching Spaces

Vincent Engelen, Karel Kreijns, and Azusa Nakata

1 Introduction

In the last chapter of the book, we present the ideas and recommendations for hybrid teaching arrangement and technical setups by referring to projects for designing and implementing 'hybrid classroom' at universities and organizations providing continuous university-level education in the Netherlands.[1]

In the previous chapters we discussed the full spectrum of hybrid learning encompassing the knowledge and skills needed to be successful in hybrid learning (Chapter "Teacher Educators' Digital Competence for Hybrid Teaching", Pedaste et al.), where to pay attention to when designing hybrid learning (Chapter "Constructing a Hybrid Learning Design Framework: A Group Concept Mapping Study", Stoyanov et al.), and its operational, pedagogical, and technological implications (Chapter "A Social Perspective on Hybrid Learning", Kreijns et al.). This chapter is going more in depth about the various configurations of hybrid learning settings in higher education institutions (HEIs) and how these configurations can be deployed by the technological setups applying industry standards. The general definition of hybrid learning adopted in the book is that hybrid learning is a learning

[1] For more information about the project, please see the SURF website https://www.surf.nl/en/themes/online-blended-education/educational-spaces

V. Engelen (✉)
Continuing Medical Education, DeusExMedica, Lanaken, Belgium
e-mail: vincent@dexm.be

K. Kreijns
Faculty of Educational Sciences, Open Universiteit, Heerlen, The Netherlands

A. Nakata
Faculty of Education and Psychology, University of Oulu, Oulu, Finland

A. Nakata et al. (eds.), *Hyb-IT-up!*,
https://doi.org/10.1007/978-3-031-99743-3_18

situation where both remote and in-person students are mixed when they attend classes and lectures, participate in discussions, and collaborate on projects in small groups. This definition, however, does not detail what is meant by mixed and leaves this open for interpretation. Therefore, it is needed that the first section of this chapter will go more in depth about possible configurations of hybrid learning setting. The second section will discuss the various technology standards and equipment needed to realize the different hybrid learning configurations.

2 Configurations of Hybrid Learning Settings

According to Raes et al. (2020), we may distinguish between a Hybrid Virtual Classroom (HVC) and a Remote Classroom (RC). In the HVC, the teacher and a group of students are in the physical classroom, while remote individual learners participate synchronously via video conferencing platforms such as Zoom or Microsoft Teams. By contrast, the RC involves the teacher teaching either from a physical classroom or a personal workspace, connecting with remote student groups who are co-located at one or multiple external locations. While HVC and RC represent the most common configurations for hybrid learning, other configurations are possible as well. For example, we may have a combination of HVC and RC, thus, where the teacher and several students are in the same physical classroom and mixed with remote individual students as well as with remote co-located students. For example, a single classroom might integrate both remote individual students (as in HVC) and remote co-located student groups (as in RC). Locations that are at educational institutions tend to be formal and the technology setup is the responsibility of the educational institution. Locations that are outside the education institutions, however, tend to be informal; the technology setup is largely dependent on who owns these locations. For example, if a student is joining from home, the students' personal equipment determines the setup. If the student is joining from, for example, Starbucks then the only setup possible is the laptop with a built-in camera and microphone.

Furthermore, hybrid learning settings are within the space of all possible settings that one can achieve with communication technology. This space of all possible settings includes fully online learning settings and settings that allow teachers and students to be mobile and distributed in several locations. In the case of the latter, one may think of a field trip to an art museum. Figure 1 and Table 1 give an overview of examples of the possibilities and how a teacher, a single student, or several students may be distributed over one or multiple locations. Note that the different configurations are either the result of a deliberate design process to fulfil several requirements laid out by the educational institution or that the configuration is the result of the situation that is determined by contextual factors such as the Covid-19 pandemic forcing teachers and students to work from their homes. Note also, that in this chapter the hybrid learning configurations also include fully online learning as an extreme configuration of hybrid learning.

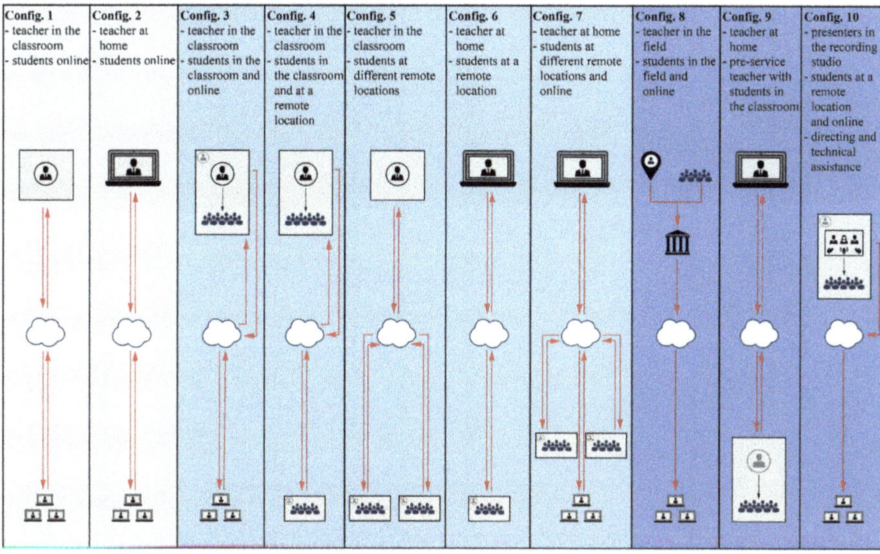

Fig. 1 Example hybrid learning configurations

3 Industry Standards and Performance Metrics for Hybrid Learning Settings

The different configurations of the hybrid learning settings, as described in the above sections, require different technological setups that concern the selection, position, and size of the screens as well as the characteristics of the microphones and cameras. To ease selection, several industrial standards exist to guide the technological setups with respect to room layouts, screen sizes, viewing directions, lighting and sound.

When designing hybrid learning environments that meet the evolving needs of higher education, it is crucial to rely on standards that provide a stable foundation amidst rapidly changing technology. For instance, the Audio, Video, and Control Architectural Drawing Symbols standard (ANSI/AVIXA) provides a universal language for audiovisual (AV) design, allowing architects and engineers to interpret AV system designs without ambiguity. This foundational clarity will remain essential no matter what new tools emerge. Similarly, the Projected Image System Contrast Ratio (PISCR) standard sets enduring benchmarks for visual contrast, ensuring that information displayed in hybrid classrooms is clear and legible across varied lighting conditions. This chapter focuses on AVIXA standards that is used in designing a hybrid classroom in the Hague, in the Netherlands, providing related guidelines for selecting technological setups. However, it should be noted that the industrial standard can only be applied to formal rooms; no standards exist for home setups.

Table 1 An overview of example hybrid learning configurations

			Teacher(s)						Individual student					Student groups						
Configuration	Teaching mode	Classroom type	Classroom	Lecture hall	Office	Location inside institute	Location outside institute	Home	Classroom	Lecture hall	Location inside institute	Location outside institute	Home	Classroom	Lecture hall	Same location inside institute	Same location outside institute	Multiple locations inside institute	Multiple locations outside institute	Multiple locations inside and outside the institute
1	Fully online	Virtual classroom	D		A	A					A	A	D							
2	Fully online	Virtual classroom						D			A	A	D							
3	Hybrid	HVC	D								A	A	D	D						
4	Hybrid	RC and one remote location	D											D		A	A			
5	Hybrid	RC and multiple remote locations	D		A	A												A	D	A
6	Hybrid	RC and one remote location						D								A	D			
7	Hybrid	Mixed HVC and RC						D			A	A	D					A	D	A
8	Hybrid	Field trip					D				A	A	D				D			
9	Fully online	Remote coaching				D	A	A	D											
10	Hybrid	HVC with one or more presenters		D							A	A	D		D					

D = default selection
A = alternative selection
HVC = hybrid virtual classroom (Raes et al., 2020)
RC = remote classroom (Raes et al., 2020)

3.1 Audio

The Audio Coverage Uniformity (ACU) standard describes how uniformly sound is produced in a room by a sound installation. This is crucial for hybrid classrooms, where both in-person and remote students are present. It is important to ensure that hybrid classrooms meet the ACU standard, and in-person and remote students have good audio experience by hearing the sound in a similar way. This includes:

- Sound coverage: everyone in the room hears the sound uniformly.
- Volume: sound is clear for both in-person and remote students.
- Sound quality: clear and intelligible sound without echoes or reverberation.
- Sound treatment measures: adding sound-absorption or acoustic panels to prevent echoes and reverberation.
- Sound system power: the appropriate amount of power to ensure even sound coverage and keep the audio intelligible.

In hybrid learning environments, much emphasis is placed on delivering high image quality, but this is only one part of the overall learning experience. No matter how sharp and clear the picture may be, it loses its value if the audio quality is poor. Good audio quality is therefore essential for clear communication and understanding. It should be ensured that the chosen technology meets the highest audio standards. Echoes, background noise, or poorly tuned microphones can seriously hamper the learning experience. This means that, in addition to investing in the right video solutions, sufficient attention should also be given to quality microphones, speakers, and sound reinforcement systems to create an optimal learning environment where both visuals and sound are aligned.

3.2 Light

According to the AVIXA Lighting Guide,[2] the color temperature in a video conferencing room should range from 3200 K to 6500 K. A lower color temperature (around 3200 K) creates a warmer and more intimate atmosphere, while a higher color temperature (around 6500 K) evokes a cooler and more productive environment. Ensuring a constant color temperature in the virtual classroom space is important for maintaining consistent image quality and accurate color display on the screen.

Using the correct and consistent color temperature is required for providing a pleasant and uniform image for video conference participants. This also applies to light glare on screens for classroom participants. If a light source is near the

[2] AVIXA, Inc. (2018). *Recommended practice for lighting performance for small to medium-sized videoconferencing rooms* (ANSI/IES/AVIXA RP-38-17).

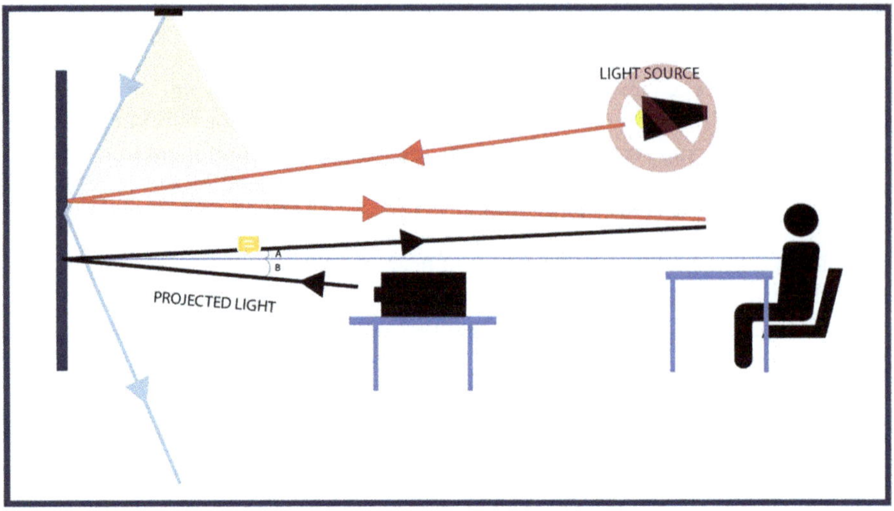

Fig. 2 Ambient (off-axis) light source

projector or at a similar angle to the screen, the light from the projector is reflected toward the viewing area (Fig. 2).

Unlike a regular projection screen, which reflects light in all directions, Ambient Light Rejection screens (ALR screens), selectively reflect light in the direction of an audience. ALR screen technology uses microstructures and layered optical filters to direct light effectively. For our purposes, there are only two "desirable directions" in which a screen can reflect light: towards the audience and away from the audience. Obviously, we want to see the image from our projector, so light that falls directly on an ALR screen is reflected toward the viewers. However, we do not want ambient light on our screens. Therefore, light hitting an ALR screen at an odd or greater angle (such as oblique light from a window, studio lights, or classroom lighting) is directed away from the viewers. They reduce or eliminate the negative effects of ambient light, giving a clear and sharp image without glaring or blurring (Fig. 3).

3.3 *Space and Screen*

An important aspect of interpreting hybrid classrooms is the screen that allows in-person students to participate in hybrid education. (TU Delft, 2018). Before diving into display technology specifications, it is necessary to highlight some advancements that may transform the screen experience in the future.

First, the next generation of Teams Rooms—the Front Row setting—requires a different display size. Front Row changes the layout of the Teams meeting and removes the feeling that your remote peers are not there. The online participants are lined up at the bottom of the screen, putting them at eye level in the classroom, making it feel much more natural to talk to them. Other changes have also been made to the layout to improve the quality of the hybrid education space. Above the Front Row, the presentation is in the middle, and either side can display, for example, the agenda, chat, or task list as desired. This allows you to see all the important components of the lesson at a glance. Showing students on both sides of the screen could potentially support the feeling of equal student participation. Note, however, that the statements here require closer examination (e.g., whether remote peers are feeling present or absent), for example by performing some research.

A 21:9 aspect ratio seems to be the ideal ratio for this version (Fig 4). However, it is desirable to have a flexible, sustainable option that can endure over time.

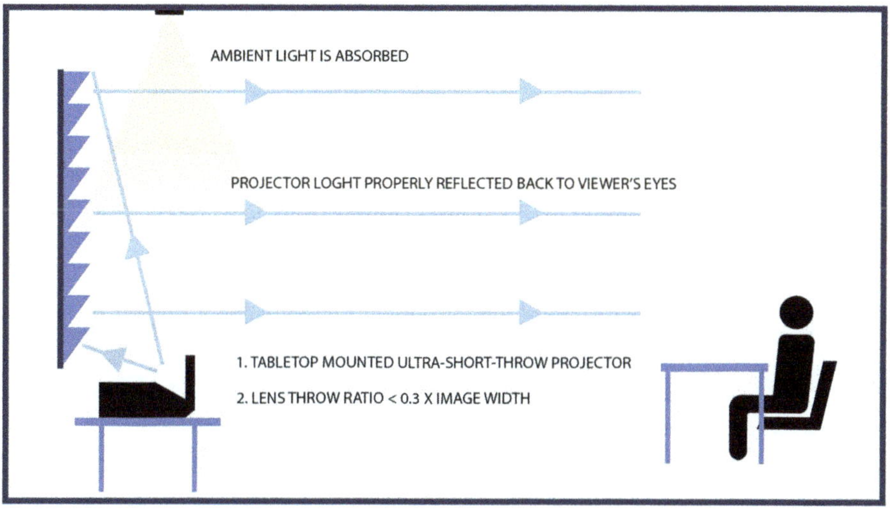

Fig. 3 Ambient light rejection screen explained

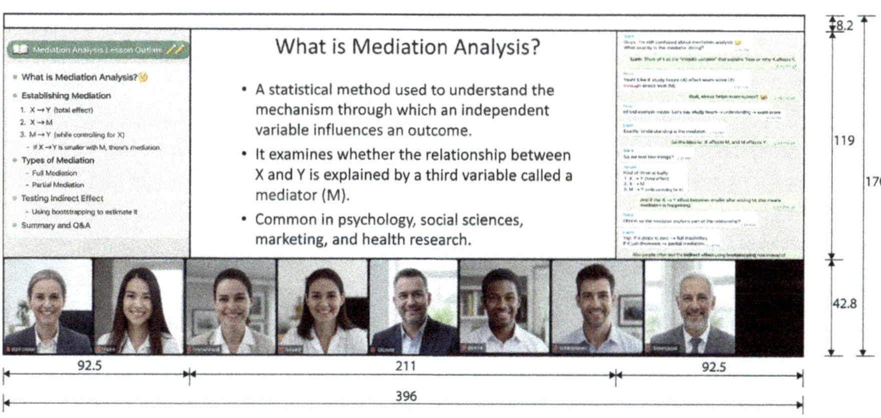

Fig. 4 ALR screen setup 21:9 ratio operating as a 21:9 ratio

Subsequently, the ability to deviate from the 21:9 aspect ratio in the setup should be a requirement. Thus, a 21:9 projection screen should allow for a 16:9 projection or alternatively for two 16:9 screens side by side, creating a 32:9 setup (see Fig. 5).

The size of a screen is determined by the room's clear height. This clear height is the open space between the finished floor and the ceiling without obstructions from pendant lights, structural elements, suspended ceilings, additional floor elements or HVAC (Heating, Ventilation and Air Conditioning) systems. HVAC systems refer to the ducts, units, and other mechanical equipment installed near the ceiling that can reduce the usable vertical space in a room. To implement a hybrid classroom, an ideal setup would include a raised floor or podium to hide the cables, connections, and power supplies. Figure 6 shows the example implementation of the raised floor and the placement of a screen. If we were to provide 18 cm for the raised floor, the maximum height of the screen would be 92 cm and the clear height would be 252 cm

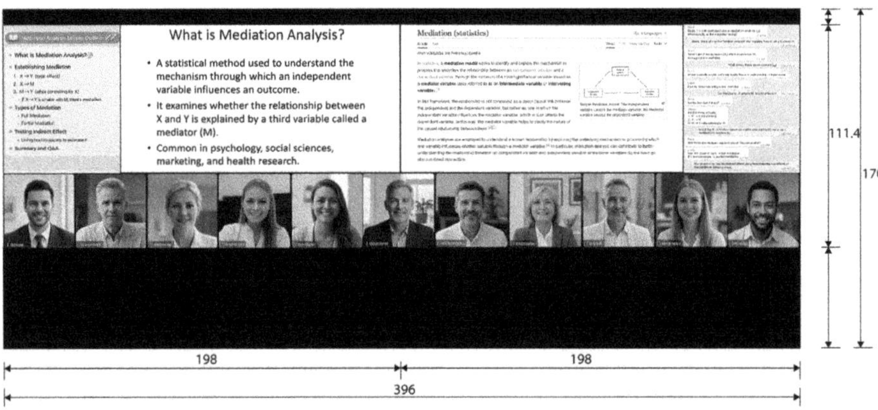

Fig. 5 ALR screen setup 21:9 ratio operating as a 32:9 ratio or 2 × 16:9 ratio

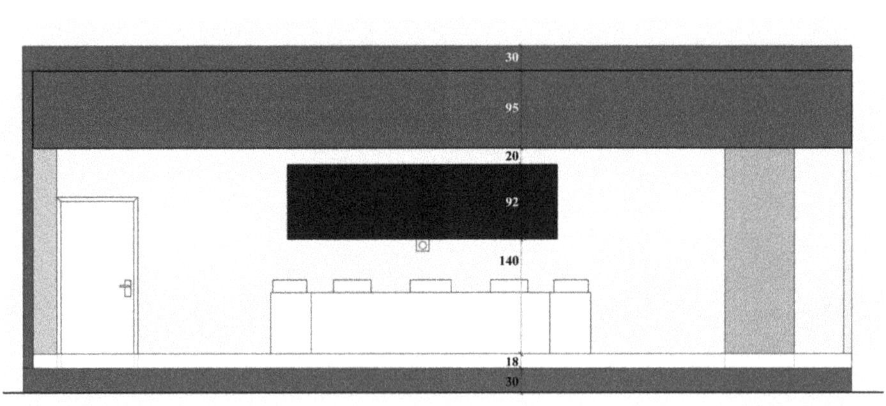

Fig. 6 Educational space presentation wall 32:9 ratio

(20 + 92 + 140 cm), instead of 270 cm. The size of raised floor impacts the size of the screen that can be hung there, according to the DISCAR standard.

Considering this, we recommend choosing ALR screens with Ultra Short Throw (UST) projectors. Unlike TVs, projectors aren't designed for direct viewing. Instead of emitting light straight into our eyes, they reflect light off a surface—usually a screen. The challenge, however, is that screens don't just reflect the projector's light; they also reflect ambient light, which can reduce image clarity. If a room cannot be completely darkened, such as a cinema auditorium, ambient light will reflect off a white screen, causing glare and blurring the image from the projector. Ambient light is not just a problem during the day. Light from a projector can scatter and reflect off light-coloured walls, creating ambient light in an otherwise dark room.

4 Conclusion

In conclusion, the chapter highlights the various configurations of hybrid learning settings that can be found in higher education institutions. Hybrid learning configuration needs to be set up based on the students' primary learning needs—whether it is mastering learning contents or interacting with other students to solve a problem—and technology should be carefully chosen to fulfil the purpose (Bell et al., 2014). We expect that the given example configurations will help a reader choose a right combination of pedagogical and technological arrangement to meet their own unique learning contexts. The chapter also shows how industry standards can be applied to help selecting the technological setups such as room layouts, screen sizes, viewing directions, lighting, and sound. By adopting standardized approaches to audio, lighting, and classroom layout while maintaining adaptability in technology and pedagogy, educational institutions can provide effective learning environments for all students. Standardization also helps minimize usability issues that often arise from the rapid evolution of technologies (Bell et al., 2014; Raes et al., 2020). Researching and recommending home setups to optimize student social presence and telepresence and engagement (see Chapter "A Social Perspective on Hybrid Learning") is an area not covered in this chapter, but will be a key focus of our future work to promote the success of hybrid learning.

Acknowledgments We acknowledge Aïcha Bidouch's work on creating graphics of Figures to ensure the better resolution and formatting.

Appendix

Overview of Key Audiovisual and Lighting Standards for System Design

Audio, Video, and Control Architectural Drawing Symbols

The Audio, Video, and Control Architectural Drawing Symbols standard (ANSI/AVIXA) establishes a set of symbols to be used in architectural drawings for AV systems. This standard ensures that all parties involved in an AV project, including architects, engineers, and AV integrators, can interpret system designs accurately. The uniform symbols minimize misunderstandings and streamline project coordination.

Source: AVIXA. (2010). Audio, video, and control architectural drawing symbols (ANSI/AVIXA). AVIXA, Inc.

Cable Labeling for Audiovisual Systems

The Cable Labeling for Audiovisual Systems guideline defines a standardized approach to labeling AV cables. Clear labeling is essential for efficient troubleshooting, maintenance, and upgrades. By following these guidelines, AV professionals can reduce installation errors and ensure that each cable is easily identifiable, especially in complex AV installations.

Source: AVIXA. (2015). Cable labeling for audiovisual systems. AVIXA, Inc.

PISCR (Projected Image System Contrast Ratio)

The Projected Image System Contrast Ratio (PISCR) standard (ANSI/AVIXA) specifies minimum contrast ratio requirements for projected images in various environments. This standard is crucial for maintaining image clarity and readability, especially in rooms with challenging lighting conditions. By meeting these contrast ratios, AV systems can deliver visuals that are easy for audiences to view and interpret.

Source: AVIXA. (2011). Projected image system contrast ratio (ANSI/AVIXA). AVIXA, Inc.

Audio Coverage Uniformity

The Audio Coverage Uniformity standard (ANSI/AVIXA) ensures even sound distribution across an audience area. This standard is essential in environments where clear and consistent audio coverage is critical, such as conference rooms, lecture halls, and performance spaces. Proper adherence to audio coverage uniformity standards helps to prevent audio "hot spots" and "dead spots" in AV installations.

Source: AVIXA. (2017). Audio coverage uniformity (ANSI/AVIXA). AVIXA, Inc.

DISCAS: Display Image Size

The DISCAS (Display Image Size) guideline provides standards for determining appropriate display sizes based on room dimensions and viewer distances. Adhering to the DISCAS guideline ensures that all audience members have an unobstructed view and can read displayed content comfortably. This is particularly relevant in educational and corporate environments where screen legibility is critical.

Source: AVIXA. (2016). DISCAS – Display image size. AVIXA, Inc.

DISCAS: Display Image Size for 2D Content in AV Systems

A subset of the broader DISCAS guideline, DISCAS—Display Image Size for 2D Content in AV Systems (ANSI/AVIXA) focuses specifically on display requirements for 2D content in professional AV installations. This standard is vital for ensuring that image size and clarity are optimized for presentations, video playback, and digital signage.

Source: AVIXA. (2016). DISCAS - Display image size for 2D content in AV systems (ANSI/AVIXA). AVIXA, Inc.

CIBSE: Society of Light and Lighting

The Society of Light & Lighting, a division of the Chartered Institution of Building Services Engineers (CIBSE), provides guidelines for lighting design in various environments. Their standards emphasize efficient lighting solutions that balance energy consumption with optimal visual conditions. These guidelines are instrumental for AV professionals who need to integrate lighting that enhances video conferencing, presentations, and other AV-dependent activities.

Source: Chartered Institution of Building Services Engineers. (n.d.). Society of light & lighting. CIBSE.

AV Rack Design

The AV Rack Design guide from AVIXA offers best practices for organizing and maintaining AV equipment racks. Proper rack design facilitates system maintenance, improves airflow for equipment cooling, and ensures efficient cable management. This standard is crucial for AV installations in both temporary and permanent setups.

Source: AVIXA. (2010). AV rack design. AVIXA, Inc.

AV Implementation Handbook

The AV Implementation Handbook (ANSI/AVIXA) provides comprehensive guidelines for deploying AV systems, from initial planning through final implementation. It covers essential considerations such as system testing, quality assurance, and client handover. This handbook is a valuable resource for AV professionals involved in large-scale installations.

Source: AVIXA. (2010). AV implementation handbook (ANSI/AVIXA). AVIXA, Inc.

Video Conferencing Lighting

The Video Conferencing Lighting guideline from AVIXA provides standards for achieving optimal lighting conditions during video conferences. Proper lighting is essential for clear video quality and participant visibility, especially as remote work and virtual meetings become increasingly common. This guideline covers both natural and artificial lighting considerations to enhance the video conferencing experience.

References

Bell, J., Sawaya, S., & Cain, W. (2014). Synchromodal classes: Designing for shared learning experiences between face-to-face and online students. *International Journal of Designs for Learning, 5*(1).

Raes, A., Detienne, L., Windey, I., & Depaepe, F. (2020). A systematic literature review on synchronous hybrid learning: Gaps identified. *Learning Environments Research, 23*(3), 269–290.

TU Delft. (2018). *Cookbook education spaces: Requirements for Education Spaces TU Delft Campus* (version 2.0). Retrieved from https://storage.googleapis.com/tudesc/docs/Cookbook_Education_Spaces.pdf

Toward an Integrated Understanding of Designing for Hybrid Learning and Teaching

Annelies Raes

1 The Changing Landscape in Higher Education

The educational landscape has undergone significant transformation over the past decades due to technological advancements, ranging from the widespread availability of the internet to the proliferation of sophisticated digital tools and platforms. These developments have often fueled high expectations for profound changes in education. Think about the MOOCs which emerged after the turn of the century and had a peak in 2012, often called the year of the MOOC (Jordan & Goshtasbpour, 2022). Looking back at these technological evolutions, we had to conclude that MOOCs are not the holy grail. This educational approach places high demands on the motivation and self-regulated learning skills of students, often resulting in high dropout rates (Littlejohn et al., 2016). Additionally, effective use of MOOCs requires specific digital competencies from teachers (Zhang et al., 2021).

The global pandemic further highlighted both the potential and the limitations of online and distance education, revealing that learning is fundamentally social in nature. Yet, various factors such as health issues, family responsibilities, or work obligations can hinder participation in traditional learning environments. Hybrid education seeks to bridge these gaps by combining the strengths of online and on-site learning, thereby expanding educational opportunities across borders.

To answer the question for flexibility and accessibility in education, different modes of education are nowadays combined, resulting in an educational landscape of merging modalities (Irvine, 2020), distinguishing delivery modes in terms of their synchronicity and modality (Ebner & Gegenfurtner, 2019). Although the landscape is changing, what remains at the core of educational innovation is the

A. Raes (✉)
Centre for Instructional Psychology and Technology, Faculty of Psychology and Educational Sciences, KU Leuven, Leuven, Belgium
e-mail: annelies.raes@kuleuven.be

A. Nakata et al. (eds.), *Hyb-IT-up!*,
https://doi.org/10.1007/978-3-031-99743-3_19

thoughtful design of learning environments (Goodyear, 2015; Kirschner, 2015; Laurillard, 2012) that are inclusive, effective, and sustainable.

This handbook embraces the importance of design by structuring itself around three key pillars: foundational theories to understand learning and teaching within this new educational landscape, design approaches for specific courses and programs within the context of hybrid education, and practical implementations of hybrid scenarios. The three parts are intertwined and interconnected. The theoretical concepts, elaborated and grounded in the field in the first part of the book, are retaken from a design perspective in the second part and exemplified from a practical point of view in the third part. Pedaste, Leijen, and Saks for example introduce their Teacher Educators' Digital Competence Framework for Hybrid Teaching in the first part (Chapter "Teacher Educators' Digital Competence for Hybrid Teaching") which is used as an analytical lens to cluster research-based guidelines during the co-design workshop described by Moreira et al. (Chapter "Competence-Driven Guidelines for Hybrid Teaching"). At the same level, Santos et al. describe the co-design process of the micro-course on hybrid learning competences for higher education students (Chapter "Co-designing a Micro-course on Hybrid Learning Competencies for Higher Education Students") based on the underlying theory on social presence presented by Kreijns et al. in Chapter "A Social Perspective on Hybrid Learning".

In what follows, I want to guide you through the comprehensive journey from conceptual foundations, through design strategies, to practical implementations. Rather than merely summarizing these contributions, this discussion will frame them through a micro-ecological lens, positioning hybrid education as a dynamic, co-evolving system involving learners, teachers, tools, pedagogies and spaces (Borge & Mercier, 2019; Damşa et al., 2019; Markauskaite et al., 2023). The micro-ecological perspective views hybrid education as a dynamic, interconnected ecosystem where learning unfolds across multiple social planes: the individual, the small group, and the broader classroom community (Dillenbourg, 2013). Unlike traditional approaches that focus on isolated cognitive processes or group collaboration, this perspective acknowledges that learning is distributed across these interconnected levels.

From this viewpoint, the learning environment functions much like a natural ecosystem where diverse elements - teachers, students, technologies, and instructional designs - continuously interact. Changes in one aspect can ripple across the learning environment, affecting various components. For example, in a hybrid learning scenario, if remote students cannot hear questions asked by students physically present in the classroom, it is not just a technical problem but a broader disruption of the learning ecology. This breakdown in communication affects not only the remote students' ability to participate, but also the teacher's orchestration efforts, the students' perception of inclusion, and the overall culture around accessibility and engagement.

Moreover, the micro-ecological perspective emphasizes that learning is shaped by interactions, not merely by the transmission of content. It focuses on how students negotiate meaning, how technological tools mediate discussions, and how teachers adapt their guidance in response to emerging challenges. This perspective resonates with the focus of several chapters throughout the book. For instance, Kreijns, Santos, and Weinberger (Chapter "A Social Perspective on Hybrid Learning") emphasize the importance of social presence and telepresence in fostering a cohesive learning environment where both in-person and remote students feel integrated. Similarly, Ahola, Nakata, and Järvenoja (Chapter "Regulation of Learning: Cognition, Motivation and Emotion") highlight the role of self-regulation, co-regulation, and socially shared regulation in hybrid learning environments, emphasizing how collaborative processes are dynamically co-constructed through interaction, which is practically described in Chapter "Hybrid Problem-Based Learning with Work-Life Clients: A Context of the Educational Technology Project Course" of Kojo et al. on hybrid problem-based learning. The focus on teacher orchestration of complex learning environments, as discussed by Amarasinghe et al. (Chapter "Orchestration Load of Hybrid Teaching"), further underscores the need for adaptive instructional strategies that respond to emergent challenges across different modalities. These chapters, among others, illustrate how hybrid education involves the continuous negotiation and adaptation of interactions across diverse social planes.

Finally, a key insight from this perspective is the role of the teacher as an orchestrator of learning, managing and responding to the complex, shifting dynamics of interactions in the educational ecosystem (Ortega-Arranz et al., 2024; Dillenbourg et al., 2018). The importance of teacher orchestration directly relates to the need for specific teacher competences in navigating hybrid learning environments as discussed by Pedaste et al. (Chapter "Teacher Educators' Digital Competence for Hybrid Teaching"), presenting their Teacher Educators' Digital Competence Framework for Hybrid Teaching.

From a micro-ecological perspective, hybrid education is not a static model to be implemented but a continuously evolving negotiation between actors, including students, teachers, and technological tools, within the learning environment. Each chapter in the book contributes to understanding how these elements interact and influence one another within diverse hybrid learning contexts.

2 The Need for Conceptual Pillars

The first part of the book, *Conceptual Pillars of Hybrid Teaching and Learning in Higher Education*, presents a foundational understanding of hybrid education by discussing critical concepts and theoretical frameworks that underpin its practice. Comprising four chapters, this section explores how teacher and student constructs contribute to the complexity and potential of hybrid learning environments.

The core of Chapter "A Social Perspective on Hybrid Learning" by Kreijns, Santos, and Weinberger focuses on understanding social presence and telepresence in hybrid learning environments. Kreijns et al. (2022, p. 1) defines social presence as "the psychological phenomenon of perceiving other persons in technology-mediated communication as ‘real’ and with whom one can connect.” Different theories underlie Kreijns’ definition, which are outlined in the chapter. By using this comprehensive model of social presence, reflection emerges on the antecedents of social presence revealing that the degree of social presence is not solely determined by telecommunication technology, but also by different communication styles and behaviors taken up by both the teacher and the peers. Based on this theory, prior research is analyzed showing that many design guidelines for hybrid education which have been shared in the field (including the one in my own research; Raes, 2022) could be explained by the comprehensive model of social presence (Kreijns et al., 2024). The chapter makes clear that in hybrid education, different perspectives are always present: the perspective of the remote student and the perspective of the on-site, face-to-face student. To better understand the perception of the on-site students and teachers, Social Presence Theory is crucial, whereas from the perspective of the remote student, Telepresence Theory plays a significant role. As stated in the chapter, while social presence is about transporting others to ‘here’, telepresence is about transporting oneself to ‘there.’ The chapter emphasizes that both types of presence are essential for effective hybrid learning environments and should be mutually reinforcing, considering suggestions for pedagogy, social aspects and technological aspects. This threefold division bears a resemblance to Goodyear’s Activity-Centered Analysis and Design (ACAD) framework (Goodyear et al., 2021), which is frequently applied in research on hybrid education to illustrate the interrelatedness of different elements in learning environments. The ACAD framework distinguishes between three interdependent layers: Epistemic Design (tasks and activities designed to promote learning), Social Design (social structures and roles that support learning interactions), and Set Design (the physical and digital environments that afford learning opportunities) which relate to the pedagogical, social, and technological suggestions. When viewed through a micro-ecological lens, the interaction between remote and in-person students is shaped not only by the technological infrastructure but also by the pedagogical strategies employed to foster inclusivity and interaction.

Chapter “Regulation of Learning: Cognition, Motivation and Emotion” by Ahola, Nakata, and Järvenoja also addresses the learner’s experience within hybrid environments but does this from the theory on regulation of the cognitive and affective dimensions of learning, including self-, co- and socially shared regulation (Järvelä & Hadwin, 2024). As noted in the introduction, MOOCs could not meet the expectations. The main reason is that many students do not have the necessary regulation skills to navigate successfully in these learning environments or that the environments did not include additional support (Kirschner et al., 2006). The chapter puts forth guidelines to support regulation skills through various means including cognitive scaffolding and motivational encouragement. Yet, while teachers may design learning environments with particular intentions - such as fostering social presence or supporting collaboration - students do not always engage with these environments as intended. This observation resonates with the concept of instructional disobedience (Elen, 2020), where learners actively or passively deviate from the designed learning paths. From a micro-ecological perspective, this divergence should not be seen merely as a design flaw but as an inevitable aspect of a dynamic learning ecosystem. Learners navigate their own paths within hybrid environments, responding to cognitive, emotional, and motivational challenges in ways that are often unpredictable and context dependent. To train a set of core competencies enabling higher education students to thrive in hybrid learning contexts, Santos et al. developed a micro-course (Chapter "Co-designing a Micro-Course on Hybrid Learning Competencies for Higher Education Students") which is highlighted further.

While Chapters "A Social Perspective on Hybrid Learning" and "Regulation of Learning: Cognition, Motivation and Emotion" rather focus on the student's perspective, Chapters "Teacher Educators' Digital Competence for Hybrid Teaching" and "Orchestration Load of Hybrid Teaching" focus on the teacher's perspective. Chapter "Teacher Educators' Digital Competence for Hybrid Teaching" by Pedaste, Leijen, and Saks introduces a Teacher Educators' Digital Competence Framework for Hybrid Teaching based on the analysis of prior competence frameworks which were not specifically developed for hybrid education. The framework's distinction between generic, contextual, and transformative competences aligns well with the idea of hybrid education as an evolving system. Generic competences address individual teacher skills, while contextual competences involve interactions within specific educational settings. Transformative competences, which consider broader societal and environmental impacts, underscore the fluid and interconnected nature of hybrid teaching. By situating teacher competence within a broader system of interactions, the framework supports the idea that effective hybrid teaching depends on the teacher's ability to adapt and co-evolve within diverse learning ecologies.

Amarasinghe and colleagues extend this perspective in Chapter "Orchestration Load of Hybrid Teaching" by examining the concept of orchestration load and its multifaceted elements in hybrid teaching. Their analysis highlights how teacher orchestration is directly influenced by the diverse and often conflicting demands of managing synchronous hybrid environments. The chapter more specifically focuses on Computer-Supported Collaborative Learning scenarios which are already very challenging to manage in a non-hybrid setting (Prieto et al., 2018). By comparing teacher experiences within on-site, online, and synchronous hybrid learning settings, the authors demonstrate how tools, pedagogies, and spaces intersect to influence teacher orchestration load. This chapter illustrates how orchestration load emerges from the continuous negotiation between technological affordances, pedagogical goals, and student needs. Rather than seeing orchestration as a static challenge to be solved, it becomes a processual activity that evolves through feedback loops and ongoing reflection.

The conceptual pillars discussed in this part of the book lay the groundwork for examining how design and practice intersect in hybrid learning environments.

3 Co-Design and Stakeholder Involvement

The second part of the book, *Unlocking the Potential of Hybrid Teaching and Learning in Higher Education through Co-Design*, shifts from foundational concepts to examining how hybrid learning environments are actively designed and implemented in collaboration with various stakeholders. This emphasis on co-design acknowledges that hybrid education is not a top-down process but an ongoing negotiation involving teachers, students, instructional designers, technology developers, and institutional leaders.

In Chapter "Constructing a Hybrid Learning Design Framework: A Group Concept Mapping Study", Stoyanov et al. share their development of a Hybrid Learning Design Framework using Group Concept Mapping involving stakeholders from various universities. This framework aims to provide structure where isolated methods have previously lacked cohesion. The framework is intended to be operational and adaptable across various hybrid environments, aligning with foundational concepts of hybridity that emphasize integration of diverse learning methods, spaces, and activities. Although the framework identifies important clusters of guidelines (e.g. facilitating collaborative learning and individualizing learning and teaching), teachers will need additional, more fine-grained guidelines to effectively design for learning in hybrid scenarios. More specifically, in addition to the higher-level guidelines, I would suggest the script theory of guidance (Fischer et al., 2013) to support the facilitation of collaborative learning, and theory on digital personalized learning (Van Schoors et al., 2021) revealing which elements within the learning environment could be personalized (e.g. target, source, method, and outcomes).

As mentioned in the introduction, Moreira et al. (Chapter "Competence-Driven Guidelines for Hybrid Teaching") build upon the competence framework presented in Chapter "Teacher Educators' Digital Competence for Hybrid Teaching" making a distinction between generic, contextual, and transformative competences. A co-design workshop with 16 teachers and researchers in education resulted in 45 guidelines which were categorized into three categories. However, as mentioned by the authors, continuous research is needed to refine these guidelines and evaluate their effectiveness in authentic practice.

Both Chapter "Enhancing Hybrid Teaching with Collaborative Online International Learning" (Balula) and Chapter "Co-designing a Micro-Course on Hybrid Learning Competencies for Higher Education Students" (Santos et al.) do not solely focus on the importance of designing for hybrid learning, but go a step further, showcasing Collaborative Online International Learning (COIL) within the landscape of hybrid education aligning with the global educational objective of inclusive, high-quality education fostering meaningful intercultural interactions. Santos et al. present how they developed and co-designed a micro-course on hybrid learning competences of students in which higher education students were active participants in the design process. This co-design process builds upon the theory-based guidelines on social presence and self-regulation presented in first part "*Conceptual Pillars of Hybrid Teaching and Learning in Higher Education*".

A key insight from this part is the recognition that designing for hybrid learning involves balancing diverse and sometimes conflicting stakeholder needs. Teachers, for instance, may prioritize pedagogical coherence and feasibility, while students may value accessibility, flexibility, and meaningful interaction. Technology developers may focus on creating scalable tools, while institutional leadership often emphasizes strategic alignment and sustainability. These competing interests must be harmonized through a process of negotiation and adaptation through different feedback loops which are critical in effective co-design.

Rather than assuming a one-size-fits-all solution, the handbook stresses the consideration of contextual factors in the design process. While certain principles of hybrid learning design may be generalizable, their implementation is always mediated by local conditions, such as institutional culture, technological infrastructure, and disciplinary norms. This context-dependence is further illustrated and elaborated in third part "*Experience-Based Cases of Hybrid Teaching and Learning*".

4 From Experimental Practices to Sustainable Practice

The third part of the handbook, including ten chapters, presents a series of practices in hybrid education demonstrating the diversity of contexts in which hybrid learning scenarios are implemented, each aiming for different learning goals and supported by various tools and strategies. The chapters illustrate hybrid education across different disciplines and domains, including problem-based learning with work-life clients (Kojo et al., Chapter "Hybrid Problem-Based Learning with Work-Life Clients: A Context of the Educational Technology Project Course") health education (Pramila-Savukoski et al., Chapter "Collaborative Hybrid Learning in Developing Health Sciences Competence"), vocational training (Wagner et al., Chapter "Hybrid Teaching and Learning in the Context of Vocational Secondary Education"), lifelong learning (Vasconcelos, Chapter "Fostering Tourism and Hospitality Students' Language and Career Skills: A Blended and Hybrid Approach"), adult education (Firssova et al., Chapter "Experimenting with Hybrid Learning in Distance Education: Experiences, Results, and Lessons Learned") and interdisciplinary collaboration (Virkus, Chapter "Telepresence Robots and Chatbots in Hybrid Teaching and Learning: A Case of Interdisciplinary Focused Environment"). Whereas most chapters focus on the experience from the teacher and student perspective stressing for example the need for pedagogical safety (Pramila-Savukoski et al.), self-regulated learning (Kojo et al.) and required preparation (Firssova et al.), four chapters also explicitly draw attention on the infrastructure needed to support hybrid scenarios based on the guidelines for social presence and supporting teacher orchestration. The final chapter of Engelen et al. (Chapter "Hybrid Classroom Scenarios and Academic Teaching Spaces") presents different configurations of the hybrid learning settings, requiring different technological setups with respect to room layouts, screen sizes, viewing directions, lighting and sound. This complex interplay is also described more concretely in Keulemans and Raes (Chapter "A Next Generation Hybrid Classroom: Facilitating Mixed-Modality Collaborative Learning in a Hybrid Context") presenting the design of the hybrid collaboration room making mixed-modality group work possible. As suggested by Kreijns et al. (Chapter "A Social Perspective on Hybrid Learning") collaboration in mixed groups could improve the social presence in higher education. Next, Pramila-Savukoski et al. (Chapter "Collaborative Hybrid Learning in Developing Health Sciences Competence") suggest to take advance of the current evolutions in Artificial Intelligence by collaborating with AI as co-orchestrator of learning scenarios, following the approach of hybrid intelligence (Cukurova, 2024; Molenaar, 2022). Finally, Virkus demonstrates in Chapter "Telepresence Robots and Chatbots in Hybrid Teaching and Learning: A Case of Interdisciplinary Focused Environment" how innovative technologies such as telepresence robots and virtual assistants can enhance hybrid learning. It highlighted how these technologies can act as co-orchestrators within the educational ecosystem, providing personalized guidance and supporting interdisciplinary collaboration.

Several chapters illustrate the differences in operationalization of hybrid education as discussed in the introduction. Both Keulemans et al. (Chapter "Connecting in All Ways: A Case on Synchronous Hybrid Education Using a Flipped Classroom Approach") and Ramos et al. (Chapter "Shaping Sustainable Urban Landscapes Through Picturebooks: An Interdisciplinary COIL Journey") situate synchronous hybrid education within a blended approach combining asynchronous online learning with synchronous on-site or hybrid learning consecutively, following the principle of the flipped classroom. Firssova et al. (Chapter "Experimenting with Hybrid Learning in Distance Education: Experiences, Results, and Lessons Learned") even describe how a former distance education context experiments with hybrid learning as an alternative to fully online classes, showing positive findings.

Together, these chapters highlight the diversity of hybrid learning implementations across contexts, disciplines, and objectives. They also reveal a common challenge: the need to design hybrid learning environments that are inclusive, interactive, and capable of fostering meaningful connections between participants. While these practices showcase creative and context-sensitive approaches, they are frequently not yet fully integrated into the institutional educational policy. This experimental character can be attributed to the novelty of hybrid learning, the rapid pace of technological change, and the need for flexible, adaptive solutions. However, for hybrid education to move from isolated initiatives to a sustainable model, a more systematic and institution-wide approach will be necessary. This includes embedding hybrid practices within strategic planning, policy development, and institutional support structures. Building on the e-capacity model (Vanderlinde & van Braak, 2010), it will be crucial to establish leadership commitment and robust digital infrastructure that support consistent and scalable hybrid learning. As Santos et al. argue in Chapter "Co-designing a Micro-Course on Hybrid Learning Competencies for Higher Education Students", effective hybrid education requires strategic planning and organizational readiness, which remain rather underdeveloped in the current volume. Without this shift from pioneering experimentation to structured integration, hybrid education risks remaining a series of disparate and short-lived projects rather than becoming a core element of educational practice.

5 Future Directions

On the one hand, Gil et al. (2022) outlined that hybridity is here to stay, on the other hand, different scholars also acknowledged that hybrid is hard (Graves et al., 2024), as also noticed in Chapter "Orchestration Load of Hybrid Teaching" of Amarasinghe et al. The current handbook, developed within the Hyb-IT-up project, provides valuable insights into the theories informing the design of hybrid education, giving also an insight in the current state of the art of practices of hybrid learning environments. However, the identified gaps also highlight areas where further research, conceptual development, and practical refinement are necessary. To advance the field of hybrid education, several future directions should be prioritized.

First, there is a pressing need for more experimental research aimed at understanding the effectiveness of specific strategies and tools within hybrid learning environments. Kreijns et al. explicitly mention that they used the term 'suggestions' for improving social presence because there is a lack of research providing solid evidence-based guidelines, as also explicitly mentioned in the final chapter (Engelen et al.). Let this be a call for future research. Virkus's description of the virtual chatbot as a co-orchestrating tool in hybrid learning scenarios presents a promising avenue for empirical investigation. Research could explore how such tools facilitate interaction, feedback, and support, particularly in mixed groups where learners are distributed across physical and digital spaces. Additionally, Keulemans and Raes (Chapter "A Next Generation Hybrid Classroom: Facilitating Mixed-Modality Collaborative Learning in a Hybrid Context") describe the hybrid collaboration room, specifically designed to enhance collaboration between in-person and remote students and to investigate teacher orchestration (load) from the researcher cockpit. Comparative studies could examine whether social presence and feelings of telepresence are higher in mixed-group collaboration facilitated by this hybrid classroom compared to one-mode groups. Furthermore, the strategies for self-regulation, co-regulation, and socially shared regulation discussed by Ahola et al. (Chapter "Regulation of Learning: Cognition, Motivation and Emotion") offer fertile ground for further investigation. Specifically, experimental research could assess to what extent these strategies can support group work in hybrid learning contexts and enhance learning outcomes. Moreover, future research could use the micro-ecological approach to investigate the teacher orchestration of different hybrid scenarios.

Second, the need for conceptual clarity in hybrid education is apparent throughout the book and I realized that my prior work also contributed to this confusion. Engelen et al. (Chapter "Hybrid Classroom Scenarios and Academic Teaching Spaces") for example refer to our systematic review (Raes et al., 2020) in which we used the concepts of 'hybrid virtual classroom' and 'remote classroom'. However, after advancing insight and reflections in the research field, we had to conclude that these concepts did not make sense as hybrid includes the combination of on-site and remote or virtual students. Nowadays we refer to hybrid classrooms connecting individuals and/or groups of students. This example shows that knowledge is socially constructed in our field and shows the need to be open towards each other as a research and learning community. This handbook also shows that hybrid learning is operationalized differently across chapters, encompassing various combinations of on-site, online, synchronous, and asynchronous modalities. While this diversity is reflective of the flexibility and adaptability of hybrid education, it also introduces complexity and potential confusion. For instance, Chapter "Orchestration Load of Hybrid Teaching" highlights how teacher orchestration load differs significantly between on-site, online, and synchronous hybrid CSCL situations. Without clear conceptual definitions, comparisons between studies or practices become challenging, and the interpretation of learning and teaching variables within the complex ecosystem of hybrid education may be compromised. Agreeing upon a shared conceptual framework that accounts for these variations is essential for enhancing both research coherence and practical application.

Additionally, it will be important to address the gap in the institutional or organizational perspective. Without addressing the role of institutional readiness and support, the potential for hybrid learning to evolve from a necessity during the pandemic to an intentional instructional design for learning will remain limited.

6 Final Quotes

As the chapters in this book demonstrate, hybrid education presents an array of possibilities for enhancing learning across diverse contexts, from teacher training and interdisciplinary collaboration to vocational education and international learning experiences. Yet, the journey toward effective hybrid education is far from straightforward. Moving from experimental initiatives to sustainable practices requires not only innovative pedagogical strategies and technological advancements but also intentional instructional design for learning that is firmly rooted in theoretical frameworks. As Fischer and Wolf (2015) aptly stated in their reflection on MOOCs, "The future of learning and education is not out there to be discovered (as Columbus discovered America) - but it has to be designed" (p. 9). This call for intentional design grounded in robust theoretical frameworks that acknowledges the complexity and dynamism of hybrid learning environments.

Moreover, as higher education institutions strive to scale these innovative practices into sustainable models, a crucial caveat remains that hybrid education should not only be accessible but also inclusive. While technological advancements can broaden access, true inclusion requires ensuring that all participants, regardless of their physical location, are genuinely engaged and valued within the learning environment. As Vernā Myers noted, "*Diversity is being invited to the party. Inclusion is being asked to dance.*" As hybrid education continues to evolve, ensuring that all learners could actively participate, contribute, and thrive will be essential for its long-term success.

References

Borge, M., & Mercier, E. (2019). Towards a micro-ecological approach to CSCL. *International Journal of Computer-Supported Collaborative Learning, 14*(2), 219–235. https://doi.org/10.1007/s11412-019-09301-6

Cukurova, M. (2024). The interplay of learning, analytics and artificial intelligence in education: A vision for hybrid intelligence. *British Journal of Educational Technology, 56*, 469–488. https://doi.org/10.1111/bjet.13514

Damşa, C., Nerland, M., & Andreadakis, Z. E. (2019). An ecological perspective on learner-constructed learning spaces. *British Journal of Educational Technology, 50*(5), 2075–2089. https://doi.org/10.1111/bjet.12855

Dillenbourg, P. (2013). Design for classroom orchestration. *Computers & Education, 69*, 485–492. https://doi.org/10.1016/J.COMPEDU.2013.04.013

Dillenbourg, P., Prieto, L. P., & Olsen, J. K. (2018). Classroom orchestration. In *International handbook of the learning sciences* (pp. 180–190). Routledge.

Ebner, C., & Gegenfurtner, A. (2019). Learning and satisfaction in webinar, online, and face-to-face instruction: A meta-analysis. *Frontiers in Education, 4*. https://doi.org/10.3389/feduc.2019.00092

Elen, J. (2020). "Instructional disobedience": A largely neglected phenomenon deserving more systematic research attention. *Educational Technology Research and Development, 68*, 2021–2032. https://doi.org/10.1007/s11423-020-09776-3

Fischer, F., Kollar, I., Stegman, K., & Wecker, C. (2013). Toward a script theory of guidance in computer-supported collaborative learning. *Educational Psychologist, 48*(1), 56–66. https://doi.org/10.1080/00461520.2012.748005

Fischer, G., & Wolf, K. (2015). *What can residential, research-based universities learn about their core competencies from MOOCs (Massive Open Online Course)?* Retrieved from https://l3d.colorado.edu/wp-content/uploads/2016/04/Bremen-Wolf-MOOCS.pdf

Gil, E., Mor, Y., Dimitriadis, Y., & Köppe, C. (Eds.). (2022). *Hybrid learning spaces*. Springer.

Goodyear, P. (2015). Teaching as design. *HERDSA Review of Higher Education, 2*, 27–50. Retrieved from www.herdsa.org.au/publications/journals/

Goodyear, P., Carvalho, L., & Yeoman, P. (2021). Activity-centred analysis and design (ACAD): Core purposes, distinctive qualities and current developments. *Educational Technology Research and Development, 69*, 445–464. https://doi.org/10.1007/s11423-020-09926-7

Graves, J. L., Hasan, E., & Varao-Sousa, T. L. (2024). Understanding the hybrid classroom in economics: A case study. *International Review of Economics Education, 45*, 100282. https://doi.org/10.1016/j.iree.2023.100282

Irvine, V. (2020). The landscape of merging modalities. *Educause Review, 4*, 40–58. Retrieved from https://er.educause.edu/articles/2020/10/the-landscape-of-merging-modalities

Järvelä, S., & Hadwin, A. (2024). Triggers for self-regulated learning: A conceptual framework for advancing multimodal research about SRL. *Learning and Individual Differences, 115*, 102526. https://doi.org/10.1016/j.lindif.2024.102526

Jordan, K., & Goshtasbpour, F. (2022). JIME virtual special collection – 2012 to 2022: The decade of the MOOC. *Journal of Interactive Media in Education, 2022*(1), 1. https://doi.org/10.5334/jime.757

Kirschner, P. A. (2015). Do we need teachers as designers of technology enhanced learning? *Instructional Science, 43*(2), 309–322. https://doi.org/10.1007/s11251-015-9346-9

Kirschner, P. A., Sweller, J., & Clark, R. E. (2006). Why minimal guidance during instruction does not work: An analysis of the failure of constructivist, discovery, problem-based, experiential, and inquiry-based teaching. *Educational Psychologist, 41*(2), 75–86.

Kreijns, K., Xu, K., & Weidlich, J. (2022). Social presence: Conceptualization and measurement. *Educational Psychology Review, 34*(1), 139–170. https://doi.org/10.1007/s10648-021-09623-8

Kreijns, K., Yau, J., Weidlich, J., & Weinberger, A. (2024). Towards a comprehensive framework of social presence for online, hybrid, and blended learning. *Frontiers in Education, 8*, 14. https://doi.org/10.3389/feduc.2023.1286594

Laurillard, D. (2012). *Teaching as a design science*. Routledge. https://doi.org/10.4324/9780203125083

Littlejohn, A., Hood, N., Milligan, C., & Mustain, P. (2016). Learning in MOOCs: Motivations and self-regulated learning in MOOCs. *The Internet and Higher Education, 29*, 40–48. https://doi.org/10.1016/J.IHEDUC.2015.12.003

Markauskaite, L., Carvalho, L., & Damşa, C. (2023). Ecological perspectives on learning and methodological implications for research and design. In C. Damşa, A. Rajala, G. Ritella, & J. Brouwer (Eds.), *Re-theorizing learning and research methods in learning research*. Routledge, EARLI Series.

Molenaar, I. (2022). Towards hybrid human-AI learning technologies. *European Journal of Education, 57*(4), 632–645. https://doi.org/10.1111/ejed.12527

Ortega-Arranz, A., Amarasinghe, I., Martínez-Monés, A., Asensio-Pérez, J. I., Dimitriadis, Y., Corrales-Astorgano, M., & Hernández-Leo, D. (2024). Collaborative activities in hybrid learning environments: Exploring teacher orchestration load and students' perceptions. *Computers & Education, 219*, 105105. https://doi.org/10.1016/J.COMPEDU.2024.105105

Prieto, L. P., Sharma, K., Kidzinski, L., & Dillenbourg, P. (2018). Orchestration load indicators and patterns: In-the-wild studies using mobile eye-tracking. *IEEE Transactions on Learning Technologies, 11*(2), 216–229. https://doi.org/10.1109/TLT.2017.2690687

Raes, A. (2022). Exploring student and teacher experiences in hybrid learning environments: Does presence matter? *Postdigital Science and Education, 4*, 138–159. https://doi.org/10.1007/s42438-021-00274-0

Raes, A., Detienne, L., Windey, I., & Depaepe, F. (2020). A systematic literature review on synchronous hybrid learning: Gaps identified. *Learning Environments Research, 23*(3), 269–290. https://doi.org/10.1007/s10984-019-09303-z

Van Schoors, R., Elen, J., Raes, A., & Depaepe, F. (2021). An overview of 25 years of research on digital personalised learning in primary and secondary education: A systematic review of conceptual and methodological trends. *British Journal of Educational Technology, 52*(5), 1798–1822. https://doi.org/10.1111/BJET.13148

Vanderlinde, R., & van Braak, J. (2010). The e-capacity of primary schools: Development of a conceptual model and scale construction from a school improvement perspective. *Computers & Education, 55*(2), 541–553. https://doi.org/10.1016/J.COMPEDU.2010.02.016

Zhang, J., Gao, M., & Zhang, J. (2021). The learning behaviours of dropouts in MOOCs: A collective attention network perspective. *Computers & Education, 167*, 104189. https://doi.org/10.1016/J.COMPEDU.2021.104189

GPSR Compliance
The European Union's (EU) General Product Safety Regulation (GPSR) is a set of rules that requires consumer products to be safe and our obligations to ensure this.

If you have any concerns about our products, you can contact us on

ProductSafety@springernature.com

In case Publisher is established outside the EU, the EU authorized representative is:

Springer Nature Customer Service Center GmbH
Europaplatz 3
69115 Heidelberg, Germany

www.ingramcontent.com/pod-product-compliance
Ingram Content Group UK Ltd.
Pitfield, Milton Keynes, MK11 3LW, UK
UKHW022203220926
475873UK00003B/30
9783031997426